Sir George Everest.

MAN AND MOUNTAIN

THE PIONEERS OF EVEREST

IM ANGESICHT DES GIGANTEN

DIE PIONIERE DES MOUNT EVEREST

DE MENS EN EEN REUS

DE PIONIERS VAN DE EVEREST

HOMBRES CONTRA UN GIGANTE

LOS PIONEROS DEL EVEREST

YVES DE CHAZOURNES

ÉDITIONS
PLACE DES
VICTOIRES

The publisher wishes to thank Jamie Owen at the RGS for his receptiveness and kindness.

6, rue du Mail - 75002 Paris.
www.victoires.com
Editorial coordination: Yohann Thibaudault
Design, layout and cover: Alessandro Fiore, Roma, Italia
Translations and revision: Textcase, Utrecht

ISBN (English): 978-2-8099-0278-5
ISBN (German): 978-2-8099-0277-8
ISBN (Dutch): 978-2-8099-0279-2

Printed in China

Picture credits:
© Royal Geographical Society, London
© Swiss Foundation for Alpine Research, Zürich: all the pictures of the 1952 expedition (P.388 to 409).

Created and distributed in cooperation with Frechmann Kolón GmbH
www.frechmann.com

P. 6-7: Tibetan plateau looking towards the Himalayas. / Hochland von Tibet mit Blick auf das Himalaya-Gebirge. / Tibetaanse plateau met uitzicht op het Himalaya-gebergte. / Meseta tibetana mirando hacia el Himalaya. © Roger Cracknell / Royal Geographical Society

P. 10-11: Aerial view of Everest and the Himalayan Range. / Luftaufnahme des Mount Everest und den Himalaya-Gebirgszug. / Overzichtsfoto van de Everest en de Himalaya. / Vista aérea del Everest y de la cordillera del Himalaya. © David Constantine / Royal Geographical Society

P. 12-13: Lhotse and Nuptse viewed from Pumori / Lhotse und Nuptse vom Pumori aus gesehen / De Lhotse en de Nuptse gezien vanaf de Pumori / Lhotse y Nuptse vistos desde Pumori, 1953.

P. 36-37: Bamboo bridge, Tibet. / Brücke aus Bambus, Tibet. / Brug van bamboe, Tibet. / Puente de bambú, El Tibet. (John B. Noel Collection).

P. 74-75: Preliminary Map to illustrate the route of the 1921 Mount Everest Expedition, 1921. / Vorläufige Karte zur Veranschaulichung der Route der Mount Everest-Expedition, 1921. / Routekaart waarmee de Everest-expeditie in 1921 van start ging. / Mapa preliminar que ilustra la ruta de la expedición de 1921 al Monte Everest, 1921.

P. 79: A wayside chorten with Ama Dablam beyond, Nepal. / Ein Chörten, ein Kultbau des Buddhismus, mit Ama Dablam im Hintergrund, Nepal. / Een boeddhistisch gedenkteken (chorten) met de Ama Dablam erachter, Nepal. / Un chorten en el camino con la montaña Ama Dablam de fondo, Nepal. © John Noble / Royal Geographical Society

P. 116-117: Tibetan women. / Tibetanische Frau. / Tibetaanse vrouwen. / Mujeres tibetanas. (John B. Noel Collection).

P. 121: Khumbu Glacier, Nepal. / Der Khumbu-Gletscher, Nepal. / Khumbu-gletsjer, Nepal. / Glaciar de Khumbu, Nepal. © Roger Cracknell / Royal Geographical Society

P. 206: Children from the village of Hurikot, in Dolpo (Western Nepal). / Kinder aus dem Dorf Hurikot in Dolpo (westliches Nepal). / Kinderen van het plaatsje Hurikot, in Dolpo (West-Nepal). / Niños del pueblo de Hurikot, en Dolpo (Nepal occidental). © Steve Razzetti / Royal Geographical Society

P. 207: Bhotias from Mustang in the province of Nari (Western Tibet) / Bhotias aus Mustang in der Provinz Nari (westliches Tibet) / Bhotia's uit Mustang in de provincie Nari (West-Tibet) / Bhotias de Mustang en la provincia de Nari (El Tíbet occidental), H.A. Oldfield, 1852-1860.

P. 242-243: Lhotse South Face (Nepal) / Südwand des Lhotse (Nepal) / Zuidzijde van de Lhotse (Nepal) / Cara sur del Lhotse (Nepal), 1953.

P. 247: Ice peak in Imja Valley / Eisbedeckte Gipfel im Imja-Tal / Piek van ijs in de Imja-vallei / Pico helado en el valle del Imja, 1953.

P. 300-301: The Solu Khumbu Glacier flows from the Everest Ice Fall ; its waters are the start of the Dudh Kosi River / Der Solu Khumbu-Gletscher ergießt sich vom Eisbruch des Mount Everest. Aus ihm entspringt der Dudh Kosi-Fluss / De gletsjer Solu Khumbu stroomt van de Everest-ijsval; met dit water begint de rivier Dudh Kosi / El glaciar de Solu Khumbu fluye desde la cascada de hielo del Everest; en sus aguas empieza el río Dudh Kosi (Nepal). © John Noble / Royal Geographical Society

P. 325: Mount Makalu photographed by Edmund Hillary / Der Makalu, Fotografie von Edmund Hillary / De Makalu gefotografeerd door Edmund Hillary, / El Monte Makalu fotografiado por Edmund Hillary, Nepal, 1953.

P. 352: Temple of Devi Bhairari at Nagarkot near Kathmandu / Tempel von Devi Bhairari in Nagarkot bei Kathmandu / De tempel Devi Bhairari in Nagarkot nabij Kathmandu / El Templo de Devi Bhairari en Nagarkot, cerca de Katmandú (Nepal), H.A. Oldfield 1854.

P. 353:
Above / Oben / Boven / Arriba: Tibetans and their sheep, in front of the stupa of a Buddhist temple at Bodhnath, near Kathmandu / Tibeter und ihre Schafe, vor der Stupa eines Buddhistischen Tempels in Bodhnath nahe Kathmandu / Tibetanen en hun schapen voor de stupa van een boeddhistische tempel in Bodhnath, nabij Kathmandu / Tibetanos y sus ovejas, delante del estupa de un templo budista en Bodhnath, cerca de Katmandú (Nepal), H.A. Oldfield, 1852-1860.

Below / Unten / Onder / Abajo: Buddhist temple in the centre of 'Eetaka Vihr' at Kathmandu / Buddhistischer Tempel im Zentrum von „Eetaka Vihr“ in Kathmandu / Boeddhistische tempel in het centrum van Eetaka Vihr, Kathmandu. / Templo budista en el centro de “Eetaka Vihr” en Katmandú, H.A. Oldfield, 1857.

P. 357: Camp beneath Mount Chomolonzo, Kama Valley (Tibet). Photo by Stephen Venables. / Lager unter dem Chomo Lönzo, Kama-Tal (Tibet). Foto von Stephen Venables. / Kamp aan de voet van de Chomolonzo, Kama-vallei (Tibet). Gefotografeerd door Stephen Venables. / Campamento debajo del Monte Chomolonzo, valle del Kama (El Tíbet). Fotografía de Stephen Venables.

P. 382-383: The Thyangboche Monastery with the Kwangde range of mountains behind / Das Kloster von Tengboche mit dem Kwangde-Gebirgszug im Hintergrund / Het klooster Thyangboche met de bergketen Kwangde erachter / El Monasterio Thyangboche con la cadena montañosa de Kwangde detrás, 1953.

P. 387: The South East ridge. View south-west over Nuptse from the site of the Swiss tent. Edmund Hillary, 29th May 1953. / Der Südostgrat. Blick nach Südwesten über den Nuptse vom Standort des Zelts der Schweizer aus. Edmund Hillary, 29. Mai 1953. / De zuidoostelijke bergkam. Zuidwestelijk uitzicht op de Nuptse van bij de Zwitserse tent. Edmund Hillary, 29 mei 1953. / La cresta del sureste. Vista suroeste sobre Nuptse desde el emplazamiento de la tienda de campaña suiza. Edmund Hillary, 29 de mayo de 1953.

P. 410-411: Mount Everest. / Der Mount Everest. / De Everest. / Monte Everest. © Roger Cracknell / Royal Geographical Society

P. 510-511: Panorama of Everest, Nuptse and the Khumba icefall at sunset. / Panorama des Mount Everest, des Nuptse und des Khumbu-Eisbruchs bei Sonnenuntergang. / Panorama van de Everest, de Nuptse en de Khumba-ijsval bij zonsondergang. / Vista del Everest, Nuptse y la cascada de hielo de Khumba al atardecer. © Michael Hughes / Royal Geographical Society

CONTENTS

INHALT

INHOUD

ÍNDICE

The Conquerors of the "Third Pole"

Whether or not one likes mountains, whether one prefers sea level or plains to the vertigo of altitude, it is difficult to remain unaffected by the beauty of the peaks, glaciers, rocks and landscapes depicted in this book. Whether or not one admires the alpinists, these "conquerors of the useless" in search of unique sensations that cannot be experienced anywhere else, or in quest of the absolute, silence, fullness, it is impossible to deny the courage, the desire to surpass themselves, the sacrifices made by the men whose stories are told on the following pages.

The difficult conquest of Everest by adventurers, British for the most part, was one of the last dreams of mankind, along with the exploration of the poles and the first steps on the moon. After the victory in 1953 of New Zealander Edmund Hillary and Sherpa Tenzing Norgay, supported by a courageous British team, other exploits would be accomplished in reaching the Roof of the World, starting with the ascent without oxygen in 1978 of the American Peter Habeler and the Italian Reinhold Messner; the same Messner who would repeat the journey alone two years later.

In less than sixty years, 15,000 Alpinists with varying degrees of talent have attempted to reach the summit of Everest and more than 4,500 have succeeded – sometimes at the cost of their lives. In 1996 alone, 15 people died on the descent. Today, expeditions are organised regularly to clean up the slopes of Everest that are cluttered with old oxygen canisters, detritus, bottles and rubbish left from campsites. The various routes to reach the Roof of the World have become, exaggerating slightly, common via ferrata, lined with fixed ropes, pitons and metal ladders.

At the start of the 20th century it was, it hardly needs to be said, quite different, when the British attacked Everest then. The mountaineers climbed in tweed jackets, hobnail boots and wore felt hats. When they rested at their base camp, they wore colonial helmets while drinking tea. It is this past era that the Royal Geographical Society's remarkable photography collection brings to life, from the first British attempts to the final victory; without forgetting the roped Helvetians, who came close to managing the feat some months earlier. The photos from the Swiss Foundation for Alpine Research that are reproduced in this book bear witness to the courage of these Genevan alpinists to whom in 1953, incidentally, the British dedicated "half of the victory".

Die Bezwinger des „dritten Pols"

Ganz gleich, ob Sie ein Liebhaber der Berge sind, ob Sie die unendliche Weite des Meeres oder der Ebene dem Schwindel der Höhe vorziehen – die erhabene Schönheit der Gipfel, Gletscher, Felsen und Landschaften in diesem Bildband wird Sie nicht unberührt lassen. Sie mögen Bewunderung oder Gleichgültigkeit für die von dem französischen Alpinisten Lionel Terray als „Eroberer des Unnützen" bezeichneten Bergsteiger empfinden, diese Himmelsstürmer auf ihrer rastlosen Suche nach anderenorts unerreichbaren Sinneseindrücken. Doch niemand kann den Mut dieser Männer, ihren Willen, über sich selbst hinauszuwachsen, und die Opfer, die sie gebracht haben, in Abrede stellen.

Die schwierige Erstbesteigung des Mount Everest durch eine Gruppe mehrheitlich britischer Abenteurer war neben der Erforschung der Pole und den ersten Schritten auf dem Mond einer der letzten unerfüllten Träume der Menschheit. Dem Erfolg des Neuseeländers Edmund Hillary und des Sherpa Tenzing Norgay im Jahre 1953 folgten weitere herausragende Leistungen: 1978 erreichten der Österreicher Peter Habeler und der Italiener Reinhold Messner das Dach der Welt erstmals ohne Sauerstoff, und nur zwei Jahre später gelang Messner der Aufstieg im Alleingang.

Insgesamt machten sich seither rund 15.000 Bergsteiger daran, den Gipfel des Everest zu erstürmen. Mehr als 4500 gelang es, doch einige kostete es das Leben. Allein 1996 starben 15 Personen beim Abstieg vom Gipfel. Heute werden regelmäßig Expeditionen veranstaltet, um die Hänge des Mount Everest von alten Sauerstoffflaschen, Getränkedosen und Lagerresten zu säubern. Die verschiedenen Routen zum Dach der Welt sind zu ganz gewöhnlichen Vie *Ferrate* geworden, zu von Seilen, Felshaken und Metallleitern gesäumten Klettersteigen.

Bei den ersten Besteigungsversuchen der Briten zu Beginn des 20. Jahrhunderts war natürlich alles noch ganz anders. Die Bergsteiger wagten sich in Tweedjacketts, in mit Nägeln beschlagenen Schuhen und mit einem Filzhut auf dem Kopf an den Aufstieg. Bei der Rast im Basislager trugen sie zur Teestunde einen Kolonialhelm. Dieses längst vergangene Zeitalter wird in den Fotografien aus der Sammlung der Royal Geographical Society wieder lebendig, die die frühen Expeditionen wie auch den endgültigen Erfolg dokumentieren. Die schweizerischen Seilschaften, die es im Vorjahr fast zum Gipfel geschafft hätten, sollen dabei nicht unerwähnt bleiben. Fotografien der Fondation Suisse pour la Recherche Alpine zeugen vom Mut dieser Genfer Bergsteiger, denen die Briten 1953 „die Hälfte ihres Erfolges" widmeten.

De veroveraars van de 'derde pool'

Of u nu een liefhebber van bergen bent of niet, dan wel de voorkeur geeft aan de zee of een vlakte op duizelingwekkende hoogte, het is heel moeilijk ongevoelig te blijven voor de schoonheid van de toppen, de gletsjers, de rotsen en de landschappen die u in dit boek zult ontdekken. Of u alpinisten, die 'dwaze strijders', op zoek naar ongekende sensatie of naar zuiverheid, stilte en ongereptheid, nu bewondert of niet, de moed, de bereidheid het eigen leven op het spel te zetten, de opofferingen van de mensen waarover het op de volgende pagina's gaat, zijn niet te ontkennen.

De moeizame verovering van de Everest door voornamelijk Britse avonturiers was een van de laatste dromen van de mensheid, naast de verkenning van de poolgebieden en de eerste stap op de maan. Na de triomf van de Nieuw-Zeelander Edmund Hillary en de Sherpa Tenzing Norgay in 1953, bijgestaan door een zeer ervaren Brits team, zijn er andere topprestaties geleverd op het 'Dak van de wereld', vooral de beklimming zonder zuurstof in 1978 door de Oostenrijker Peter Habeler en de Italiaan Reinhold Messner, dezelfde Messner die deze prestatie twee jaar later als solitaire klimmer herhaalde.

In minder dan zestig jaar tijd hebben ongeveer 15.000 ervaren alpinisten geprobeerd de top van de Everest te bereiken en meer dan 4500 van hen zijn daarin geslaagd, hoewel een aantal dat met hun leven moest bekopen. Alleen al in 1996 kwamen 15 personen om tijdens de afdaling. Tegenwoordig worden er regelmatig expedities georganiseerd om de hellingen van de Everest te ontdoen van oude zuurstofflessen, vuilnis, touwklossen en overblijfselen van kampementen. De verschillende routes naar het 'Dak van de wereld' zijn, om het enigszins te overdrijven, verworden tot gewone vias ferratas (ijzeren wegen), gemarkeerd met permanente touwen, rotshaken en metalen ladders.

Het ging er anders aan toe aan het begin van de 20ste eeuw, toen de Britten op de Everest worstelden. Zij klommen in jassen van tweed, bespijkerde schoenen en een vilten hoed op het hoofd. Pauzerend in hun basiskamp droegen zij een tropenhelm terwijl zij thee dronken. Dat verleden laat de fotocollectie van de *Royal Geographical Society* herleven, vanaf de eerste Britse pogingen tot aan hun triomf, en, niet te vergeten, van de Zwitsers die enkele maanden eerder dicht bij de zege waren. De foto's van de Zwitserse Stichting voor Alpenonderzoek getuigen van de moed van deze Zwitserse alpinisten, aan wie de Britten in 1953 niet voor niets de 'halve zege' hebben toegekend.

Los conquistadores del «tercer polo»

Nos guste o no la montaña, prefiramos el nivel del mar o de la llanura al vértigo de la altitud, es difícil permanecer insensible ante la belleza de las cumbres, los glaciares, las rocas y los paisajes que descubrirá en esta obra. Admire o no a los escaladores, estos «conquistadores de lo inútil» a la búsqueda de sensaciones no experimentadas en ninguna otra parte, o en busca de lo absoluto, del silencio y de la plenitud, es imposible negar la valentía, la voluntad de superación de sí mismos y los sacrificios llevados a cabo por los hombres de los que se habla en las siguientes páginas.

La difícil conquista del Everest por parte de estos aventureros, británicos en su mayoría, era uno de los últimos sueños del hombre, junto con la exploración de los polos y los primeros pasos sobre la luna. Tras la victoria del neozelandés Edmund Hillary y del sherpa Tenzing Norgay, apoyados por un valioso equipo británico en 1953, se lograrán otras proezas para culminar el Techo del mundo, comenzando por el ascenso sin oxígeno en 1978 del austriaco Peter Habeler y del italiano Reinhold Messner; el mismo Messner que reiterará la proeza en solitario dos años más tarde.

En menos de sesenta años, 15.000 alpinistas más o menos experimentados, han intentado coronar la cumbre del Everest y más de 4500 lo han logrado, a veces pagando por ello con sus vidas. Solamente en 1996, 15 personas perecen en el descenso. Actualmente se organizan expediciones para limpiar las vertientes del Everest abigarradas de viejas botellas de oxígeno, detritus, botellines y vestigios de campamentos. Los diferentes itinerarios para llegar al Techo del mundo se han convertido en vulgares vías ferratas, jalonadas de cuerdas fijas, pitones y escaleras metálicas.

Hay que decir que todo era diferente a principios del siglo XX, cuando los británicos organizaban las expediciones al Everest. Los montañeros escalan con chaqueta de tweed, zapatos con clavos y sombreros de fieltro sobre la cabeza. Cuando descansan en su campamento base, suelen beber té con el casco colonial puesto. La distinguida colección fotográfica de la Royal Geographical Society nos hace revivir esta época pasada, caracterizada por los primeros intentos británicos hasta conseguir la victoria; sin olvidar las cordadas helvéticas, que rozaron muy de cerca la proeza unos meses antes. Las fotografías de la Fundación suiza para la búsqueda alpina, que se reproducen en este libro, ponen de manifiesto la valentía de estos alpinistas de Ginebra a los que, por otra parte, los británicos dedicaron en 1953 «la mitad de la victoria».

A Giant is Born, it Will be Called Everest!
Ein Gigant namens Everest ist geboren!
Een reus is geboren, hij heet Everest!
Ha nacido un gigante, ¡se llamará Everest!

In 1823 George Everest, *Surveyor General* of the Indies, founded the geodesic service that would undertake to note down the summits of the Himalayan mountain chain. The British and Indian surveyors were not able to approach those territories closed off to foreigners, in particular Tibet, Nepal and the small neighbouring kingdoms of Sikkim and Bhutan. They were therefore restricted to making their scholarly triangulation calculations at great distances from the summits they are observing. They used bulky theodolites that each required a dozen porters to move them. In 1843 George Everest was replaced by Andrew Waugh and, some years later, his stewards were intrigued by a summit, well hidden behind Mount Kangchenjunga, which for ten years seemed to them to be the highest mountain on the planet. They provisionally call it *Peak B*. The biggest of the theodolites is moved to different places to compare the results that seem to indicate that the summit is higher than any other.

The geodesy service headquarters was at that time located in the town of Dehra Dun, nestled at the foot of the Indian part of the Himalayas. This is where all the data collected on site is sent. Meanwhile, a deputy director has begun to set out a new system classifying the highest summits in the Himalayas. Peak B becomes Peak XV and Kangchenjunga is then known as Peak IX.

The story goes that one day in 1852 the chief geometer, Radhanath Sikhdar, rushed into Andrew Waugh's office shouting: "Sir, I have discovered the highest mountain on the planet!" Meticulously detailed trigonometric calculations will be carried out for many months and years and it will not be until March 1856 that the whole world will find out the secret: Peak XV has an altitude of 8,839 metres. In homage to his predecessor, Andrew Waugh suggests naming it Everest, confirming that there is no local name for this mountain. Ancient Tibetan writings do however make reference to the Tibetan name *Chomolungma*, which, according to the transcriptions, means: *Goddess Mother of the Winds* or *Goddess Mother of the World*. The Tibetans still call it this today. On the Nepalese side, the highest summit on the planet, at an altitude recalculated to be 8,848 metres (and even 8,850 according to other measures), has the more recent name of *Sagamartha* ("Head of Heaven").

In 1865, after many hesitations, the name *Everest* is officially accepted by the London Royal Geographical Society (RGS), the prestigious scholarly society that has encouraged and organised most of the British expeditions in the world since 1830.

The first to flirt with the idea of climbing this mysterious and formidable mountain is Clinton Thomas, president of the Alpine Club. Francis Younghusband, a soldier, mountaineer and future president of the RGS, passes close to Everest in 1903, during a military expedition. In 1911, after conquering a summit of 7,128 metres, Alexander Kellas is convinced that Everest is not impregnable, and he advocates using the services of the Sherpa people, who, as he had discovered during his ascents, are especially tough. Two years later, a daredevil captain 23 years old, John Noel, secretly enters Tibet and succeeds in coming within fewer than 60 kilometres of Everest. It is he who, the day after the Great War, will convince the Royal Geographical Society to launch a reconnaissance mission on the mountain. The real starting trigger for the British expeditions is the creation in 1920 of the Joint Everest Committee, jointly between the RGS and the Alpine Club, at soon as the very young Dalai Lama of the time decides to grant the British authorisation to enter Tibet and to approach the sacred mountain, *Chomolungma*.

It marks the start of a long journey of almost thirty-five years towards the highest summit in the world. Before the war, the British saw victory slip from their grasp at both the North and South poles, first by the Americans, then by the Norwegians. This time, there is no question of leaving the conquest of the *third pole* for anyone else to claim. In 1921, the adventure can finally begin!

Im Jahre1823 übernimmt George Everest, der spätere *„Generallandvermesser Indiens"*, die Leitung des *Great Trigonometric Survey of India*. Bestandteil der Vermessungsarbeiten ist auch die Aufnahme der Gipfel des Himalayagebirges. Den britischen und indischen Landvermessern bleibt allerdings wie allen Ausländern der Zugang zu bestimmten Territorien in diesem Gebiet verwehrt, insbesondere zu Tibet, Nepal und den kleineren benachbarten Königreichen Sikkim und Bhutan. Sie sind daher gezwungen, ihre gelehrten trigonometrischen Berechnungen aus großer Entfernung zu den Gipfeln durchzuführen. Als Messinstrumente verwenden sie sperrige Theodoliten, von denen jeder nur mit zwölf Trägern von der Stelle bewegt werden kann. 1843 wird George Everest von Andrew Waugh als Generallandvermesser abgelöst. Nur wenige Jahre später wenden Landvermesser ihre Aufmerksamkeit einem Gipfel zu, der sich weit hinter dem Kangchendzönga verbirgt und in dem sie schon seit zehn Jahren den höchsten Berg der Erde vermuten. Sie nennen ihn vorerst *Gipfel B* und bewegen den größten der Theodoliten

Advance party of Sherpas climbs on ahead over avalanche snow above Zemu Chu, Sikkim, 1907-1911.
Träger bewegen sich auf dem Schnee einer abgegangenen Lawine über dem Zemu Chu vorwärts, Sikkim, 1907-1911.
Dragers onderweg naar boven over lawinesneeuw op de Zemu Chu, Sikkim, 1907-1911.
Culis subiendo por una avalancha de nieve sobre el Zemu Chu, Sikkim, 1907-1911.

mehrfach von der Stelle, um Messungen aus verschiedenen Winkeln vorzunehmen: Alle Messergebnisse scheinen darauf hinzudeuten, dass der Gipfel höher ist als alle anderen, bekannten Gipfel.
Das Hauptquartier der Landvermesser befand sich damals in der Stadt Dehradun, am Fuße der indischen Seite des Himalaya. Dort werden alle Gebietsaufnahmen gesammelt. In der Zwischenzeit hat ein Stellvertreter des Direktors mit der Erstellung einer neuen Nomenklatur der höchsten Gipfel des Himalaya begonnen. Der Gipfel B wird zum Gipfel XV, und der Kangchendzönga wird von nun an unter der Bezeichnung Gipfel IX geführt.
Der Überlieferung nach soll der leitende Landvermesser Radhanath Sikhdar eines Tages im Jahr 1852 mit der Bemerkung *„Sir, ich habe den höchsten Berg der Erde entdeckt!"* ins Büro Andrew Waughs gestürzt sein. Während der folgenden Monate und Jahre werden weitere sorgfältige trigonometrische Berechnungen durchgeführt. Erst im März 1856 sollte die ganze Welt das Geheimnis erfahren: Gipfel XV ist 8.839 Meter hoch. Andrew Waugh schlägt vor, ihn zu Ehren seines Vorgängers *Everest* zu nennen. Ihm zufolge ist vor Ort kein anderer Name gebräuchlich, doch einige alte Handschriften aus Tibet erwähnen den Namen *Chomolungma*, was in der Umschrift *„Muttergöttin der Winde"* oder *„Muttergöttin der Welt"* bedeutet. Noch heute nennen die Tibeter den Mount Everest so. Auf der nepalesischen Seite erhält der mit 8.848 Metern (nach anderen Messungen gar 8.858 Meter) höchste Gipfel der Erde später den Namen *Sagamartha* („Kopf des Himmels").
1865 wird der Name Mount Everest nach langem Zögern von der Royal Geographical Society (RGS) in London offiziell bestätigt. Seit 1830 hatte die prestigeträchtige Gesellschaft die meisten britischen Expeditionen in der Welt gefördert und organisiert.
Der erste, der mit der Idee einer Besteigung des geheimnisumwobenen, beunruhigenden Bergs spielt, ist Clinton Thomas, der Präsident des *Alpine Club*. Francis Younghusband, britischer Offizier, Bergsteiger und künftiger Präsident der RGS, gelangt bei einer Militärexpedition im Jahre 1903 in die Nähe des Mount Everest. 1911 kommt Alexander Kellas, nachdem ihm die Besteigung eines Gipfels von 7.128 Metern Höhe gelungen ist, zu der Überzeugung, dass der Everest sich bezwingen lässt. Er hat angeraten , die Dienste des Volkes der Sherpa in Anspruch zu nehmen, das er während seiner Bergbesteigungen entdeckt hat und für besonders zäh und widerstandsfähig hält. Zwei Jahre später reist der wagemutige, erst 23 Jahre alte Captain John Noel heimlich nach Tibet. Ihm gelingt es, sich dem Berg auf weniger als 60 Kilometer zu nähern, und er ist es auch, der nach dem Ersten Weltkrieg die Royal Geographical Society davon überzeugt, eine Erkundungsmission zum Mount Everest zu schicken. Den endgültigen Anstoß zu der britischen Expedition gibt die Gründung des Joint Everest Committee im Jahre 1920 durch die RGS und den Alpine Club, nachdem die Entscheidung des noch sehr jungen damaligen Dalai Lama bekannt wird, den Briten die Genehmigung zur Einreise nach Tibet und die Annäherung an den heiligen Berg der Tibeter, den *Chomolungma*, zu gestatten.
Es ist der Beginn eines sehr langen Aufstiegs zum höchsten Gipfel der Welt, der fast 35 Jahre dauert. Vor dem Krieg hatten sich die Briten beim Wettrennen zum Nordpol und schließlich auch zum Südpol jeweils den Sieg wegschnappen lassen, erst von einem Amerikaner, dann von einem Norweger. Auf keinen Fall können sie die Bezwingung des *„dritten Pols"* ebenfalls anderen überlassen. 1921 kann das Abenteuer endlich beginnen.

In 1823 richt George Everest, rijkslandmeter in India, de geodetische dienst op die de toppen van de Himalayaketen gaat opmeten. De Britse en Indiase aardmeetkundigen mogen zich niet begeven in landen die zijn gesloten voor vreemdelingen, in het bijzonder Tibet, Nepal en hun kleine buurlanden Sikkim en Bhutan. Ze zien zich dan ook gedwongen de driehoeksmetingen op grote afstand van de onderzochte toppen te verrichten. Daarbij werken ze met grote theodolieten, voor de verplaatsing waarvan per theodoliet twaalf dragers nodig zijn. In 1843 wordt George Everest opgevolgd door Andrew Waugh en een aantal jaren later concentreert diens werk zich op een top die verscholen gaat achter de Kanchenjunga, die tien jaar lang als de hoogste berg van de planeet is beschouwd. Ze noemen de top voorlopig 'piek B'. De grootste theodoliet wordt een aantal keren verplaatst om de resultaten te toetsen, die erop lijken te wijzen dat deze top hoger is dan alle andere toppen.
Het hoofdkantoor van de geodetische dienst is dan gevestigd in de plaats Dehra Dun, gelegen aan de voet van het Indiase gedeelte van de Himalaya. Daar komen alle meetresultaten binnen. Ondertussen is een directieassistent begonnen met het herbenoemen van de hoogste Himalaya-toppen. Piek B wordt piek XV en de Kanchenjunga zal voortaan piek IX heten.
Volgens de verhalen stormde op een dag in 1852 hoofdlandmeetkundige Radhanath Sikhdar het kantoor van Andrew Waugh binnen met

Kellas and his Sherpas, Sikkim, 1907-1911.
Kellas und seine Träger, Sikkim, 1907-1911.

Kellas en zijn dragers, Sikkim, 1907-1911.
Kellas y sus culis, Sikkim, 1907-1911.

de boodschap: 'Meneer, ik heb de hoogste berg van de planeet ontdekt!' Gedurende de maanden en jaren die volgden, zouden er nog diverse driehoeksmetingen ter controle worden uitgevoerd voordat in maart 1856 het nieuws wereldkundig wordt gemaakt: piek XV heeft een hoogte van 8839 meter. Als eerbetoon aan zijn voorganger, stelt Andrew Waugh voor de top 'Everest' te noemen, waarmee hij het deed voorkomen alsof de lokale bevolking geen naam had voor deze berg. Oude Tibetaanse geschriften maken echter melding van de Tibetaanse naam *Chomolungma*, wat 'Moedergodin van de wind' of 'Moedergodin van de aarde' betekent. Deze naam wordt door de Tibetanen nog altijd gebruikt. De hoogste top van de planeet, waarvan de hoogte na herberekeningen op 8848 meter (en volgens andere metingen zelfs op 8850 meter) is vastgesteld, heeft in Nepal de nieuwe naam Sagamartha (Top van de hemel).
In 1865 wordt na veel aarzeling de naam Everest officieel geaccepteerd door de Royal Geographical Society (RGS) in Londen, de prestigieuze wetenschappelijke sociëteit die sinds 1830 de meeste Britse expedities financiert en organiseert.
De eerste die het idee koestert om deze mysterieuze en gevaarlijke berg te beklimmen, is Clinton Thomas, voorzitter van de in Groot-Brittannië gevestigde *Alpine Club*. Soldaat en klimmer Francis Younghusband, die later voorzitter van de RGS zal worden, komt in 1903 dicht in de buurt van de Everest tijdens een militaire expeditie. In 1911 raakt Alexander Kellas, die is gekomen om een top van 7128 meter te overwinnen, ervan overtuigd dat de Everest niet onneembaar is en hij adviseert een beroep te doen op de diensten van de bijzonder sterke Sherpa's, die hij ontdekte tijdens zijn beklimmingen. Twee jaar later gaat een stoutmoedige kapitein van 23 jaar, John Noel, clandestien Tibet in en slaagt erin om de Everest tot op een afstand van minder dan 60 kilometer te naderen. Hij is degene die, in de nadagen van de Eerste Wereldoorlog, de RGS ervan zal overtuigen een verkenningsexpeditie naar deze berg te organiseren. De echte aanzet tot de Britse expedities is de oprichting van het gezamenlijke Everest-comité van de RGS en de Alpine Club in 1920, waarbij meespeelde dat de toenmalige Tibetaanse autoriteiten de Britten het recht hadden gegeven Tibet binnen te gaan en hun heilige berg, de *Chomolungma*, te bezoeken.

Dit vormt het begin van een lange aanloop van bijna vijfendertig jaar naar de hoogste top van de wereld. Voor de oorlog zagen de Britten zich verslagen door de Amerikanen en vervolgens door de Noren op respectievelijk de Noord- en Zuidpool. Deze keer zullen zij zich de ontdekking van de 'derde pool' niet door anderen laten ontnemen. En in 1921 kan het avontuur eindelijk beginnen.

En 1823, George Everest, «*agrimensor general*» de las Indias, funda el servicio geodésico que se encargará de elaborar una relación de las cumbres de la cadena del Himalaya. Los topógrafos británicos e indios no pueden acercarse a los territorios cerrados a los extranjeros, en particular, el Tíbet, Nepal y sus pequeños reinos vecinos de Sikkim y Bután. Por tanto, se ven obligados a realizar sus cálculos científicos de triangulación a distancias muy grandes de las cumbres que observan. Utilizan teodolitos voluminosos que precisan cada uno de ellos unos doce portadores para ser desplazados. En 1843, George Everest es reemplazado por Andrew Waugh y, unos años después, despierta su curiosidad una cumbre, oculta en la lejanía detrás del Monte Kangchenjunga que desde hace diez años pensaban que era la montaña más alta del planeta. La llamaron provisionalmente *pico B*. Desplazan el teodolito más grande a varios lugares para comparar los resultados que parecen indicar que esta cumbre es más alta que ninguna otra.
El cuartel general del servicio de geodesia se encuentra por aquel entonces en la ciudad de Dehra Dun, escondida al pie de la parte india del Himalaya. Es allí adonde llegan todas las lecturas efectuadas sobre el terreno. Mientras tanto, un adjunto del director comienza a redactar una nueva nomenclatura de las cumbres más altas del Himalaya. El pico B se convierte en el pico XV y el Kangchenjunga es conocido entonces con la apelación de pico IX.
La anécdota cuenta que un día del año 1852, el topógrafo jefe Radhanath Sikhdar entró precipitadamente en el despacho de Andrew Waugh gritando: «*¡Señor, he descubierto la montaña más alta del planeta!*». Se efectuarán cálculos trigonométricos minuciosos durante meses y años, pero el secreto no se dará a conocer al mundo entero hasta marzo de 1856: el Pico XV tiene una altitud de 8839 metros. En homenaje a su predecesor, Andrew Waugh propone llamarlo Everest, afirmando que

Sherpas, 1907-1911.
Sherpa-Träger, 1907-1911.

Sherpadragers, 1907-1911.
Culis *sherpas*, 1907-1911.

esta montaña no tiene ningún nombre local. No obstante, los antiguos escritos del Tíbet mencionan el nombre tibetano de *Chomolungma*, que según las transcripciones quiere decir «diosa madre de los vientos» o «*diosa madre del mundo*». Es el nombre que en la actualidad le siguen dando los tibetanos. En el lado nepalés, la cumbre más alta del planeta, de una altitud reevaluada de 8848 metros (e incluso 8850 según otras mediciones), lleva el nombre más reciente de *Sagamartha* («la cabeza del cielo»).

En 1865, tras muchas dudas, el nombre Everest es oficialmente aceptado por la Royal Geographical Society (RGS), de Londres la prestigiosa sociedad científica que fomenta y organiza la mayor parte de las expediciones británicas en el mundo desde 1830.

El primero en acariciar la idea de escalar esta montaña misteriosa e inquietante es Clinton Thomas, presidente del *Alpine Club*. Francis Younghusband, soldado montañero y futuro presidente de la RGS, se acerca al Everest en 1903 durante una expedición militar. En 1911, es Alexander Kellas quien, al llegar a vencer una cumbre de 7128 metros, se convence de que el Everest no es inexpugnable, y recomienda utilizar los servicios del pueblo *sherpa*, particularmente resistente, que ha descubierto durante sus ascensos. Dos años después, un temerario capitán de 23 años, John Noel, penetra clandestinamente en el Tíbet y logra acercarse a menos de 60 kilómetros del Everest. Es él quien, al día siguiente de la Gran Guerra, convence a la Royal Geographical Society de poner en marcha una misión de reconocimiento en la montaña. El verdadero arranque de las expediciones británicas podemos situarlo en 1920 con la creación de un comité conjunto del Everest, entre la RGS y el Alpine Club, tan pronto como se conoce la decisión del jovencísimo dalái lama de aquella época de conceder autorización a los británicos para penetrar en el Tíbet y acercarse a su montaña sagrada, el *Chomolungma*.

Es el inicio de una larga marcha de alrededor de treinta y cinco años hacia la cumbre más alta del mundo. Antes de la guerra, los británicos han visto cómo se les esfumaba la victoria, primero en el Polo Norte, y después en el Polo Sur, a manos de los americanos y los noruegos, respectivamente. Esta vez no es cuestión de dejar a otros la conquista del «*tercer polo*». Y en 1921, ¡por fin puede comenzar la aventura!

Sir Francis Younghusband (1863-1942).

Sir William Martin Conway (1856-1937).

Sherpas on a peak in Sikkim, photographed by Alexander Kellas, 31st December 1911. Kellas was the first to realise the exceptional capacity of the Sherpa people to live at high altitude.

Sherpas auf einem Gipfel in Sikkim, Aufnahme von Alexander Kellas, 31. Dezember 1911. Kellas erkannte als erster die außergewöhnlich große Belastbarkeit der Sherpa in großen Höhen.

Sherpa's op een piek in Sikkim gefotografeerd door Alexander Kellas op 31 december 1911. Kellas ontdekte als eerste het uitzonderlijke uithoudingsvermogen van Sherpa's op grote hoogte.

Sherpas en un pico de Sikkim fotografiados por Alexander Kellas, el 31 de diciembre de 1911. Este último fue el primero que se percató de las excepcionales capacidades de la gente *sherpa* a elevadas altitudes.

Kellas outside his tent, India, 1907-1911.

Kellas neben seinem Zelt, Indien, 1907-1911.

Kellas bij zijn tent, India, 1907-1911.

Kellas y su tienda de campaña, India, 1907-1911.

Porters preparing camp en route to the Kangchenjunga region (8,586m), border between India and Nepal, 1907-1911.

Träger bei der Vorbereitung eines Lagers auf dem Weg zum Kangchendzönga (8586 m) im Grenzgebiet zwischen Indien und Nepal, 1907-1911.

Dragers richten een kamp in onderweg naar de Kangchenjunga-regic (8586 m) bij ce grens van India en Nepal, 1907-1911.

Portadores preparando el campamento en la ruta hacia la región de Kangchenjunga (8586 m), frontera entre India y Nepal, 1907-1911.

Camping in snow high up in the Himalayas, 1907-1911.

Hochlager im Himalaya auf Schnee, 1907-1911.

Hoog Himalaya-kamp op de sneeuw, 1907-1911.

Campamento en el Alto Himalaya, 1907-1911.

 A GIANT IS BORN, IT WILL BE CALLED EVEREST! – EIN GIGANT NAMENS EVEREST IST GEBOREN!

Testing out a pulley system in a Sikkimese village, India, 1907-1911.

Testen eines Flaschenzugsystems in einem Dorf in Sikkim, Indien, 1907-1911.

Testen van een katrolsysteem in een Sikkimees dorp, India, 1907-1911.

Probando una polea en el pueblo de Sikkimese, India, 1907-1911.

Himalayan peak, Tibet, 1907-1911.

Gipfel im Himalaya, Tibet, 1907-1911.

Piek in Himalaya, Tibet, 1907-1911.

Pico del Himalaya, El Tíbet, 1907-1911.

Captain Rawling with his surveying equipment, 1903-1904.

Captain Rawling mit seinen Vermessungsgeräten, 1903-1904.

Kapitein Rawling met zijn meetapparatuur, 1903-1904.

El capitán Rawling con su equipo de topografía, 1903-1904.

Mountain camp, Tibet, 1907-1911.

Berglager, Tibet, 1907-1911.

Kamp in gebergte, Tibet, 1907-1911.

Campamento en la montaña, El Tibet, 1907-1911.

Camp with a view of Pauhunri (7,065m), Sikkim, 1907-1911.

Lager mit Blick auf den Pauhunri (7065 m), Sikkim, 1907-1911.

Kamp met uitzicht op de Pauhunri (7065 m), Sikkim, 1907-1911.

Campamento a la vista de Pauhunri (7065 m), Sikkim, 1907-1911.

The party ropes up to pass along a snowy ridge, 1907-1911.

Seilschaft an einem schneebedeckten Grat, 1907-1911.

Met touwen verbonden over een besneeuwde kam, 1907-1911.

Avanzando atados a lo largo de una cadena nevada, 1907-1911.

The Langpo Peak viewed from the South (6,954m).

Der Langpo-Gipfel von Süden aus (6954 m).

Langpo-top gezien vanaf het zuiden (6954 m).

El Pico Langpo desde el sur (6954 m).

Alexander Mitchell Kellas on a plateau amidst snowy peaks, Sikkim, 1907-1911.

Alexander Mitchell Kellas auf einem Plateau vor verschneiten Gipfeln, Sikkim, 1907-1911.

Alexander Mitchell Kellas op een plateau tussen besneeuwde toppen, Sikkim, 1907-1911.

Alexander Mitchell Kellas en una meseta en medio de picos nevados, Sikkim, 1907-1911.

Camp on the Tibetan Plateau, 1913.

Lager im Hochland von Tibet, 1913.

Kamp op het Tibetaanse plateau, 1913.

Campamento en la meseta tibetana, 1913.

Howard-Bury's camp on the Tibetan Plateau near Phari, one of the coldest and highest cities in the world (4,500m), with Chomolhari in the distance.

Howard-Burys Lager bei Phari im Hochland von Tibet, einer der kältesten und höchsten Städte der Welt (4500 m), mit dem Chomolhari im Hintergrund.

Howard-Burys kamp op het Tibetaanse plateau bij Phari, een van de koudste en hoogstgelegen nederzettingen ter wereld (4500 m), met in de verte de Chomolhari.

Campamento de Howard-Bury en la meseta tibetana, cerca de Phari, una de las ciudades más frías y más altas del mundo (4500 m), con Chomolhari a lo lejos.

Sunrise on Mount Kamet (7,756m) from near the Kharian Pass.

Sonnenaufgang am Kamet (7756 m), in der Nähe des Kharian-Passes aufgenommen.

Zonsopgang op de Kamet (7756 m) gezien van bij de Kharian-pas.

Amanecer en el Monte Kamet (7756 m) desde cerca del Paso Kharian.

Group including Captain Noel, 1913.

Gruppenfoto mit Captain Noel, 1913.

Expeditieleden met kapitein Noel, 1913.

Grupo con el capitán Noel, 1913.

A precarious bamboo bridge crossing during Captain Noel's expedition, 1913.

Eine bedenklich instabil wirkende Brücke aus Bambus, aufgenommen während Captain Noels Expedition, 1913.

Gevaarlijke oversteek via een bamboebrug tijdens de expeditie van kapitein Noel, 1913.

Cruce sobre un precario puente de bambú durante la expedición del capitán Noel, 1913.

Two expedition members examine a crevasse, 1913.

Zwei Expeditionsteilnehmer bei der Untersuchung einer Gletscherspalte, 1913.

Twee expeditieleden onderzoeken een spleet, 1913.

Dos miembros de la expedición examinan una grieta, 1913.

The Potala photographed by Captain Rawling, 1904.

Der Potala-Palast, Aufnahme von Captain Rawling, 1904.

De Potala gefotografeerd door kapitein Rawling, 1904.

El Potala fotografiado por el capitán Rawling, 1904.

Camp on Chomiomo (6,829m), 1907-1911.

Lager auf dem Chomiomo (6829 m), 1907-1911.

Kamp op de Chomiomo (6829 m), 1907-1911.

Campamento en Chomiomo (6829 m), 1907-1911.

Camp beneath rocky peaks to the west of the Khariam glacier, Gahrwal, 1907-1911.

Lager unterhalb von Felsgipfeln westlich vom Khariam-Gletscher, Garhwal, 1907-1911.

Kamp onder rotspieken ten westen van de Khariam-gletsjer, Gahrwal, 1907-1911.

Campamento bajo los picos de una roca al oeste del glaciar Khariam, Gahrwal, 1907-1911.

Village children, Sikkim, 1907-1911.

Kinder in der Nähe eines Dorfs, Sikkim, 1907-1911.

Dorpskinderen, Sikkim, 1907-1911.

Niños del pueblo, Sikkim, 1907-1911.

Dzongpen at Kampa, Tibet, 1913.

Dzongpen am Kampa-Pass, Tibet, 1913.

Dzongpen in Kampa, Tibet, 1913.

Dzongpenn en Kampa, El Tibet, 1913.

Pauhunri (7,126m), photographed by Alexander Kellas, 1907-1911.

Pauhunri (7126 m), Aufnahme von Alexander Kellas, 1907-1911.

De Pauhunri (7126 m) gefotografeerd door Alexander Kellas, 1907-1911.

Pauhunri (7126 m) fotografiado por Alexander Kellas, 1907-1911.

1921

The Pioneers of Everest
Die Pioniere des Everest

Shortly before Christmas 1920, the British, who are on good terms with the Tibetan authorities, receive authorisation to carry out an initial reconnaissance expedition, leaving from Tibet. The Everest dream starts to take shape. This mission is entrusted to Lieutenant-Colonel Charles Howard-Bury, a renowned Irish mountaineer. He chooses for his team a 53-year-old Scot, Alexander Kellas, who, before the war, was first to discover the extraordinary capacity of the Sherpa people to carry heavy loads at very high altitude. Three other climbers join him: a second Scot, Harold Raeburn, who will lead the ascents, and two of the best of the new generation of alpinists, Guy Bullock and, above all, George Mallory, 35 years old, a climbing virtuoso. To complete the expedition, which is ready to leave Darjeeling, Sikkim, in May 1921, the team also includes a geologist, a botanist, a renowned mountaineer doctor and, finally, a cartographer. This group of pioneers will start off with a cohort of Nepalese Sherpas and around a hundred mules, to be replaced later on with a herd of yaks. The long column will cover close to 500 kilometres in five weeks, travelling across Sikkim and then the Tibetan plateau.
On 6 June, at an altitude of 5,250 metres and very close to the majestic fort of Kampa Dzong, Alexander Kellas dies of a heart attack. His friends dig a makeshift tomb for him on the side of the mountain. And there, for the first time, Everest heaves into view in a gap in the clouds. Harold Raeburn will shortly abandon the mission in his turn and return to Sikkim with the group's doctor. For weeks, George Mallory and his teammate Guy Bullock try one path after another, before climbing the immense Rongbuk glacier that descends on both sides of the ridges of the northern face of Everest. At the end of June they establish their base camp at more than 5,000 metres altitude near the Rongbuk monastery, which is inhabited by around twenty lamas. The surface of the glacier is a tempestuous sea of seracs and crevasses. The two British alpinists have with them sixteen porters led by a Sirdar. They teach their men to use ropes and ice axes. At 5,900 metres the two climbers spy the North Col, below Everest. Their instinct tells them that this is the best way to the summit. But how to meet up with this famous col? They then make a fatal interpretative error, which will make them lose further precious weeks: a spur of ice from the Rongbuk glacier that they thought ran straight actually bends sharply, distancing them from their goal.
For their part, the other members of the group spend weeks mapping out the area, which will significantly help the two alpinists, Mallory and Bullock, to realise where they went wrong. Despite the weather deteriorating, they very quickly start researching anew to find the access route to the North Col. The ascent is planned for the end of the monsoon. On 20 September 1921, with fourteen Sherpas, the two young Britons begin the climb up to the col. By 23 September the little column is in a bad state. The previous night the temperatures dropped to -34°C and the wind nearly destroyed the camp! In the morning several Sherpas are unable to continue. On 24 September Mallory and Bullock leave again with three Sherpas who break a trail. The small group arrives at its goal before midday. From the North Col the ascent to the summit of Everest seems feasible to them, but they are out of breath. The two men descend again, their mission is complete. This time there is no debate: the path to the highest summit in the world is open.

Kurz vor Weihnachten 1920 wird den Briten, die gute Beziehungen zum Dalai Lama unterhalten, die Genehmigung erteilt, eine erste Erkundungsexpedition von Tibet aus zu starten. Der Traum, den Mount Everest zu erzwingen, nimmt erste Formen an. Zum Leiter dieser Expedition wird Lieutenant-Colonel Charles Howard-Bury ernannt, ein namhafter irischer Bergsteiger. Er nimmt den 53-jährigen Schotten Alexander Kellas in sein Expeditionsteam auf. Er hatte, als erster, noch vor dem Ersten Weltkrieg, die außergewöhnliche Fähigkeit des Sherpa-Volkes, um in sehr großen Höhen schwere Lasten zu tragen, entdeckt. Außer Kellas gehören Howard-Burys Gruppe drei weitere Bergsteiger an: ein zweiter Schotte, Harold Raeburn, als Leiter der Besteigungsversuche und zwei der besten Bergsteiger der neuen Generation, Guy Bullock und natürlich der 35-jährige Klettervirtuose, George Mallory. Weitere Teilnehmer der Expedition, die sich im Mai 1921 bereit machen, Darjeeling im indischen Staat Sikkim zu verlassen, sind ein Geologe, ein Botaniker, ein Mediziner, der sich auch als Bergsteiger einen Namen gemacht hat, und ein Kartograf. Diese Gruppe Pioniere setzt sich mit einer Kohorte nepalesischer Sherpas und rund hundert Maultieren, die später durch eine Herde Yaks ersetzt werden, in Bewegung. Die lange Kolonne legt innerhalb fünf Wochen fast fünfhundert Kilometer zurück und durchquert zunächst Sikkim und anschließend die tibetische Hochebene.
Am 6. Juni erleidet Alexander Kellas bei der Durchquerung eines Engpasses auf 5.250 Metern Höhe, nahe der majestätischen Festung Kampa

De pioniers van de Everest
Los exploradores del Everest

Dzong, einen Herzanfall und stirbt. Seine Freunde bereiten ihm am Berghang ein notdürftiges Grab. Und dann, zum ersten Mal, als die Wolkendecke aufbricht, können sie einen Blick auf den Mount Everest erhaschen. Auch Harold Raeburn muss bald aufgeben und kehrt mit dem Arzt der Gruppe nach Sikkim zurück. Während der folgenden Wochen probieren George Mallory und sein Teamgefährte Guy Bullock unablässig eine Route nach der anderen aus, bevor sie schließlich den gewaltigen Rongpu-Gletscher besteigen, der sich auf beiden Seiten des Grats von der Nordwand des Mount Everest erstreckt. Ende Juni schlagen sie ihr Basislager auf mehr als 5.000 Metern Höhe, in der Nähe des Rongpu-Klosters auf, wo damals etwa zwanzig Lamas lebten. Die Oberfläche des Gletschers ist ein bizarres, chaotisches Meer aus Eiszacken und Gletscherspalten. Die beiden britischen Bergsteiger werden von sechzehn Trägern begleitet, von einem Sirdar angeführt, und lehren ihnen Seile und Eispickel zu gebrauchen. Auf 5.900 Metern Höhe erblicken sie den Nordpass des Mount Everest und erahnen, dass dies der Weg ist, der zum Gipfel führt. Doch wie können sie diesen Pass erreichen? Beim Versuch, diese Frage zu beantworten, unterläuft ihnen eine fatale Fehleinschätzung, die ihnen weitere kostbare Wochen Zeit kostet: Eine Zunge des Rongpu-Gletschers, die ihrer Ansicht nach geradlinig verläuft, macht in Wirklichkeit einen abrupten Knick und führt sie von ihrem Ziel fort.
Die übrigen Mitglieder der Gruppe haben seit Wochen die Gegend kartografiert. Ihre Arbeit trägt in erheblichem Maße dazu bei, dass die beiden Bergsteiger Mallory und Bullock ihre Fehler erkennen. Rasch unternehmen sie trotz der sich verschlechternden Wetterlage neue Vorstöße und finden schließlich den Zugang zum Nordpass. Die Besteigung ist für das Ende des Monsun vorgesehen. Am 20. September 1921 brechen die beiden jungen Briten mit vierzehn Sherpas Richtung Nordpass auf. Schon am 23. hat sich der Zustand der kleinen Kolonne verschlechtert. In der vorhergehenden Nacht war die Temperatur bis auf -34°C gesunken, und der Wind hätte zudem fast das Lager hinweg geblasen. Am Morgen fühlen sich viele der Sherpas außerstande, weiter aufzusteigen. Am 24. September wagen Mallory und Bullock mit drei Sherpas, die die Spur weisen, einen erneuten Versuch. Noch vor dem Mittag erreicht die kleine Truppe ihr Ziel. Vom Nordpass aus scheint ihnen die Besteigung des Mount Everest möglich, aber, sie geraten außer Atem. Die beiden Männer steigen wieder ab, ihre Mission ist abgeschlossen: Diesmal gibt es keinen Zweifel, der Weg zum höchsten Gipfel der Welt steht offen.

Vlak voor Kerstmis 1920 kregen de Britten, die goede betrekkingen onderhielden met de lokale autoriteiten, toestemming voor een eerste verkenningsexpeditie vanuit Tibet. Hiermee nam de Everest-droom concrete vorm aan. De missie wordt toevertrouwd aan luitenant-kolonel Charles Howard-Bury, een gerenommeerde Ierse bergbeklimmer. In zijn team neemt hij Alexander Kellas op, een Schot van 53 jaar, die als eerste, voor de oorlog, tot de ontdekking kwam dat de Sherpa's bijzonder geschikt zijn om zware vracht op grote hoogte te dragen. Naast hem kiest hij nog drie andere klimmers: een tweede Schot, Harold Raeburn, die de beklimmingen zou leiden, en twee van de beste alpinisten van de nieuwe generatie, Guy Bullock en de 35-jarige virtuoze bergbeklimmer George Mallory. Een geoloog, een botanist, een bekwame arts en een cartograaf completeren het team, waarna de expeditie in mei 1921 kon vertrekken vanuit Darjeeling in Sikkim. Deze pioniers beginnen aan de tocht met een groep Nepalese Sherpa's en een honderdtal ezels die later zouden worden vervangen door jaks. De lange colonne zal ongeveer 500 kilometer afleggen in vijf weken, trekkend door de Sikkim en vervolgens over het Tibetaanse plateau.
Op 6 juni, bij de doortocht van een engte op 5250 meter hoogte in de buurt van het majestueuze fort Kampa Dzong, overlijdt Alexander Kellas aan een hartaanval. Zijn vrienden begraven hem eervol op de berghelling. Daar zien ze voor het eerst de Everest tussen de wolken opdoemen. Harold Raeburn verlaat al snel de expeditie. Hij moet terugkeren naar Sikkim met de arts van de groep. In de weken die volgen doen George Mallory en zijn teammaat Guy Bullock diverse verwoede pogingen alvorens daadwerkelijk de immense Rongbuk-gletsjer te beklimmen, die door verschillende sleuven aan de noordzijde van de Everest omlaaggglijdt. Eind juni, op meer dan 5000 meter hoogte zetten zij hun basiskamp op, vlak bij het klooster van Rongbuk, waar circa twintig lama's leven. Het gletsjeroppervlak is een verraderlijk meer van ijsverheffingen en sleuven. De twee Britse alpinisten laten zich vergezellen door dertien dragers onder aanvoering van een sirdar. Zij worden verder begeleid door mannen die touwen en pikhouwelen aanreiken. Op 5900 meter hoogte nemen de twee de noordelijke bergpas waar, verzonken in de Everest. Gevoelsmatig gaan ze ervan uit dat dit het punt is waarlangs de top kan worden bereikt. Maar hoe bereiken ze deze fameuze pas? Ze maken vervolgens een kapitale inschattingsfout en verliezen opnieuw kostbare weken: een gletsjertong van

Rongbuk die zij recht achtten, maakt in werkelijkheid een scherpe bocht en leidt hen weg van het doel.
De andere leden van de groep hebben op hun beurt wekenlang de omgeving in kaart gebracht, waardoor Mallory en Bullock meer zicht krijgen op hun vergissingen. Al zeer snel, ondanks het verslechterende weer, ondernemen zij nieuwe zoektochten naar de doorgang via de noordelijke pas. De afdaling staat gepland voor het einde van de moesson. Op 20 september 1921 beginnen de twee jonge Britten met veertig Sherpa's aan de klim naar de pas. Enkele dagen later, op 23 september, is de kleine colonne er slecht aan toe. De voorgaande nacht vroor het 34 graden en de stormachtige wind verwoestte het kamp volledig. Die ochtend zijn veel Sherpa's niet in staat verder te gaan. Op 24 september gaan Mallory en Bullock weer op pad met drie Sherpa's als gids. Voor de middag bereikt de kleine groep het doel. Via de noordelijke pas lijkt de klim naar de top van de Everest haalbaar, maar ze zijn uitgeput. De twee mannen dalen weer af, hun missie is voltooid: de poort naar de hoogste top van de wereld staat open.

Justo antes de la Navidad de 1920, los británicos que tienen buenas relaciones con el dalái lama reciben la autorización para realizar una primera expedición de reconocimiento con salida desde el Tíbet. El sueño del Everest comienza a tomar forma. Se encarga esta misión al teniente coronel Charles Howard-Bury, montañero irlandés de renombre. Para formar parte de su equipo elige a un escocés de 53 años, Alexander Kellas, que es el primero en descubrir, antes de la guerra, la extraordinaria capacidad del pueblo *sherpa* de llevar cargas pesadas a una altitud muy elevada. Junto con él, otros tres escaladores: un segundo escocés, Harold Raeburn, que dirige los ascensos, y dos de los mejores alpinistas de la nueva generación, Guy Bullock y especialmente George Mallory, de 35 años, virtuoso de la escalada. Para completar la expedición, preparada para salir de Darjeeling, en Sikkim, en este mes de mayo de 1921: un geólogo, un botánico, un prestigioso médico montañero y, por último, un cartógrafo. Este grupo de pioneros se pone en marcha con una cohorte de *sherpas* nepaleses y un centenar de mulas sustituidas posteriormente por manadas de yaks. La larga columna recorre cerca de 500 kilómetros en cinco semanas, atravesando primeramente el Sikkim y después la meseta tibetana.
El 6 de junio, en el paso de un desfiladero de 5250 metros de altitud, muy cerca del majestuoso fuerte de Kampa Dzong, Alexander Kellas muere a causa de un infarto. Sus amigos cavan una tumba improvisada en el flanco de la montaña. Y allí, por primera vez, el Everest aparece ante ellos en un claro que se abre entre las nubes. A su vez, Harold Raeburn abandona pronto y debe volver al Sikkim con el médico del grupo. Durante varias semanas, George Mallory y su compañero de equipo, Guy Bullock, prueban sin descanso una vía tras otra antes de volver a escalar el inmenso glaciar de Rongbuk que baja por un lado y por el otro de las crestas de la cara norte del Everest. A finales del mes de junio, establecen su campamento base a más de 5000 metros de altitud, cerca del monasterio de Rongbuk, donde viven unos veinte lamas. La superficie del glaciar es un mar caótico de seracs y grietas. Los dos alpinistas británicos van acompañados de dieciséis portadores dirigidos por un Sirdar. Enseñan a sus hombres a utilizar cuerdas y piolets. A 5900 metros, los dos escaladores divisan el Collado Norte, a un nivel inferior del Everest. Tienen la intuición de que es por allí por donde hay que pasar para alcanzar la cima. ¿Pero cómo llegar a este famoso collado? Es entonces cuando cometen un error fatal de interpretación, que les hace perder unas cuantas semanas preciosas: una lengua del glaciar de Rongbuk, que pensaban que era rectilínea, forma, en realidad, un codo brusco y los aleja de la meta.
Por su parte, los otros miembros del grupo han trazado desde hace semanas la cartografía de los lugares, lo que ayudará considerablemente a los dos alpinistas Mallory y Bullock a reconocer sus errores. Muy pronto, y pese a que el tiempo empeora, emprenden nuevas búsquedas para encontrar por fin la vía de acceso al Collado Norte. El ascenso está previsto para finales del monzón. El 20 de septiembre de 1921, con catorce *sherpas*, los dos jóvenes británicos culminan el ascenso hacia el collado. El 23, la pequeña columna se encuentra maltrecha. La noche anterior, la temperatura ha sido de -34 °C y el viento ha estado a punto de echar abajo el campamento. Y por la mañana, varios *sherpas* no son capaces de avanzar. El 24 de septiembre, Mallory y Bullock vuelven a partir con tres sherpas que siguen el rastro. Antes del mediodía, la pequeña tropa llega a su destino. Desde el Collado Norte, el ascenso hasta la cima del Everest les parece factible, pero están sin aliento. Los dos hombres vuelven a descender, su misión ha terminado: esta vez es la definitiva, la vía hacia la cumbre más alta del mundo está abierta.

Map showing exploration of the Everest region, including the point reached by John Noel in 1913 (64 km from Mount Everest) and the planned itinerary for the 1921 expedition.

Karte des Mount Everest-Gebiets mit einer Darstellung der unternommenen Erkundungsversuche, einschließlich des 1913 von John Noel erreichten Punkts (64 km entfernt vom Mount Everest) und der für 1921 vorgesehenen Route.

Omgevingskaart van de Everest met het punt dat John Noel in 1913 bereikte (op ruim 64 kilometer afstand van de Everest) en de geplande route voor de expeditie in 1921.

Mapa que muestra la exploración de la región del Everest, incluyendo el punto alcanzado por John Noel en 1913 (a 64 km del Monte Everest) y el itinerario planificado para la expedición de 1921.

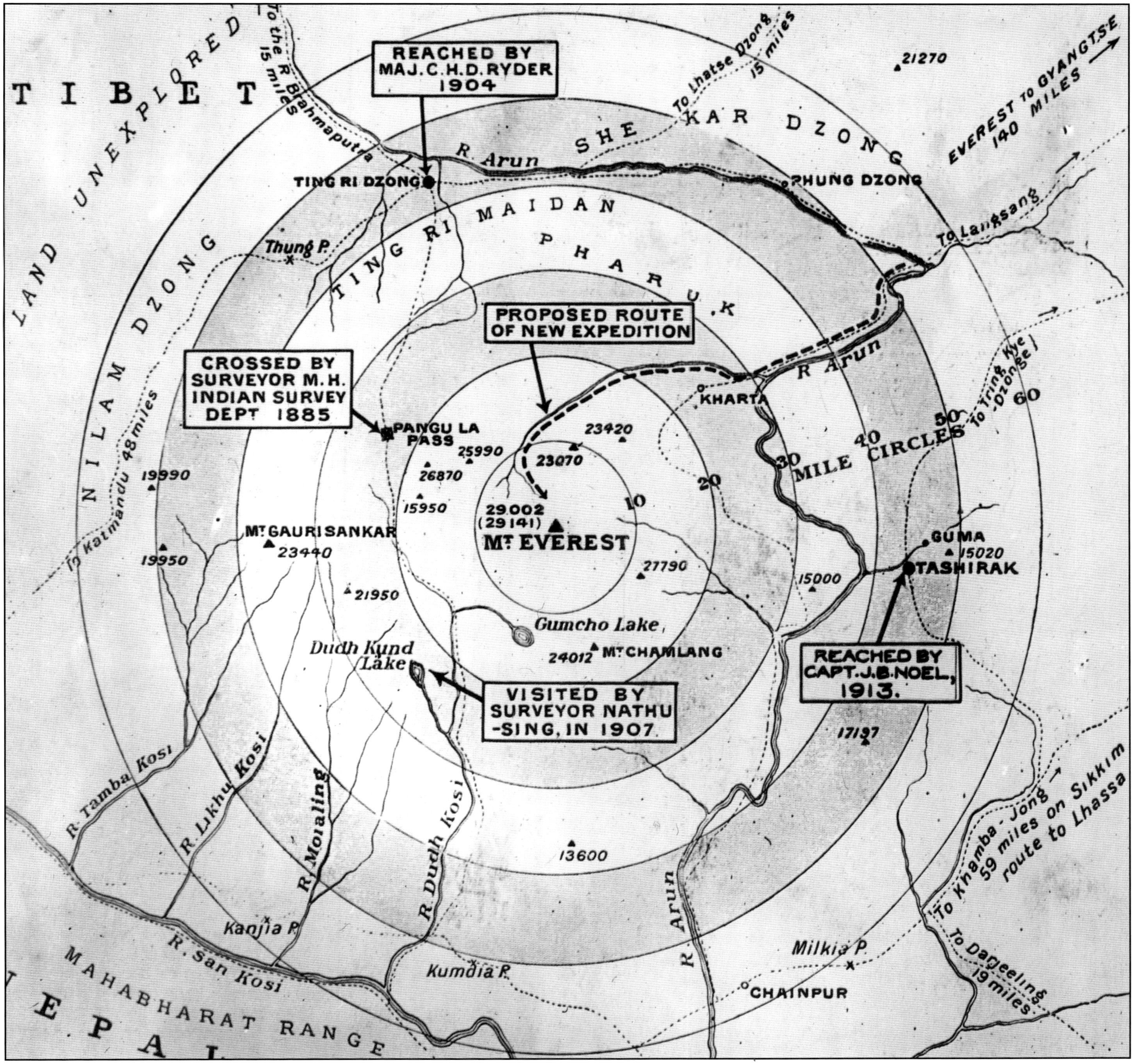
TIBET
LAND UNEXPLORED
To the R. Brahmaputra 15 miles
REACHED BY MAJ. C. H. D. RYDER 1904
To Lhatse Dzong 15 miles
21270
EVEREST TO GYANGTSE 140 MILES
SHE KAR DZONG
R. Arun
TING RI DZONG
PHUNG DZONG
TING RI MAIDAN
To Langsang
Thung P.
NILAM DZONG
TING RI
PHARUK
PROPOSED ROUTE OF NEW EXPEDITION
CROSSED BY SURVEYOR M. H. INDIAN SURVEY DEPT 1885
KHARTA
PANGU LA PASS
23420
25990
23070
26870
MILE CIRCLES
10
20
30
40
50
60
To Trink Kye Dzonge
To Katmandu 48 miles
19990
15950
29002 (29141)
Mt. EVEREST
Mt. GAURISANKAR
23440
GUMA
15020
TASHIRAK
19950
27790
15000
21950
Gumcho Lake
Dudh Kund Lake
24012
Mt. CHAMLANG
REACHED BY CAPT. J. B. NOEL, 1913.
VISITED BY SURVEYOR NATHU-SING, IN 1907
17197
R. Tamba Kosi
R. Likhu Kosi
R. Moraling
R. Dudh Kosi
To Khamba-Jong 59 miles on Sikkim route to Lhassa
13600
R. Arun
Kanjia P.
R. San Kosi
Milkia P.
To Dargeeling 19 miles
Kumdia P.
CHAINPUR
MAHABHARAT RANGE
NEPAL

Tibetan women.

Tibetaanse vrouwen.

Tibeterin.

Mujeres tibetanas.

Admiring group of Tibetans at Lingga.

Tibetaanse bewonderaars in Lingga.

Eine Gruppe tibetischer Bewunderer bei Lingga.

Grupo admirado de tibetanos en Lingga.

Bales of wool coming down through Sikkim from Tibet.

Wollballen aus Tibet beim Transport durch Sikkim.

Balen wol uit Tibet worden via Sikkim getransporteerd.

Fardos de lana bajando a través de Sikkim desde El Tibet.

Loading yaks.

Beladen von Yaks.

Beladen jaks.

Cargando los yaks.

Pack animals.

Packtiere.

Lastdieren.

Bestias de carga.

The Lamas of the Kharta Monastery (Gandenchofel Monastery).

Die Lamas des Kharta-Klosters (Gandenchofel-Kloster).

De monniken van het Kharta-klooster (Gandenchofel-klooster).

Los lamas del Monasterio Kharta (Monasterio Gandenchofel).

Interpreters Gyalzen Kazi (left) and Chittan Wangdi (right).

De tolken Gyalzen Kazi (links) en Chittan Wangdi (rechts).

Die Dolmetscher Gyalzen Kazi (links) und Chittan Wangdi (rechts).

Los intérpretes Gyalzen Kazi (a la izquierda) y Chittan Wangdi (a la derecha).

The Dzongpen of Kharta and his wife.

De Dzong Pen van Kharta met zijn vrouw.

Der Dzongpen von Kharta und seine Ehefrau.

El Dzongpen de Kharta y su esposa.

Khampa Dzong.

The battlements at Kampa Dzong.

Vestingmuren van Kampa Dzong.

Die Festungsmauern von Kampa Dzong.

Las almenas en Kampa Dzong.

Dr A.M. Kellas, who died during the expedition.

Dokter A.M. Kellas, die omkwam tijdens de expeditie.

Dr. Alexander M. Kellas, der während der Expedition verstarb.

El Dr. A.M. Kellas, que murió durante la expedición.

Headstone for Dr Kellas' grave at Kampa Dzong, 30th October 1921.

Dokter Kellas' stenen graf in Kampa Dzong, 30 oktober 1921.

Grabstein für Dr. Kellas bei Kampa Dzong, 30. Oktober 1921.

La lápida de la tumba del Dr. Kellas en Kampa Dzong, el 30 de octubre de 1921.

Camera belonging to Alexander F. R. Wollaston and taken on the 1921 Mount Everest Expedition. It was used to take photographs at an altitude of 6,820m.

Alexander F. R. Wollastons camera, gebruikt tijdens de expeditie van 1921. Er zijn foto's mee gemaakt op 6820 meter hoogte.

Alexander F. R. Wollastons Kamera, mit der während der Mount Everest-Expedition von 1921 Aufnahmen auf einer Höhe von 6.820 m gelangen.

La cámara de Alexander F. R. Wollaston utilizada durante la expedición de 1921 al Monte Everest. Tomó fotografías a una altitud de 6820 m.

The Alpine Club leaving Phari.
Guy Bullock and George Mallory riding mules.

Mitglieder des Alpine Clubs verlassen Phari. Guy Bullock und George Mallory auf dem Rücken von Maultieren.

De Alpine Club verlaat Phari.
Guy Bullock en George Mallory op ezels.

El Alpine Club saliendo de Phari.
Guy Bullock y George Mallory a lomos de las mulas.

Descending from Carpo-Ri at the head of Kama Valley.

Abstieg vom Carpo-Ri im oberen Teil des Kama-Tals.

Afdaling van de Carpo-Ri aan het begin van de Kama-vallei.

Descendiendo desde Carpo-Ri en la punta del Valle Kama.

A team member in the foreground, with Mount Everest (East side) in the distance.

Ein Expeditionsteilnehmer im Vordergrund, der Mount Everest (Ostseite) im Hintergrund.

Een teamlid op de voorgrond en de Everest (oostzijde) op de achtergrond.

Un miembro del equipo en primer plano, con el Monte Everest (lado este) a lo lejos.

Taking a nap in a mountain landscape.

Ein Nickerchen in der Berglandschaft.

Een dutje doen in een berglandschap.

Echando una siesta con un paisaje de montaña.

Summit of Mount Everest from the north-east, photograph taken with a telephoto lens.

Gipfel des Mount Everest von Nordosten gesehen (Telefotografie)

Top van de Everest, gezien vanuit het noordoosten, met telelens.

Cumbre del Monte Everest desde el noreste, telefotografía.

Resting at the base of an ice pinnacle.

Pauze aan de voet van een ijspiek.

Rast am Fuße eines Eisturms.

Descansando en la base de una cumbre helada.

George Mallory descending a rocky ridge.

George Mallory, afdalend van een rotsrichel.

George Mallory beim Abstieg von einem Felsgrat.

George Mallory descendiendo por una cadena rocosa.

Members of the 1921 Everest Expedition at the Camp at 5,273 m (from left to right): Bullock, Morshead, Wheeler and Mallory (back row); Heron, Wollaston, Howard-Bury and Raeburn (front row). Kellas was missing, due to his having died along the way.

Mitglieder der Mount Everest-Expedition von 1921 im Lager auf 5273 m Höhe (von links nach rechts): Bullock, Morshead, Wheeler und Mallory (hintere Reihe), Heron, Wollaston, Howard-Bury und Raeburn (vordere Reihe). Kellas fehlt, weil er auf dem Weg gestorben war.

Deelnemers aan de Everest-expeditie van 1921 in een kamp op 5273 meter hoogte (v.l.n.r.): Bullock, Morshead, Wheeler en Mallory (achter); Heron, Wollaston, Howard-Bury en Raeburn (voor). Kellas ontbreekt omdat hij onderweg was omgekomen.

Miembros de la expedición de 1921 al Everest en el campamento a 5273 m (de izquierda a derecha): Bullock, Morshead, Wheeler y Mallory (fila trasera); Heron, Wollaston, Howard-Bury y Raeburn (fila delantera). Kellas no aparece porque murió en el camino.

Major Wheeler's Photographic Survey Party.

Major Wheeler und Helfer bei fotografischen Geländeaufnahmen.

Het fotografische onderzoeksteam van majoor Wheeler.

Grupo de topografía fotográfica del mayor Wheeler.

Guy Bullock and Sherpas wearing snowshoes for the first time.

Guy Bullock und einige Träger haben zum ersten Mal Schneeschuhe angelegt.

Guy Bullock met dragers die voor het eerst sneeuwschoenen dragen.

Guy Bullock y culis con raquetas de nieve por primera vez.

Rongbuk Glacier and Mount Everest in the distance.

Der Rongpu-Gletscher mit dem Mount Everest im Hintergrund.

Rongbuk-gletsjer en de Everest op de achtergrond.

El Glaciar Rongbuk y el Monte Everest a lo lejos.

Looking North from an altitude of 5,200m. Base camp, Kharta Valley.

Blick nach Norden vom Basislager auf 5200 m Höhe, Kharta-Tal.

Uitzicht op het noorden vanaf het basiskamp op 5200 meter hoogte, Kharta-vallei.

Mirando al norte desde 5200 m. Campamento base, valle Kharta.

Sherpas climbing along a rocky ridge.

Träger beim Klettern an einem Felsgrat.

Dragers klimmend langs de rotsen.

Culis escalando una cadena rocosa.

Major Morshead and Gujjar Singh using the plane tabling method at 5,180m.

Major Morshead und Gujjar Singh am Messtisch auf 5180 m Höhe.

Majoor Morshead en Gujjar Singh voeren driehoeksmetingen uit op 5180 meter hoogte.

El mayor Morshead y Gujjar realizando mediciones con la plancheta a (5180 m).

Camp at 6,100m. Everest, with its wind-ravaged summit, is in the distance.

Lager auf 6100 m Höhe, Mount Everest im Hintergrund mit Wind auf dem Gipfel.

Kamp op 6100 meter hoogte. De Everest bestookt door wind op de achtergrond.

Campamento a 6100 m. El Everest en la lejanía, con viento en la cumbre.

Camp at 6,100m, with Everest in the distance.

Lager auf 6100 m Höhe, Mount Everest im Hintergrund.

Kamp op 6100 meter hoogte met de Everest op de achtergrond.

Everest vu du camp situé à 6 100 mètres d'altitude.

Camp at 6,100m in cloudy weather after snowfall.

Lager auf 6100 m Höhe bei trübem Wetter nach Schneefall.

Kamp op 6100 meter hoogte in bewolkt weer na een sneeuwbui.

Campamento a 6100 m con tiempo nuboso tras la caída de nieve.

Mount Everest with the North Peak and Col visible.

Mount Everest, Blick auf Nordgipfel und Nordsattel.

De noordelijke piek en pas van de Everest.

El Monte Everest mostrando el Collado y Pico Norte.

View of the advanced base camp at 6,490m.

Blick auf das vorgeschobene Basislager auf 6490 m Höhe.

Zicht vanaf het gevorderde basiskamp op 6490 meter hoogte.

Vista del campamento base avanzado a 6490 m.

Windy Col Camp 7,000m, looking east.

Lager am windigen Sattel (7000 m), Blick nach Osten.

Kamp in de Lhakpa La (windpas) op ongeveer 7000 meter hoogte met uitzicht op het oosten.

Campamento en el Collado Ventoso (7000 m), mirando al este.

Climbing party.

Bergsteigergruppe.

Klimploeg.

Grupo en ascenso.

Summit of Everest and the North Col from Lhakpa La (Windy Col).

Gipfel des Mount Everest und Nordsattel vom Lhakpa La (Windiger Pass) aus gesehen.

Top van de Everest en de noordelijke pas,gezien vanaf de Lhakpa La (windpas).

Cumbre del Everest y Collado Norte desde Lhakpa La (Collado Ventoso).

Storm on Everest, seen from Lhakpa La (Windy Col).

Sturm auf dem Mount Everest, aufgenommen vom Lhakpa La (Windiger Gipfel).

Storm op de Everest, gezien vanaf de Lhakpa La (windpas).

Tormenta en el Everest, vista desde Lhakpa La (Collado Ventoso).

Published by the Royal Geographical Society

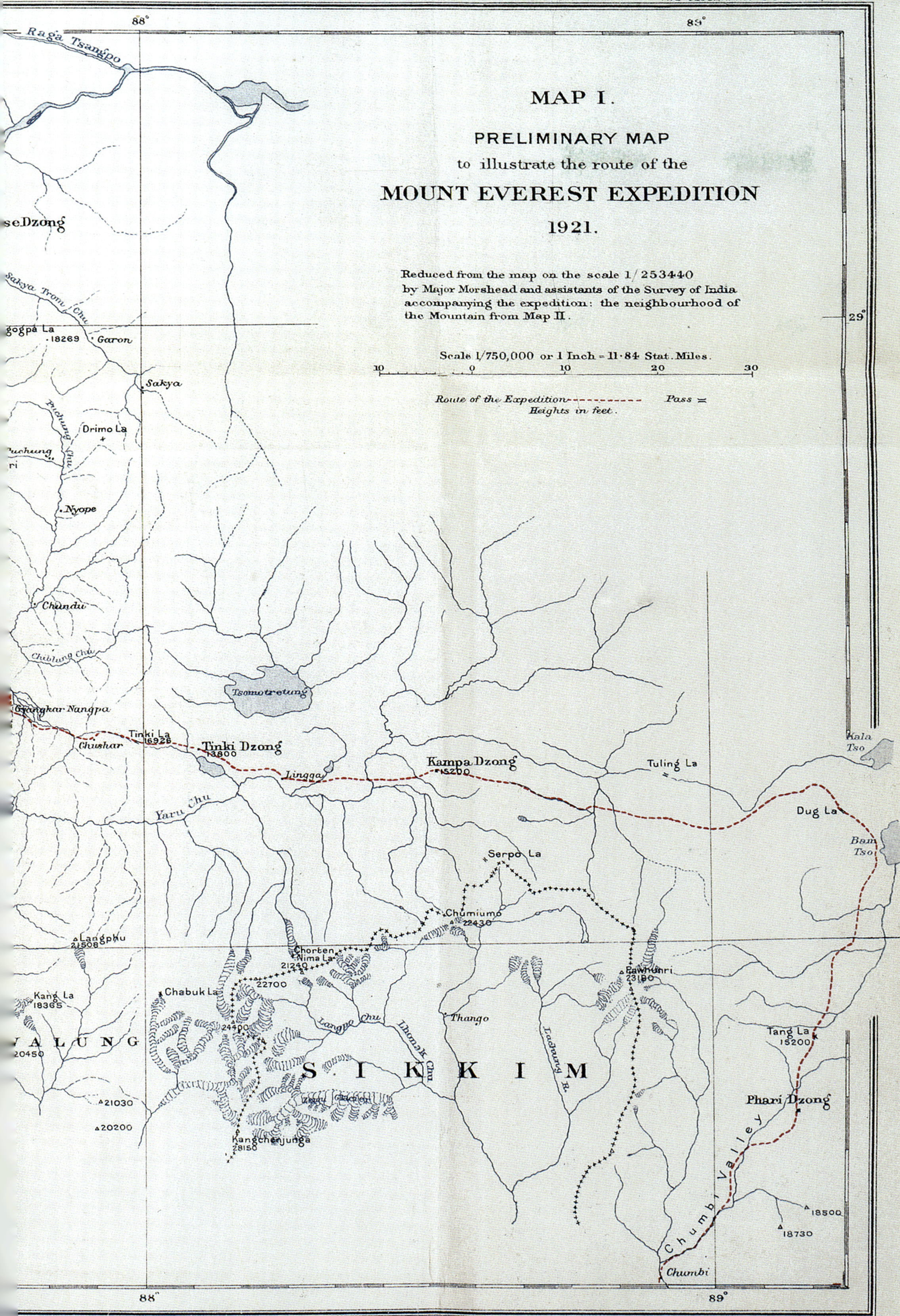
MAP I.
PRELIMINARY MAP
to illustrate the route of the
MOUNT EVEREST EXPEDITION
1921.
Reduced from the map on the scale 1/253440
by Major Morshead and assistants of the Survey of India
accompanying the expedition: the neighbourhood of
the Mountain from Map II.
Scale 1/750,000 or 1 Inch = 11·84 Stat. Miles.
10 0 10 20 30
Route of the Expedition
Pass
Heights in feet.
88°
89°
29°
28°
Raga Tsangpo
se Dzong
Sakya Trom Chu
gogpa La
18269
Garon
Sakya
Drimo La
Nyope
Chandu
Chiblung Chu
Tsomotretung
Gyangkar Nangpa
Tinki La
16926
Chushar
Tinki Dzong
13800
Lingga
Yaru Chu
Kampa Dzong
15200
Tuling La
Kala Tso
Dug La
Bam Tso
Serpo La
Chumiumo
22430
Langphu
21508
Chorten Nima La
21240
22700
Chabuk La
Kang La
18365
24400
Langpo Chu
Lhonak Chu
Thango
Lachung R.
Pawhunri
23180
Tang La
15200
S I K K I M
Phari Dzong
Chumbi Valley
20450
21030
20200
Kangchenjunga
28150
18500
18730
Chumbi

1922

First Exploits, First Victims

Erste Besteigungsversuche, erste Opfer

George Mallory, the hero of the 1921 expedition, recommences the following year, determined this time to conquer Everest. The man who is leading this mission is Charles Bruce, a dashing general who has travelled the Himalayas for thirty years. With him he takes seasoned mountaineers, among whom there are doctors and a military photographer. There is also his grand-nephew, Geoffrey Bruce, and a certain George Finch, an Australian chemist living in Switzerland, one of the best Alpinists of the age. Contrary to George Mallory, he is convinced that Everest cannot be conquered without oxygen breathing apparatus. It is he who will explain to each member of the party the workings of this very cumbersome equipment, composed of four steel cylinders and weighing close to 15 kilograms.
On 30 April 1922 the expedition arrives in the vicinity of the Rongbuk glacier. The route, which passes by the North Col at 7,000 metres, is the one that was found the previous year. On 19 May, George Mallory, Dr Somervell and two other alpinists launch an initial attack on Everest, without oxygen masks, assisted by nine porters. They suffer from the cold and experience difficulty breathing, but succeed in reaching more than 7,600 metres in order to spend the night there installed above an imposing sheer drop. The following day they are delayed by the snow that has fallen thickly and, at 8,200 metres of altitude, are forced to turn back. They nearly kill themselves on the descent.
George Finch is determined to try his luck too, but this time by taking oxygen equipment. He starts off on the morning of 24 May, accompanied by the young Bruce and a Gurkha lance-corporal. The glacial wind gathers pace during the day and turns into a raging storm as night falls. For eighteen hours straight the Alpinists in distress remain standing in order to keep hold of the tent, which the gusts of wind threaten to blow away.
Loaded up like mules, the men leave early in the morning. Suddenly Bruce cries out, he has no more oxygen. Finch catches hold of him just before he can topple over into the abyss. He jams his own mask over Bruce's mouth and repairs the apparatus. The alpinists continue forward a little further but, reaching 8,320 metres – a new record – they are forced to declare themselves beaten.
Mallory, Dr Somervell and the survivors of the first attempt have had fifteen days in which to recover from their fatigue and are ready to launch a new attack, despite the imminent bad weather. Finch wants to be part of the party too, but he cannot follow for long. The situation is worrying, it has snowed heavily on the slopes of Everest and this is an early warning sign of the monsoon. On 7 June the men begin the climb towards the North Col. The crust of snow is not solid enough to bear them and they sink in up to their knees. Suddenly, in the awe-inspiring silence of the mountain, the muffled rumble of an avalanche can be heard. The group of Britons manages to get clear, but the snowslide carries off two roped parties of Sherpas, who tumble headlong into a crevasse. Seven porters are missing. These are the first Everest deaths. At this tragedy the expedition is called off. A cairn is erected at the base camp in memory of the victims.

George Mallory, der Held der Expedition von 1921, kehrt bereits im folgenden Jahr zurück, entschlossen, den Mount Everest diesmal zu bezwingen. Zum Leiter dieser Mission wird Charles Bruce ernannt, ein gutmütiger General, der bereits seit dreißig Jahren den Himalaya bereist. Er wird von erfahrenen Bergsteigern begleitet, darunter auch Ärzte und ein Armeefotograf, sein Neffe Geoffrey Bruce und George Finch, ein australischer Chemiker, der in der Schweiz lebt und zu den besten Bergsteigern der Zeit zählt. Im Gegensatz zu George Mallory ist Finch davon überzeugt, dass der Mount Everest nicht ohne Sauerstoffgerät bezwungen werden kann. Er erklärt allen Expeditionsteilnehmern das Funktionieren dieser sperrigen Geräte mit vier Stahlzylindern, die fast 15 Kilogramm wiegen.
Am 30. April 1922 gelangt die Expedition in die Nähe des Rongpu-Gletschers. Sie folgt der Route, die in 7000 Metern Höhe über den Nordpass verläuft und im vorherigen Jahr als begehbar befunden wurde. Am 19. Mai unternehmen George Mallory, Dr. Somervell

Eerste beklimmingen, eerste slachtoffers
Primeros asaltos, primeras víctimas

und zwei andere Bergsteiger mit Hilfe von neun Trägern einen ersten Versuch, den Mount Everest ohne Sauerstoffgeräte zu bezwingen. Sie leiden unter der Kälte und haben Mühe zu atmen, doch sie gelangen bis auf eine Höhe von 7.600 Metern, wo sie die Nacht in aufgestellten Zelten verbringen, in der Nähe einer eindrucksvollen Steilwand. Am nächsten Morgen verzögert sich der weitere Aufstieg wegen des reichlichen Schneefalls, und auf einer Höhe von 8.200 Metern muss die Gruppe schließlich umkehren. Beim Abstieg entgehen die Bergsteiger nur knapp dem Tod.
George Finch ist entschlossen, sein Glück ebenfalls zu versuchen, diesmal allerdings mit Sauerstoff. Am Morgen des 24. Mai beginnt er in Begleitung des jungen Bruce und eines Gurkha-Korporals seinen Aufstieg. Im Laufe des Tages wird der eisige Wind immer stärker und wächst sich bis zum Einbruch der Dunkelheit zu einem Sturm aus. Die in Not geratenen Bergsteiger müssen achtzehn Stunden lang, stehend in ihren Zelten, verharren, damit diese nicht von den Windböen mitgerissen werden.
Beladen wie Maultiere brechen die Männer früh am nächsten Morgen auf. Bruce schreit plötzlich auf, er hat keinen Sauerstoff mehr. Finch gelingt es gerade noch, ihn festzuhalten, bevor er in den Abgrund taumelt. Er gibt Bruce seine eigene Maske und repariert das Sauerstoffgerät. Die beiden Bergsteiger gelangen noch bis auf 8.320 Meter Höhe – ein neuer Rekord – und müssen sich dann geschlagen geben.
Mallory, Dr. Somervell und die übrigen unversehrten Teilnehmer des ersten Besteigungsversuchs haben sich inzwischen vierzehn Tage lang von ihrer Erschöpfung erholt, und sind trotz der drohenden Verschlechterung der Wetterlage entschlossen, einen neuen Versuch zu wagen. Finch möchte ebenfalls dabei sein, doch er kann nicht lange mithalten. Die große Menge Schnee auf den Hügeln des Mount Everest ist beunruhigend – ein sicheres Zeichen für den bevorstehenden Monsun. Am 7. Juni beginnen die Männer mit dem Aufstieg zum Nordpass. Die Schneekruste ist nicht fest genug, um sie zu tragen, und sie sinken bis über die Knie ein. Plötzlich wird die überwältigende Stille der Berge vom dumpfen Grollen einer Lawine durchbrochen. Den Briten gelingt es, sich zu befreien, doch zwei Seilschaften, Sherpas, werden von den Schneemassen mitgerissen und stürzen in eine Spalte. Sieben Träger verlieren ihr Leben – die ersten Toten des Mount Everest. Mit dieser Tragödie ist die Expedition zu Ende. Im Basislager wird zur Erinnerung an die Toten ein Hügelgrab errichtet.

George Mallory, held van de expeditie in 1921, gaat het jaar daarna terug, vastbesloten om deze keer de Everest te bedwingen. De man die de nieuwe missie leidt, is Charles Bruce, een goedmoedige allrounder, die al dertig jaar door het Himalayagebergte trekt. Hij heeft geroutineerde klimmers bij zich, onder wie medische hulpverleners en een legerfotograaf. Verder zijn er nog zijn jongere neef Geoffrey Bruce en ene George Finch, een Australische chemicus die in Zwitserland woont en tot de beste bergbeklimmers van die tijd behoort. In tegenstelling tot George Mallory, is Charles Bruce ervan overtuigd dat de Everest niet kan worden bedwongen zonder zuurstofapparaten. Hij is dan ook degene die alle expeditieleden de werking zal uitleggen van dit hinderlijke hulpmiddel dat vier stalen cilinders heeft en bijna 15 kilogram weegt.
Op 30 april 1922 arriveert de expeditie nabij de gletsjer van Rongbuk. De geplande route via de noordelijke pas op 7000 meter is het jaar ervoor ontdekt. Op 19 mei beginnen George Mallory, dokter Somervell en twee andere alpinisten aan een eerste beklimming van de Everest, zonder zuurstofapparaten en geholpen door negen dragers. Ze lijden kou en vorderen moeizaam, maar bereiken een hoogte van ruim 7600 meter, waar ze de nacht zullen doorbrengen in tenten aan de voet van een indrukwekkende piek. De volgende dag lopen zij vertraging op in de sneeuw die met bakken tegelijk is gevallen en zien zich op 8200 meter hoogte gedwongen om terug te keren. Het scheelt niet veel of zij komen om tijdens de afdaling.
George Finch is vastbesloten eveneens een poging te wagen, maar dan met behulp van zuurstof. De ochtend van 24 mei gaat hij op

weg, samen met de jonge Bruce en een Gurkha-korporaal. De ijzige wind neemt in kracht toe naarmate de dag vordert en is tegen het vallen van de avond overgegaan in een storm. Gedurende achttien uur zijn de geplaagde alpinisten in de weer om te voorkomen dat de tent door de snijdende windvlagen wordt weggeblazen.
Bepakt als ezels trekken de mannen vroeg in de ochtend verder. Plotseling slaakt Bruce een kreet: hij heeft geen zuurstof meer. Finch is nog net op tijd bij hem. Hij bindt hem zijn eigen masker voor en maakt het apparaat van Bruce weer in orde. De alpinisten maken vervolgens weer enkele vorderingen, maar aangekomen op 8320 meter – een nieuw record – moeten zij opgeven.
Mallory, dokter Somervell en de overige deelnemers aan de eerste poging hebben veertig uur de tijd gehad om van hun vermoeidheid te herstellen en wagen een nieuwe poging, ondanks het slechte weer dat dreigt. Finch sluit zich bij de groep aan, maar houdt het niet lang vol. De grote hoeveelheid sneeuw die op de hellingen van de Everest is gevallen, is een verontrustend voorteken van de naderende moesson. Op 7 juni beginnen de mannen aan de klim via de noordelijke pas. De sneeuwlaag is niet stevig genoeg om hen te dragen. Ze zakken er tot hun knieën in weg. Ineens is daar in de indrukwekkende stilte van de berg het gedempte gerommel van een lawine. De Britten weten hun hachje te redden, maar de naar beneden razende sneeuwmassa heeft twee groepen Sherpa's een spleet in gesleurd. Zeven dragers ontbreken op het appel. Zij zijn de eerste dodelijke slachtoffers van de Everest. De expeditie eindigt met deze tragedie. In het basiskamp wordt een stenen gedenkteken voor de slachtoffers opgericht.

George Mallory, el héroe de la expedición de 1921, vuelve al año siguiente, esta vez completamente decidido a conquistar el Everest. El hombre que dirige esta misión es Charles Bruce, un general bonachón que lleva treinta años recorriendo el Himalaya. Lo acompañan una serie de montañeros curtidos, entre los que se encuentran varios médicos y un fotógrafo del ejército. También lo acompaña su sobrino nieto, Geoffrey Brice, y George Finch, químico australiano que vive en Suiza y uno de los mejores alpinistas del momento. Al contrario que George Mallory, está convencido de que no es posible coronar el Everest sin máquina de oxígeno. Por tanto, él es quien explica a los demás el funcionamiento de estos aparatos muy voluminosos, formados por cuatro cilindros de acero y con un peso aproximado de 15 kilogramos.
El 30 de abril de 1922, la expedición llega cerca del glaciar de Rongbuk. El itinerario, que pasa por el Collado Norte, a 7000 metros, es el mismo que se había localizado el año anterior. El 19 de mayo, George Mallory, el Dr. Somervell y otros dos escaladores lanzan un primer asalto al Everest, sin máscara de oxígeno y con la ayuda de nueve portadores. Padecen el frío y respiran con dificultad, pero llegan a más de 7600 metros y pasan la noche en las tiendas de campaña montadas sobre un impresionante acantilado. Al día siguiente, se retrasan debido a la abundante nieve caída durante la noche, y a 8200 metros de altitud se ven obligados a darse media vuelta. Casi se matan en el descenso.
George Finch está completamente decidido a probar suerte, pero esta vez con oxígeno. La mañana del 24 de mayo, emprende el camino, acompañado por el joven Bruce y un cabo gurkha. El viento glaciar se endurece durante la jornada hasta transformarse en tormenta al caer la noche. Durante dieciocho horas seguidas de peligro, los escaladores se afanan por mantener en pie la tienda de campaña amenazada por las borrascas.
Cargados como mulas, los hombres vuelven a salir temprano por la mañana temprano. De repente, Bruce da un grito, no les queda oxígeno. Finch lo agarra justo antes de que se precipite al vacío. Le pone su propia máscara sobre el rostro y repara su aparato. Los alpinistas siguen avanzando un poco más, pero al llegar a 8230 metros, un nuevo récord, deben darse por vencidos.
Mallory, el Dr. Somervell y los supervivientes del primer intento han tenido quince días para recuperarse del cansancio y están preparados para iniciar otro asalto, pese a la amenaza del mal tiempo. Finch también quiere formar parte de la cuadrilla, pero no puede continuar en la expedición mucho más tiempo. Es preocupante lo nevadas que están las pendientes del Everest, signo precursor del monzón. El 7 de junio, los hombres comienzan el ascenso hacia el Collado Norte. La corteza de nieve no es lo suficientemente sólida para que puedan caminar sobre ella con comodidad así que se calan hasta las rodillas. Y de repente, en el silencio estremecedor de la montaña, se oye el rugido sordo de una avalancha. El grupo de británicos logra escapar, pero el río de nieve se ha llevado consigo dos cordadas de sherpas que se precipitan en una grieta. Faltan siete portadores. Serán los primeros muertos del Everest. La expedición termina con esta tragedia. En el campamento base, se levanta un mojón en memoria de las víctimas.

On the road in Sikkim.

Unterwegs in Sikkim.

Onderweg in Sikkim.

En la carretera en Sikkim.

A group of Tibetan women spinning and weaving yak hair in the Kharta Valley.

Eine Gruppe von Tibeterinnen im Kharta-Tal beim Spinnen und Weben von Yakhaar.

Tibetaanse vrouwen spinnen en weven de wol van jaks in de Kharta-vallei.

Un grupo de mujeres tibetanas hilando y tejiendo pelo de yak en el valle de Kharta.

Dr. Howard Somervell ensures that porters have a medical examination, Kampa Dzong.

Dr. Howard Somervell unterzieht die Träger einer medizinischen Untersuchung, Kampa Dzong.

Dokter Howard Somervell onderwerpt dragers aan een medische keuring in Kampa Dzong.

El Dr. Howard Somervell somete a los portadores a una exploración médica, Kampa Dzong.

Second march from Phari.

Tweede tocht vanuit Phari.

Zweiter Fußmarsch von Phari aus.

Segunda marcha desde Phari.

Breakfast stop. Seated left to right: Wakefield, Morris, General Bruce, Karma Paul, Geoffrey Bruce, an unnamed Ghurkha, Norton.

Ontbijtpauze. Gezeten van links naar rechts: Wakefield, Morris, generaal Bruce, Karma Paul, Geoffrey Bruce, een Gurkha en Norton.

Frühstückspause, sitzend von links nach rechts: Wakefield, Morris, General Bruce, Karma Paul, Geoffrey Bruce, unbenannter Gurkha, Norton.

Parada para desayunar. Sentados de izquierda a derecha: Wakefield, Morris, General Bruce, Karma Paul, Geoffrey Bruce, *gurkha* de nombre desconocido, Norton.

Shekar Dzong monastery and village.

Het klooster en dorp van Shekar Dzong.

Kloster und Dorf Shekar Dzong.

El monasterio y el pueblo de Shekar Dzong.

Dr. Somervell crossing the rope bridge at Kharkung.

Dokter Somervell gaat over de touwbrug bij Kharkung.

Dr. Somervell bei der Überquerung einer Seilbrücke bei Kharkung.

El Dr. Somervell cruzando el puente de cuerda en Kharkung.

Leaving Shekar. Captain G. Bruce on a pony.

Abmarsch aus Shekar, Captain Bruce auf einem Pony.

Vertrek uit Shekar. Kapitein G. Bruce op een pony.

Saliendo de Shekar. El capitán G. Bruce en un poni.

Bridge across Bhong Chu, Pangla region.

Brücke über den Bhong Chu im Gebiet des Pang La.

Brug over de Bhong Chu, Pangla-regio.

Puente cruzando Bhong Chu, región de Pangla.

View of Kampa Dzong in 1922.

Blick auf Kampa Dzong im Jahr 1922.

Kampa Dzong in 1922.

Vista de Kampa Dzong en 1922.

General Bruce interviewing Jongpens, the governor of Kampa Dzong.

General Bruce im Gespräch mit Jongpens, dem Gouverneur von Kampa Dzong.

Generaal Bruce interviewt Jongpens, de gouverneur van Kampa Dzong.

El general Bruce entrevistando a Jongpens, el gobernador de Kampa Dzong.

Howard Somervell at Kampa Dzong.

Howard Somervell in Kampa Dzong.

Howard Somervell in Kampa Dzong.

Howard Somervell en Kampa Dzong.

Edward Strutt approaching Tinki.

Edward Strutt kurz vor der Ankunft in Tinki.

Edward Strutt nadert Tinki.

Edward Strutt acercándose a Tinki.

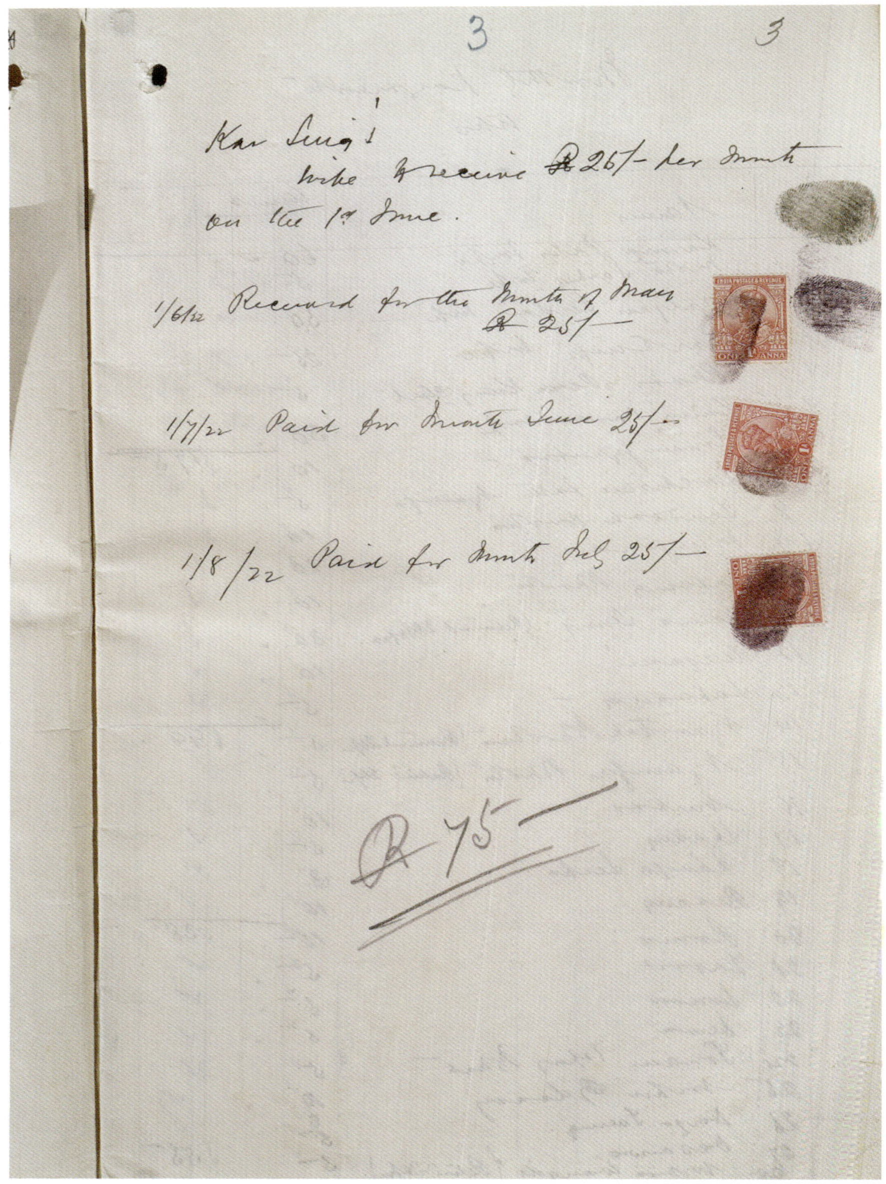

3 3

Kar Sing!
Like to receive Rs 25/- per month
on the 1st June.

1/6/22 Received for the month of May
Rs 25/-

1/7/22 Paid for month June 25/-

1/8/22 Paid for month July 25/-

Rs 75/-

Four-cylinder oxygen set used on the 1922 Mount Everest Expedition, weighing in at around 15 kilograms.

Set met vier zuurstofcilinders gebruikt tijdens de Everest-expeditie van 1922. Deze woog ongeveer 15 kilogram.

Sauerstoffgerät mit vier Zylindern und einem Gewicht von 15 kg, das während der Mount Everest-Expedition von 1922 verwendet wurde.

Cuatro cilindros de oxígeno utilizados en la Expedición al Monte Everest de 1922. Su peso aproximado era de 15 kilogramos.

Sherpa thumbprints to prove payment for work on the 1922 Mount Everest Expedition.

De duimafdruk van Sherpa's dient als betaalbewijs voor werk tijdens de Everest-expeditie van 1922.

Daumenabdrücke von Sherpas als Beleg für die erhaltene Entlohnung ihrer Arbeit während der Mount Everest-Expedition von 1922.

Huellas digitales de *sherpas* como prueba de recepción del pago por su trabajo en la Expedición al Monte Everest de 1922.

Captain Finch and the oxygen equipment he so firmly believed in.

Captain Finch und die Sauerstoffgeräte, an die er so fest glaubte.

Finch draagt een zuurstofmasker. Hij werkte onvermoeibaar aan verbetering van het systeem.

El capitán Finch y el equipo de oxígeno en el que creía con tanta firmeza.

Members of the expedition practicing oxygen gas drill.

Expeditionsmitglieder üben den Umgang mit Sauerstoffgeräten.

Leden van de expeditie tijdens een zuurstofmaskeroefening.

Miembros de la expedición practicando con el gas de oxígeno.

El capitán Finch y el equipo de oxígeno en el que creía con tanta firmeza.

Finch beim Tragen eines Sauerstoffgeräts. Er arbeitete unermüdlich an der Verbesserung des Systems.

Kapitein Finch met de zuurstofapparatuur waarin hij zoveel vertrouwen had.

Finch con el aparato de oxígeno. Trabajó sin cesar para mejorar el sistema.

Captain Noel, photographer and his photographic porters.

Der Fotograf Captain Noel und seine Träger.

Fotograaf kapitein Noel en zijn dragers.

El capitán Noel, fotógrafo y sus portadores fotográficos.

The Chief Lama of the Rongbuk monastery.

Der oberste Lama des Rongpu-Klosters.

De lama die het Rongbuk-klooster leidde.

El lama jefe del monasterio de Rongbuk.

Everest and other peaks.

Der Mount Everest und weitere Gipfel.

De Everest en andere pieken.

El Everest y otros picos.

View of mountain peaks above the clouds.

Blick auf Berggipfel über der Wolkendecke.

Bergtoppen boven de bewolking.

Vista de los picos de la montaña sobre las nubes.

View of the summit of Everest.

Blick zum Gipfel des Mount Everest.

De top van de Everest.

Vista de la cumbre del Everest.

Members of the expedition at Base Camp, 3rd May 1922. From left to right: Mallory, Finch, Longstaff, General Bruce, Strutt and Crawford (front row); Morshead, Geoffrey Bruce, Wakefield, Somervell, Morris and Norton (back row). John Noel doesn't appear, since he took the photo.

Die Expeditionsmitglieder im Basislager, 3. Mai 1922, von links nach rechts: Mallory, Finch, Longstaff, General Bruce, Strutt und Crawford (vordere Reihe), Morshead, Geoffrey Bruce, Wakefield, Somervell, Morris und Norton (hintere Reihe). John Noel ist als Fotograf nicht im Bild zu sehen.

Expeditieleden in het basiskamp op 3 mei 1922 (v.l.n.r.): Mallory, Finch, Longstaff, generaal Bruce, Strutt en Crawford (voor); Morshead, Geoffrey Bruce, Wakefield, Somervell, Morris en Norton (achter). John Noel, die de foto nam, staat er niet bij.

Miembros de la expedición en el campamento base, 3 de mayo de 1922. De izquierda a derecha: Mallory, Finch, Longstaff, General Bruce, Strutt y Crawford (fila delantera); Morshead, Geoffrey Bruce, Wakefield, Somervell, Morris y Norton (fila trasera). John Noel, que tomó la fotografía, no aparece.

Mountain ridges viewed above the clouds.

Gebirgskämme über den Wolken.

Bergkammen boven de bewolking.

Las crestas montañosas vistas sobre las nubes.

Mount Everest seen from Base Camp.

Blick auf den Mount Everest vom Basislager aus.

De Everest gezien vanuit het basiskamp.

El Monte Everest visto desde el campamento base.

Camp II at sunset, in the shelter of a 20m high vertical cliff.

Lager II bei Sonnenuntergang, im Schutz einer 20 m hohen senkrecht abfallenden Eiswand.

Kamp II bij zonsondergang, beschut door een 20 meter hoge klif.

El campamento II al atardecer, en el refugio de un precipicio de 20 m de alto.

Seracs on the East Rongbuk glacier, above Camp II.

Eiszacken des östlichen Rongpu-Gletschers über Lager II.

IJspieken van de oostelijke Rongbuk-gletsjer, boven kamp II.

Seracs del lado este del glaciar Rongbuk, sobre el campamento II.

North Col Camp and the North Peak.

Lager am Nordsattel und der Nordgipfel.

Kamp in de noordelijke pas en de noordelijke piek.

Campamento del Collado Norte y el Pico Norte.

A hole in the ice.

Eine Höhle im Eis.

Een holte in het ijs.

Un agujero en el hielo.

The advanced base camp at 6,100m.

Das vorgeschobene Basislager auf 6100 m Höhe.

Het gevorderde basiskamp op 6100 meter hoogte.

El campamento base avanzado a 6100 m.

North Col.

Der Nordsattel.

Noordelijke pas.

Collado Norte.

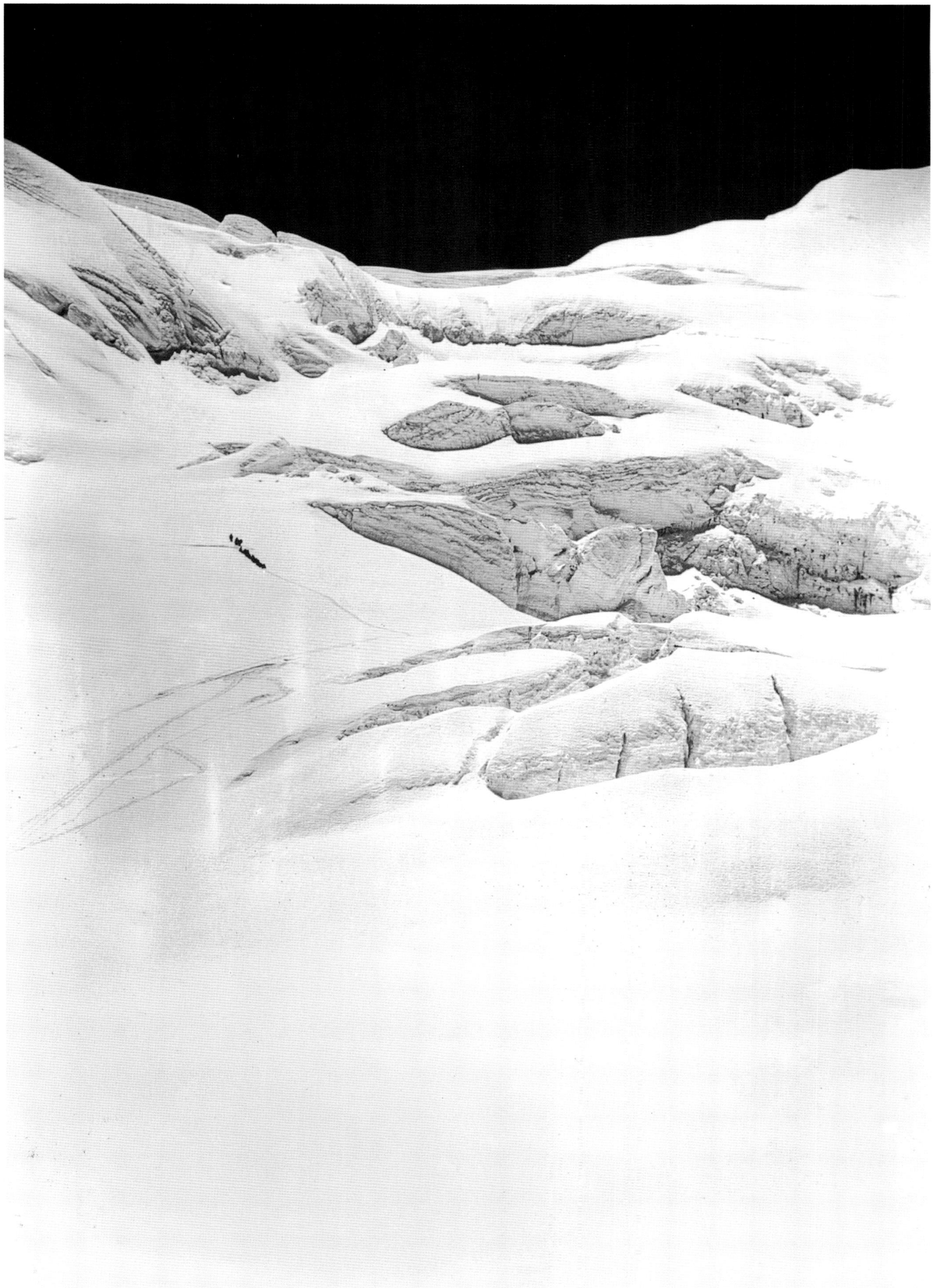

Captain John Noel films the climbing of Everest from Chang La.

Captain Noel filmt den Aufstieg zum Mount Everest von Chang La aus.

Kapitein Noel legt de beklimming van de Everest vanaf Chang La op film vast.

El capitán Noel cinematografiando el ascenso del Monte Everest desde Chang La.

Camp III and North-East shoulder of Everest, with the summit in background.

Das Lager III und die Nordostschulter des Mount Everest mit dem Gipfel im Hintergrund.

Kamp III en de noordoostelijke 'schouder' van de Everest, met de top op de achtergrond.

El campamento III y el margen noreste del Everest con la cumbre al fondo.

Descending the East Rongbuk glacier.

Abstieg über den östlichen Rongpu-Gletscher.

Afdaling van de oostelijke Rongbuk-gletsjer.

Descendiendo el lado este del glaciar Rongbuk.

Campsite on the mountain.

Lagerstätte auf dem Berg.

Kampement op de berg.

Emplazamiento del campamento en la montaña.

The way to the summit from the highest point of the final climb.

De weg naar de top gezien vanaf het hoogste punt van de eindklim.

Der Weg zum Gipfel vom höchsten Punkt des letzten Aufstiegs.

El camino hacia la cumbre desde el punto más alto del ascenso final.

Mallory and Norton approach their highest point on Everest, at 8,200m.

Mallory en Norton naderen hun hoogste punt op de Everest, op ruim 8200 meter hoogte.

Mallory und Norton nähern sich ihrem Rekord von 8200 m Höhe auf dem Mount Everest.

Mallory y Norton se acercan a su punto más alto del Everest, a 8200 m.

The British members of the second climbing party, Geoffrey Bruce and George Finch.

De Britse leden van het tweede team, Geoffrey Bruce en George Finch.

Die britischen Teilnehmer des zweiten Besteigungsversuchs, Geoffrey Bruce und George Finch.

Los miembros británicos del segundo grupo de escalada, Geoffrey Bruce y George Finch.

Bruce and Finch descending from their record climb.

Bruce en Finch afdalend na hun klimrecord.

Bruce und Finch bei der Rückkehr von ihrem Besteigungsversuch, bei dem sie einen neuen Höhenrekord erzielten.

Bruce y Finch descendiendo desde su punto de escalada récord.

Cover of the programme of the 1922 Everest Expedition film made by Captain J.B. Noel.

Omslag van het programmaboekje bij kapitein J.B. Noel's gefilmde verslag van de expeditie in 1922.

Deckblatt des Programms für den von Captain J.B. Noel gedrehten Film über die Mount Everest-Expedition von 1922.

Portada del programa de la película de Expedición del Everest de 1922 realizada por el capitán J.B. Noel.

Through the crevasses, Geoffrey Bruce decends to camp II.

Geoffrey Bruce daalt door de gletsjerspleten af naar kamp II.

Geoffrey Bruce stieg durch die Gletscherspalter ab in das Camp II.

Geoffrey Bruce desciende al campamento II a través de las grietas.

1924

Drama and Mystery on Everest
Drama und Rätsel rundum den Everest

Despite the failure of the 1922 expedition, the British are more determined than ever to succeed in climbing to the top of Everest. The team includes several experienced members, starting with General Bruce, who will not lead the expedition for long. Laid low by malaria, he will give way to his second in command, Major Norton. Those who were also there in 1922 include the mountaineer and doctor Howard Somervell, the young Geoffrey Bruce and Captain John Noel, expedition cameraman and photographer. Above all George Mallory who, at only 38, has more hats than any of them. He has just completed a lecture tour in the United States, where he gave the following response to a journalist asking him why he set so much store by Everest: "because it's there!" Andrew Irvine, a 22-year-old alpinist still studying to be an engineer, is also a member of the expedition that begins its long trek at the end of March 1924.
A bad omen, the Grand Lama of the Rongbuk monastery is too ill to lead the prayer ceremonies in honour of the expedition. Indeed, the start of the adventure at the foot of Everest is a real disaster.
In mid-May the weather improves again, but this does not last. Again, the snow falls during the day, while temperatures at night fall to -31°C. The alpinists and porters all descend in panic; only four Sherpas, in too bad a state to descend, remain captives of the North Col and are subsequently saved at the point of death.
On 2 June Mallory and Bruce launch an attack that will end in failure, as the Sherpas refuse to climb any higher. Two days later, at first light, Norton and Somervell begin their advance towards the summit. They have a choice between two routes for the final ascent: one is shorter but practically impossible due to the overhanging projections, one of which is 60 metres high and is called the *Second Step*. The other is the long diagonal crossing of the north face up to a band of yellow limestone 300 metres wide. At midday Somervell gives up and his teammate continues on alone up the mountain. He walks another 275 metres, but only climbs 30 metres. He looks at his watch: he will never have time to reach the summit and descend again. He consults the altimeter one last time: 8,573 metres! A record that will last a long time. After regrouping, the two men descend again with difficulty, without even registering their disappointment. Norton, who has not been wearing his sunglasses much, starts to lose his vision.
Arriving at the North Col they encounter Mallory, who has meanwhile gone with his porters to find oxygen cylinders at the base camp. He climbs with the young Irvine, who knows exactly how to use the breathing apparatus. Norton, who will remain completely blind for several days, must be taken back into the valley below.
The following morning, 9 June 1924, Odell climbs towards camp VI in order to carry out some scientific observations. A curtain of cloud parts to reveal the ridge summit. From a distance he spies a tiny point that moves, then another. He has the impression that the first man – Mallory, almost certainly – has, after some minutes, cleared the famous *Second Step*, which opens up the most direct path to the summit of Everest. The curtain of cloud sweeps back into place. He will never see George Mallory or Andrew Irvine again.

Trotz der gescheiterten Expedition von 1922 waren die Briten entschlossener als je zuvor, den Mount Everest zu bezwingen. Zahlreiche Altbekannte befinden sich unter den Teilnehmern der neuen Expedition, angefangen bei General Bruce, der die Leitung der Expedition allerdings nach kurzer Zeit aufgrund einer Malariaerkrankung aufgeben muss. Er gibt seinen Platz ab an seinen Stellvertreter Major Edward Norton. Zudem sind, wie schon 1922, Arzt und Alpinist Howard Somervell und der junge Geoffrey Bruce und Captain John Noel, Kameramann und Fotograf der Mission. Der erfahrenste Teilnehmer ist jedoch der erst 38-jährige George Mallory. Er hat gerade eine Konferenzreise durch die Vereinigten Staaten abgeschlossen und auf die Frage eines Journalisten, warum ihm die Besteigung des Mount Everest so wichtig sei, die berühmt gewordene Antwort „Because it's there" (Weil er da ist) gegeben. Auch Andrew Irvine, ein mit 22 Jahren noch junger Bergsteiger, der die Ingenieurschule noch nicht abgeschlossen hat, nimmt an der Expedition teil, derer lange Marsch Ende März 1924 beginnt.

Drama en mysterie op de Everest
Drama y misterio en el Everest

Die Expedition beginnt bereits unter einem schlechten Vorzeichen: Der Lama des Rongpu-Klosters ist zu krank, um die Gebetszeremonie zu Ehren der Expeditionsteilnehmer durchzuführen. Der gesamte Beginn des Abenteuers am Fuße des Mount Everest ist eine wahre Katastrophe.

Mitte Mai bessert sich das Wetter wieder, doch die Besserung ist nicht von Dauer. Tagsüber schneit es erneut, und nachts fällt die Temperatur bis auf -31°C. Die Bergsteiger und ihre Träger machen sich unter diesen katastrophalen Bedingungen an den Abstieg. Vier Sherpas bleiben jedoch aufgrund ihres schlechten körperlichen Zustands auf dem Nordpass stecken und werden in letzter Minute gerettet.

Am 2. Juni unternehmen Mallory und Bruce einen Besteigungsversuch, der erneut mit einem Fehlschlag endet: Die Sherpas verweigern den weiteren Aufstieg. Zwei Tage später beginnen Norton und Somervell bei Tagesanbruch mit dem Aufstieg. Für das letzte Stück bis zum Gipfel haben sie die Wahl zwischen zwei Routen: Zwar ist die erste Route kürzer, doch erscheint sie aufgrund von drei Vorsprüngen kaum begehbar. Die größte davon – auch als „Second Step" (Zweite Stufe) bekannt – ist fast sechzig Meter hoch. Die zweite Route ist eine lange, diagonale Traverse entlang der Nordwand, die sich bis zu einem 300 Meter langen Felsband aus gelbem Kalkstein hinzieht. Gegen Mittag gibt Somervell auf, sein Gefährte setzt seinen Weg zum Gipfel allein fort, trotz der Gefahren. Er kommt noch 275 Meter voran, legt dabei jedoch nur einen Höhenunterschied von 30 Metern zurück. Dann schaut er auf seine Uhr: Er hat niemals genügend Zeit für die Besteigung des Gipfels und den Abstieg. Ein letztes Mal schaut er auf seinen Höhenmesser: 8.573 Meter! Ein neuer Rekord, der lange Zeit nicht übertroffen wird. Nachdem Norton wieder bei seinem Gefährten angelangt ist, beginnen die beiden Männer den mühevollen Abstieg, ohne Spuren der Enttäuschung zu spüren. Norton, der seine Sonnenbrille nicht ausreichend oft getragen hat, fängt an unter Schneeblindheit zu leiden. Auf dem Nordpass angekommen, begegnen sie Mallory, der inzwischen mit Hilfe einiger Träger Sauerstoffzylinder aus dem Basislager geholt hat. In Begleitung des jungen Irvine, der mit dem Gebrauch der Atemgeräte vertraut ist, beginnen sie erneut mit dem Aufstieg. Norton hingegen ist nach ein paar Tagen vollkommen blind und muss ins Tal zurück.

Am nächsten Morgen, am 9. Juni 1924, steigt Noel Odell zum Lager VI auf, um einige geologische Untersuchungen durchzuführen. Dichte Wolken verdecken den Gipfelbereich. Als der Wolkenvorhang aufreißt, erspäht er einen kleinen Punkt, der sich fortbewegt, dann einen zweiten. Er hat den Eindruck, dass der erste Mann, zweifellos Mallory, innerhalb weniger Minuten den gefürchteten „Second Step" erklommen hat, der den direktesten Weg zum Gipfel des Mount Everest erschließt. Dann zieht sich die Wolkendecke zu. Er wird weder George Mallory noch Andrew Irvine jemals wiedersehen.

De Britten zijn ondanks de rampspoed van de expeditie in 1922 vastbeslotener dan ooit de beklimming van de Everest te volbrengen. Een aantal oudgedienden maakt opnieuw deel uit van het team, om te beginnen generaal Bruce, die niet lang aan het hoofd van de expeditie zal staan. Geveld door malaria draagt hij zijn leidersrol over aan de tweede man, majoor Norton. Verder zijn de volgende deelnemers van de expeditie in 1922 weer van de partij: dokter Howard Somervell, de jonge Geoffrey Bruce en kapitein John Noel, de cameraman en fotograaf van de missie. Ook George Mallory, de grootste waaghals van allemaal met zijn 38 jaar, is erbij. Hij belegde in de Verenigde Staten een reeks conferenties en beantwoordde de vraag van een journalist waarom de Everest hem bleef boeien, met: 'Hij is er nu eenmaal.' Verder maakt Andrew Irvine, een jonge alpinist en ingenieur-in-opleiding van 22 jaar, deel uit van de expeditie die eind maart 1924 aan de lange mars begint.

Het is een slecht voorteken dat de grootlama van het Rongbukklooster te ziek is om de gebedsceremonie ter zegening van de expeditie te leiden. De start van het avontuur aan de voet van de Everest is feitelijk een regelrecht drama.

Midden mei treedt er een weersverbetering op, maar lang houdt die niet aan. Opnieuw sneeuwt het overdag en in de nacht daalt de temperatuur naar -31°C. De aangeslagen alpinisten en hun dragers dalen weer af, met uitzondering van vier Sherpa's die te ziek zijn en achterblijven op de noordelijke pas tot ze, op sterven na dood, worden gered.
Op 2 juni ondernemen Mallory en Bruce een volgende poging, die op een mislukking uitloopt omdat de Sherpa's weigeren nog hoger te gaan. Twee dagen later beginnen Norton en Somervell in de vroege ochtend aan hun poging om de top te bedwingen. Zij hebben de keus uit twee routes voor het laatste deel van het klimtraject. De kortste route is praktisch onmogelijk vanwege uitsteeksels, waaronder een van 60 meter hoog die 'De tweede stap' wordt genoemd. De andere strekt zich langgerekt en diagonaal uit over de noordelijke zijde tot aan een 300 meter brede strook van gele kalksteen. In de middag geeft Somervell op, terwijl zijn kameraad ondanks het gevaar alleen verder de berg op gaat. Norton legt nog 275 meter af maar klimt niet meer dan 30 meter. Hij kijkt op zijn horloge en ziet dat er niet genoeg tijd resteert om de top te bereiken en weer af te dalen. Hij raadpleegt zijn hoogtemeter nog een laatste keer: 8573 meter! Een record dat lang stand zal houden. Na elkaar te hebben teruggevonden, dalen de beide mannen moeizaam maar niet teleurgesteld af. Norton, die zijn zonnebril amper heeft gedragen, begint zijn gezichtsvermogen te verliezen.
Op de noordelijke pas aangekomen, treffen ze Mallory weer, die intussen met zijn dragers zuurstofcilinders heeft gehaald in het basiskamp. Mallory klimt in gezelschap van de jonge Irvine, die uitstekend overweg kan met zuurstofapparaten. Norton, die gedurende een groot aantal uren volledig blind blijft, moet naar de vallei worden teruggebracht.
De volgende ochtend, 9 juni 1924, begeeft Odell zich naar kamp VI voor wetenschappelijke observaties. Het wolkendek opent zich rond de hoogste top. Odell ziet in de verte een bewegende kleine stip en daarna nog een. Hij meent dat het de eerste 'stip' – zeer waarschijnlijk Mallory – is gelukt om binnen enkele minuten de beruchte 'Tweede stap' te nemen op de kortste route naar de top van de Everest. Het wolkendek sluit zich weer. Daarna zal Odell noch George Mallory noch Andrew Irvine ooit weerzien.

Pese al fracaso de la expedición de 1922, los británicos están más decididos que nunca a coronar con éxito el ascenso del Everest. Varios veteranos forman parte del equipo, empezando por el general Bruce, que no permanecerá demasiado tiempo a la cabeza de la expedición. Abatido por la malaria, cederá su lugar a su segundo, el mayor Norton. Ya estaban allí en 1922: el médico montañero Howard Somervell, el joven Geoffrey Bruce y el capitán John Noel, cámara y fotógrafo de la misión. Pero, sobre todo, George Mallory, el que acumula más expediciones con solo 38 años. Acaba de terminar una ronda de conferencias en Estados Unidos, donde ha dado esta respuesta a un periodista que le ha preguntado por qué tenía tanto interés en el Everest: «¡Porque está ahí!». Andrew Irvine, un joven alpinista de 22 años, todavía alumno de ingeniería, también forma parte de la expedición que empieza su larga marcha a finales del mes de marzo de 1924.
Mal presagio, el gran lama del monasterio de Rongbuk está demasiado enfermo para celebrar las ceremonias de plegarias en honor de la expedición. Y de hecho, los inicios de la aventura al pie del Everest son una verdadera catástrofe.
A mediados de mayo, el tiempo vuelve a ser bueno, pero dura poco. De nuevo, vuelve a nevar durante días, con una temperatura de -31 °C por la noche. Los escaladores y los portadores descienden muy perjudicados; tan solo cuatro sherpas, que se encuentran demasiado mal para descender, permanecen prisioneros del Collado Norte y son rescatados posteriormente in extremis.
El 2 de junio, Mallory y Bruce lanzan un asalto que se saldará con un fracaso, ya que los *sherpas* se niegan a escalar más alto. Dos días después, a primera hora, Norton y Somervell inician su ascenso hacia la cumbre. Pueden elegir entre dos itinerarios para el ascenso final: uno más corto pero prácticamente imposible debido a los salientes, uno de ellos de 60 metros de alto, llamado el «*segundo paso*»; otro que consiste en una larga travesía en diagonal desde la cara norte hasta una banda de caliza amarilla, con 300 metros de ancho. Al mediodía, Somervell baja los brazos, su compañero continúa solo en la montaña, a pesar del peligro. Sigue caminando otros 275 metros pero únicamente sube 30 metros. Mira su reloj: no le dará tiempo de coronar la cumbre y volver a descender. Consulta por última vez el altímetro: ¡8573 metros! Un récord que ostentará durante mucho tiempo. Después de reencontrarse, los dos hombres descienden con dificultad, sin ni siquiera sentir el más mínimo atisbo de decepción. Norton, que apenas se ha puesto las gafas de sol, comienza a perder la vista.
Una vez que llegan al Collado Norte, se reencuentran con Mallory, que mientras tanto ha ido al campamento base a buscar cilindros de oxígeno con sus portadores. A su vez, emprende la subida en compañía del joven Irvine, que sabe utilizar perfectamente los respiradores. Por su parte, Norton, que quedará completamente ciego durante varios días, debe ser bajado al valle.
La mañana siguiente, 9 de junio de 1924, Odell sube en dirección al campamento VI para hacer observaciones científicas. Una pantalla de nubes deja ver la arista de la cumbre. A lo lejos, divisa un punto minúsculo que se desplaza y después otro. Tiene la impresión de que el primer hombre, muy seguramente Mallory, ha atravesado transcurridos unos minutos el famoso «*segundo paso*» que abre la vía más directa hacia la cumbre del Everest. La cortina de nubes se desplaza. Es el fin, no volverá a ver nunca más ni a George Mallory ni a Andrew Irvine.

Taking Sherpas' thumbprints.

Abnehmen der Daumenabdrücke von Angehörigen der Träger.

Familieleden van dragers plaatsen een duimafdruk.

Tomando las huellas digitales de los familiares de los culis.

Chumbi looking south,
second transport party.

Chumbi-Tal, Blick nach Süden,
zweite Transportgruppe.

Chumbi, uitzicht naar het zuiden,
tweede transport.

Chumbi mirando hacia el sur,
segundo grupo de transporte.

A loaded yak.

Ein beladener Yak.

Een beladen jak.

Un yak cargado.

Portraits of Tibetans.

Porträts von Tibetern.

Portret van Tibetanen.

Retratos de tibetanos.

Lamas at Talung , Sikkim.

Lamas in Talung, Sikkim.

Lama's in Talung, Sikkim.

Lamas en Talung, Sikkim.

Tibetan women weaving.

Tibeterinnen beim Weben.

Wevende Tibetaanse vrouwen.

Mujeres tibetanas tejiendo.

Tibetan house at the foot of a mountain range.

Tibetisches Haus am Fuße der Bergkette.

Tibetaans huis aan de voet van een bergketen.

Casa tibetana al pie de una cadena montañosa.

Fording a river.

Durchquerung eines Flusses.

Het doorwaden van een rivier.

Vadeando un río.

Campsite of the expedition at Kyebrac, on the way to the Rongshar Valley.

Lagerstätte der Expedition in Kyebrac auf dem Weg ins Rongshar-Tal.

Kampement van de expeditie in Kyebrac, op weg naar de Rongshar-vallei.

Camping de la expedición en Kyebrac, de camino al valle Rongshar.

Lhatse rope bridge over the river Tsangpo.

Lhatse-Seilbrücke über den Fluss Tsangpo.

Lhatse-touwbrug over de Tsangpo.

Puente de cuerda de Lhatse sobre el río Tsangpo.

Woman from Lhasa, Tibet, making paper.

Frauen aus Lhasa, Tibet, stellen Papier her.

Vrouwen uit Lhasa, Tibet, maken papier.

Mujeres de Lhasa, Tibet, fabricando papel.

On the march.

Auf dem Marsch.

Onderweg.

Durante la marcha.

Yaks resting.

Yaks während einer Rast.

De jaks rusten uit.

Yaks descansando.

Mules loaded with supplies en route for Everest.

Mit Vorräten beladene Maultiere auf dem Weg zum Mount Everest.

Muilezels beladen met voorraden op weg naar de Everest.

Mulas cargadas de provisiones en la ruta al Everest.

A Tibitan from Lhasa making paper from elder bark in the Rongshar Valley.

Ein Tibeter aus Lhasa stellt papier aus der Rinde des Holunderbaums her (Rongshar Tal).

Een Tibetaan uit Lhasa maakt papier van oude boomschors in de Rongshar-vallei.

Un tibetano de Lhasa fabricando papel con una corteza antigua en el valle de Rongshar.

Brigadier General Charles G. Bruce drinking chang, a local alcoholic drink.

Brigadier General Charles G. Bruce trinkt Chang, das örtliche alkoholische Getränk.

Brigadier-generaal Charles G. Bruce drinkt *chang*, een lokale alcoholische drank.

El general de brigada Charles G. Bruce bebiendo chang, una bebida local con alcohol.

Edward Shebbeare in the Zemu Gorge, in the Lachen Valley.

Edward Shebbeare in der Zemu-Schlucht im Lachen-Tal.

Edward Shebbeare op een brug in de Zemu-kloof, Lachen-vallei.

Edward Shebbeare sobre la garganta de Zemu, en el valle de Lachen.

General Bruce, Somervell and Mallory on the Tista Bridge.

General Bruce, Somervell und Mallory auf einer Brücke über die Tista.

Generaal Bruce, Somervell en Mallory op de Tista-brug.

El general Bruce, Somervell y Mallory en el Puente Tista.

Bridge over Lo Chu, near Shekar.

Brücke über den Lo Chu in der Nähe von Shekar.

Brug over de Lo Chu, nabij Shekar.

Puente sobre Lo Chu, cerca de Shekar.

Camp at the Shekar Dzong.

Lager bei Shekar Dzong.

Kamp in Shekar Dzong.

Campamento en Shekar Dzong.

Mallory bathing at Rongli.

Mallory beim Baden im Rongli.

Mallory gaat zwemmen in Rongli.

Mallory bañándose en Rongli.

Camp at the Shekar monastery.

Lager beim Kloster Shekar.

Kamp bij het klooster van Shekar.

Campamento en el monasterio Shekar.

The Shekar Dzong monastery.

Das Kloster Shekar Dzong.

Het klooster Shekar Dzong.

El Monasterio de Shekar Dzong.

Governor's tent below Shekar.

Zelt des Gouverneurs unterhalb von Shekar.

Gouverneurstent bij Shekar.

Tienda de campaña del gobernador bajo Shekar.

Line of porters and Sherpas at Base Camp, carrying equipment for climbing Everest.

Träger und Sherpas beladen mit der Ausrüstung zum Aufstieg auf den Mount Everest im Basislager.

Sherpa's stellen zich in het basiskamp op voor het dragen van klimuitrusting.

Portadores y *sherpas* alineados llevando los equipos para escalar el Everest en el campamento base.

Camp in a valley.

Lager in einem Tal.

Kamp in een vallei.

Campamento en un valle.

Camp at Tinki Dzong.

Lager in Tinki Dzong.

Kamp in Tinki Dzong.

Campamento en Tinki Dzong.

Everest seen from the Pang-La pass.

Der Mount Everest vom Pang La-Pass aus gesehen.

De Everest gezien vanuit de Pang-La-pas.

El Everest visto desde el paso Pang-La.

The Wheel of Life. Decoration inside the monastery.

Das Rad des Lebens, Dekoration im Klostergebäude.

De *Bhavacakra* (het levensrad). Decoratie in het klooster.

La rueda de la vida. Decoración del interior del monasterio.

Detail from the Wheel of Life.

Detail: Das Rad des Lebens.

Detail van de *Bhavacakra* (het levensrad).

Detalle de la Rueda de la vida.

The Dzongpen of Kharta and his wife.

Der Dzongpen von Kharta und seine Ehefrau.

De Dzong Pen van Kharta en zijn vrouw.

El Dzongpen de Kharta y su esposa.

The fortress of Kampa Dzong.

Die Festung Kampa Dzong.

Het fort Kampa Dzong.

La fortaleza de Kampa Dzong.

Expedition supplies.

Expeditionsvorräte.

Expeditievoorraad.

Provisiones de la expedición.

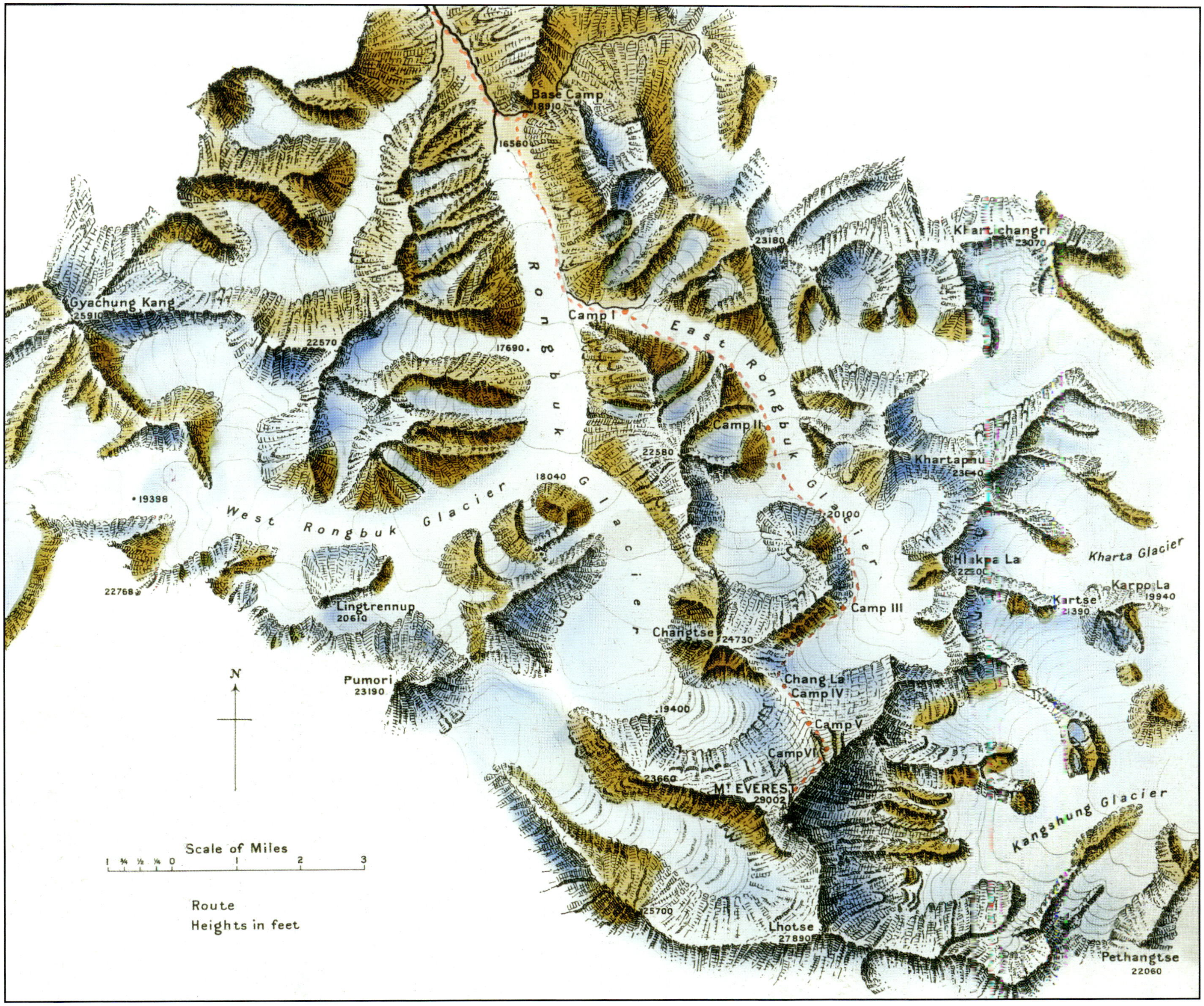

Hand-drawn map of the Rongbuk glacier and surrounding area.

Handgezeichnete Karte des Rongpu-Gletschers und seiner Umgebung.

Handgetekende kaart van de Rongbuk-gletsjer en omgeving.

Mapa dibujado a mano del glaciar Rongbuk y la zona circundante.

Members of the 1924 Mount Everest Expedition (from left to right): Irvine, Mallory, Norton, Odell and Macdonald (back row); Shabbeare, Bruce, Somervell and Beetham (front row).

Die Mitglieder der Mount Everest-Expedition von 1924 (von links nach rechts): Irvine, Mallory, Norton, Odell und Macdonald (hintere Reihe), Shebbeare, Bruce, Somervell und Beetham (vordere Reihe).

Deelnemers aan de Everest-expeditie van 1924 (v.l.n.r.): Irvine, Mallory, Norton, Odell en Macdonald (achter); Shabbeare, Bruce, Somervell en Beetham (voor).

Miembros de la Expedición del Monte Everest 1924 (de izquierda a derecha): Irvine, Mallory, Norton, Odell y Macdonald (fila trasera); Shabbeare, Bruce, Somervell y Beetham (fila delantera).

John Hazard.

Geoffrey Bruce.

Dr. T.H. Somervell.

Howard Somervell at Base Camp.

Howard Somervell im Basislager.

Howard Somervell in het basiskamp.

Howard Somervell en el campamento base.

On the way to Everest, Irvine demonstrates the "Roarer Cooker" to the Sherpa cooks.

Während der Reise zum Mount Everest demonstriert Irvine Sherpa-Köchen den „Roarer Cooker“ (Kochgerät).

Irvine demonstreert de fluitketel aan de Sherpa-koks onderweg naar de Everest.

Irvine muestra la cocina "Roarer Cooker" a los cocineros *sherpas* en ruta al Everest.

Rongbuk glacier ice and the North face of Everest.

Das Eis des Rongpu-Gletschers und die Nordseite des Mount Everest.

Rongbuk-gletsjerijs en de noordzijde van de Everest.

El hielo del glaciar Rongbuk y la cara norte del Everest.

Andrew Irvine fixing an oxygen cylinder.

Andrew Irvine bei der Reparatur eines Sauerstoffzylinders.

Andrew Irvine repareert een zuurstofcilinder

Andrew Irvine arreglando un cilindro de oxígeno.

Everest team members on the ice pinnacles of the East Rongbuk glacier.

Mitglieder der Mount Everest-Expedition inmitten der Eistürme des östlichen Rongbu-Gletschers.

Expeditieteam nabij ijspieken van de oostelijke Rongbuk-gletsjer.

Los miembros del equipo del Everest en las cumbres heladas del lado este del glaciar de Rongbuk.

Camp II on the East
Rongbuk glacier.

Lager II am östlichen
Rongpu-Gletscher.

Kamp II op de oostelijke
Rongbuk-gletsjer.

El campamento II en el
lado este del glaciar de
Rongbuk.

In the "Trough'.

Im „Trog".

In de 'trog'.

En la "depresión".

Sunset on the summit of Mount Everest.

Sonnenaufgang über dem Gipfel des Mount Everest.

Zonsondergang op de top van de Everest.

Atardecer en la cumbre del Monte Everest

Tents surrounded by ice-pinnacles.

Zelte inmitten von Eistürmen.

Tenten tussen ijspieken.

Tiendas de campaña entre cumbres de hielo.

Mount Everest in 1924.

Der Mount Everest im Jahr 1924.

De Everest in 1924.

El Monte Everest en 1924.

Team members on the ice pinnacles of the East Rongbuk glacier.

Mitglieder des Teams inmitten der Eistürme des östlichen Rongpu-Gletschers.

Expeditieteam tussen ijspieken van de oostelijke Rongbuk-gletsjer.

Los miembros del equipo en las cumbres heladas del lado este del glaciar de Rongbuk.

Near the top of the "Trough", 5th May 1924. This is one of the last images taken by Irvine before he and Mallory disappeared.

Am oberen Ende des „Trogs“, 5. Mai 1924, eines der letzten von Irvine aufgenommenen Bilder vor seinem Verschwinden.

Nabij de top van de 'trog', 5 mei 1924. Dit is een van de laatste foto's gemaakt door Irvine voor hij verdween met Mallory.

Cerca de la cima de la "depresión", 5 de mayo de 1924. Esta es una de las últimas imágenes tomadas por Irvine antes de desaparecer con Mallory.

Seracs on the Rongbuk glacier and surrounding mountains.

Eiszacken auf dem Rongpu-Gletscher und den benachbarten Bergen.

IJsformaties op de Rongbuk-gletsjer en het gebergte eromheen.

Seracs en el glaciar Rongbuk y las montañas circundantes.

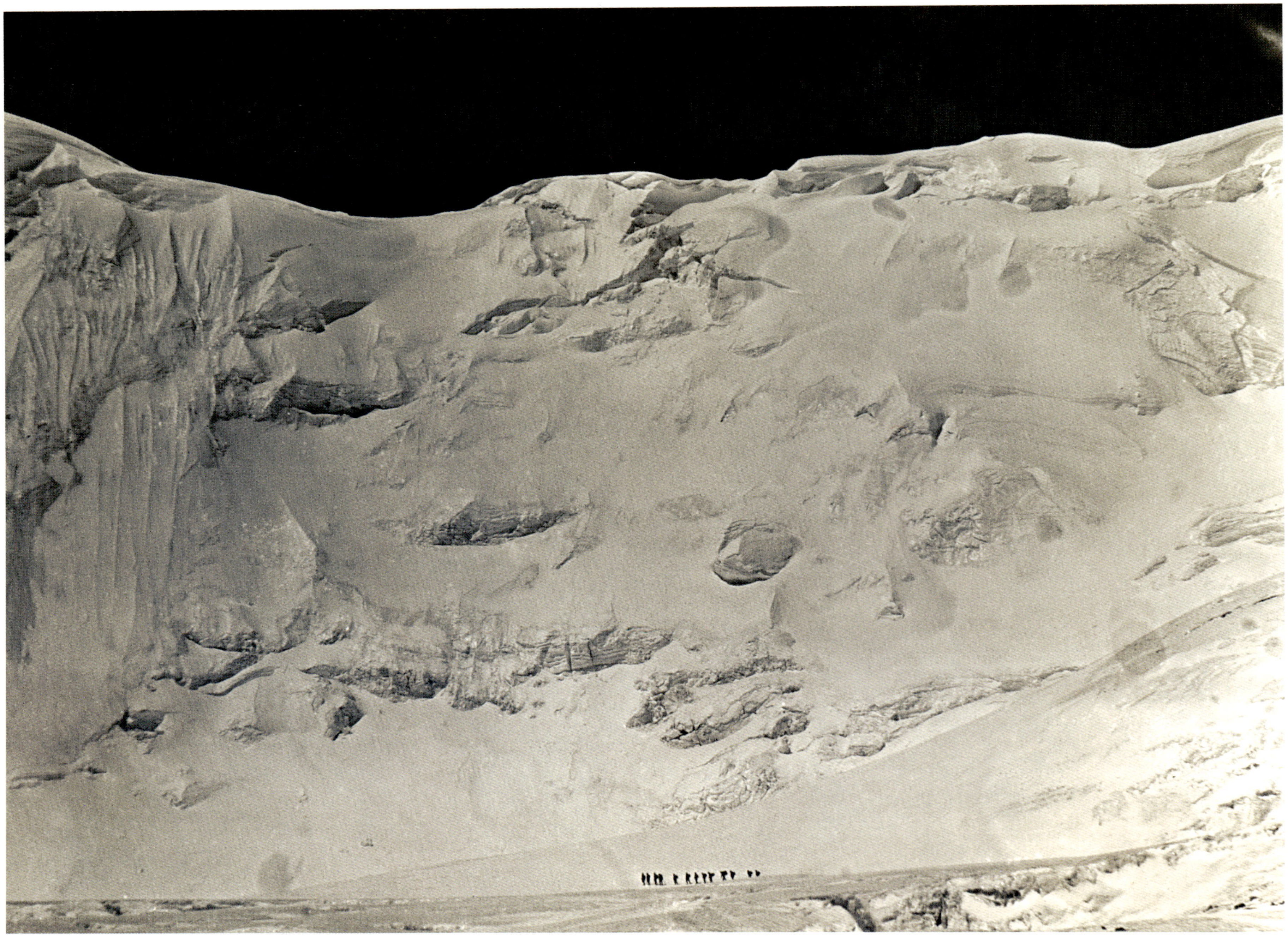

The ant-like figures of expedition members put the sheer scale of the task at hand, climbing the North Col, into perspective.

Die ameisengleichen Gestalten der Expeditionsteilnehmer bringen die schiere Größe des Vorhabens, die Besteigung des Nordsattels, in das richtige Verhältnis.

Dat de expeditieleden op mieren lijken, geeft duidelijk aan dat het een zware opgave was om de noordelijke pas te beklimmen.

Las figuras con forma de hormiga de los miembros de la expedición ofrecen una perspectiva de la gran envergadura de la tarea que les ocupa, escalando el Collado Norte.

Odell and porters climbing the North Col (known in Tibet as the Chang-La chimney).

Odell und seine Träger beim Aufstieg auf den Nordsattel (in Tibet Chang-La-Schornstein genannt).

Odell en zijn dragers beklimmen de noordelijke pas (de Chang-La-schoorsteen genoemd in Tibet).

Escalando el Collado Norte (llamado chimenea Chang-La en El Tibet) por Odell y los portadores.

Climbing the North Col.

Besteigung des Nordsattels.

Beklimming van de noordelijke pas.

Escalando el Collado Norte.

The Sherpa Namgya suffered with frostbite whilst he was stranded on the North Col.

Der Sherpa Namgya erlitt Erfrierungen, während er auf dem Nordsattel festsaß.

De Sherpa Namgya leed aan bevriezing van de huid toen hij was gestrand op de noordelijke pas.

El *sherpa* Namgya afectado por la congelación y abandonado en el Collado Norte.

Namgya drinking tea with his frostbitten hands.

Namgya mit einer Tasse Tee in seinen von Erfrierungen gezeichneten Händen.

Met bevroren handen brengt Namgya zijn kop thee naar zijn mond.

Namgya bebiendo té con las manos congeladas.

Climbing party.

Bergsteigergruppe.

Klimteam.

Grupo en ascenso.

Everest seen from a frozen lake.

Der Mount Everest von einem gefrorenen See aus gesehen.

De Everest gezien vanaf een bevroren meer.

El Everest visto desde un lago helado.

Gauri Sankar from the north-west, painted by Somervell.

Der Gauri Sankar von Nordwesten, gemalt von Somervell.

Gauri Sankar vanuit het noordwesten, geschilderd door Somervell.

Gauri Sankar desde el noroeste, pintado por Somervell.

View from camp of the summit of Everest through the clouds.

Blick auf den wolkenverhangenen Gipfel des Mount Everest vom Lager aus.

Zicht vanuit het kamp op de bewolkte Everest-top.

Vista de la cumbre del Everest a través de las nubes desde el campamento.

Norton (left) and Somervell (right) with three porters.

Norton (links) und Somervell (rechts) mit drei Trägern.

Norton (links) en Somervell (rechts) met drie dragers.

Norton (a la izquierda) y Somervell (a la derecha) con tres portadores.

Everest and the Rongbuk glacier.

Der Mount Everest und der Rongpu-Gletscher.

De Everest en de Rongbuk-gletsjer.

El Everest y el glaciar Rongbuk.

Camp II on Everest. Mount Kellas rises above at 6,850m.

Lager II auf dem Mount Everest, dahinter der Mount Kellas (6850 m).

Kamp II op de Everest. De Kellas torent boven het kamp uit met een hoogte van 6850 meter.

El campamento III en el Everest. Por encima se alza el Monte Kellas a 6850 m.

Close view of the peak of Everest.

Großaufnahme vom Gipfel des Mount Everest.

De Everest-top van dichtbij.

Vista de cerca del pico del Everest.

Camp III at 6,400m.

Kamp III op 6400 meter hoogte.

Lager III auf 6400 m Höhe.

El campamento III a 6400 m.

On the snow.

Auf dem Schnee.

Op de sneeuw.

En la nieve.

Ice pinnacles on the Rongbuk glacier.

Eistürme im Rongpu-Gletscher.

IJspieken op de Rongbuk-gletsjer.

Cumbres de hielo en el glaciar Rongbuk.

Ice pinnacles.

Eistürme.

IJspieken.

Cumbres de hielo.

Team members on the ice pinnacles of the East Rongbuk glacier.

Teammitglieder inmitten der Eistürme im Rongpu-Gletscher.

Teamleden tussen ijspieken van de Rongbuk-gletsjer.

Los miembros del equipo en las cumbres heladas del lado este del glaciar de Rongbuk.

Camp II at 6,000m.

Kamp II op 6000 meter hoogte.

Lager II auf 6000 m Höhe.

El campamento II a 6.000 m.

Norton, Shebbeare, Somervell, Mallory.

Team members moving through the ice pinnacles on the East Rongbuk glacier.

Expeditionsteilnehmer zwischen den Eistürmen im östlichen Rongpu-Gletscher.

Teamleden begeven zich tussen ijspieken van de oostelijke Rongbuk-gletsjer.

Los miembros del equipo avanzando por las cumbres heladas en el lado este del glaciar de Rongbuk.

Ice pinnacles in the East Rongbuk glacier's corridor to Everest.

Eistürme im Korridor des Rongpu-Gletschers zum Mount Everest.

IJspieken van de oostelijke Rongbuk-gletsjer in de corridor naar de Everest.

Cumbres de hielo en el pasillo del lado este del glaciar Rongbuk hacia el Everest.

An expedition member giving a talk.

Ein Expeditionsteilnehmer bei einem Vortrag am Berg.

Een expeditielid houdt een praatje.

Un miembro de la expedición dando una charla.

A river of ice and ice pinnacles.

Ein Fluss aus Eis und Eistürmen.

Een ijsrivier en ijspieken.

Un río de hielo y cumbres de hielo.

Ice pinnacles jutting through the water.

Eistürme ragen aus dem Wasser.

Boven het water uitstekende ijspieken.

Cumbres de hielo sobresaliendo por el agua.

View of Camp III and Mount Everest.

Blick auf Lager III und den Mount Everest.

Kamp III en de Everest.

Vista del campamento III y Monte Everest.

Camping on the edge of the ice pinnacles.

Lager am Rande der Eistürme.

Kamp op een helling met ijspieken.

Campamento al borde de las cumbres de hielo.

Camp IV.

Lager IV.

Kamp IV.

Campamento IV.

A tent surrounded by ice-pinnacles.

Ein Zelt inmitten von Eistürmen.

Een tent tussen ijspieken.

Una tienda de campaña entre cumbres de hielo.

On the edge of a crevasse.

Am Rande einer Gletscherspalte.

Op de rand van een gletsjerspleet.

Al borde de una grieta.

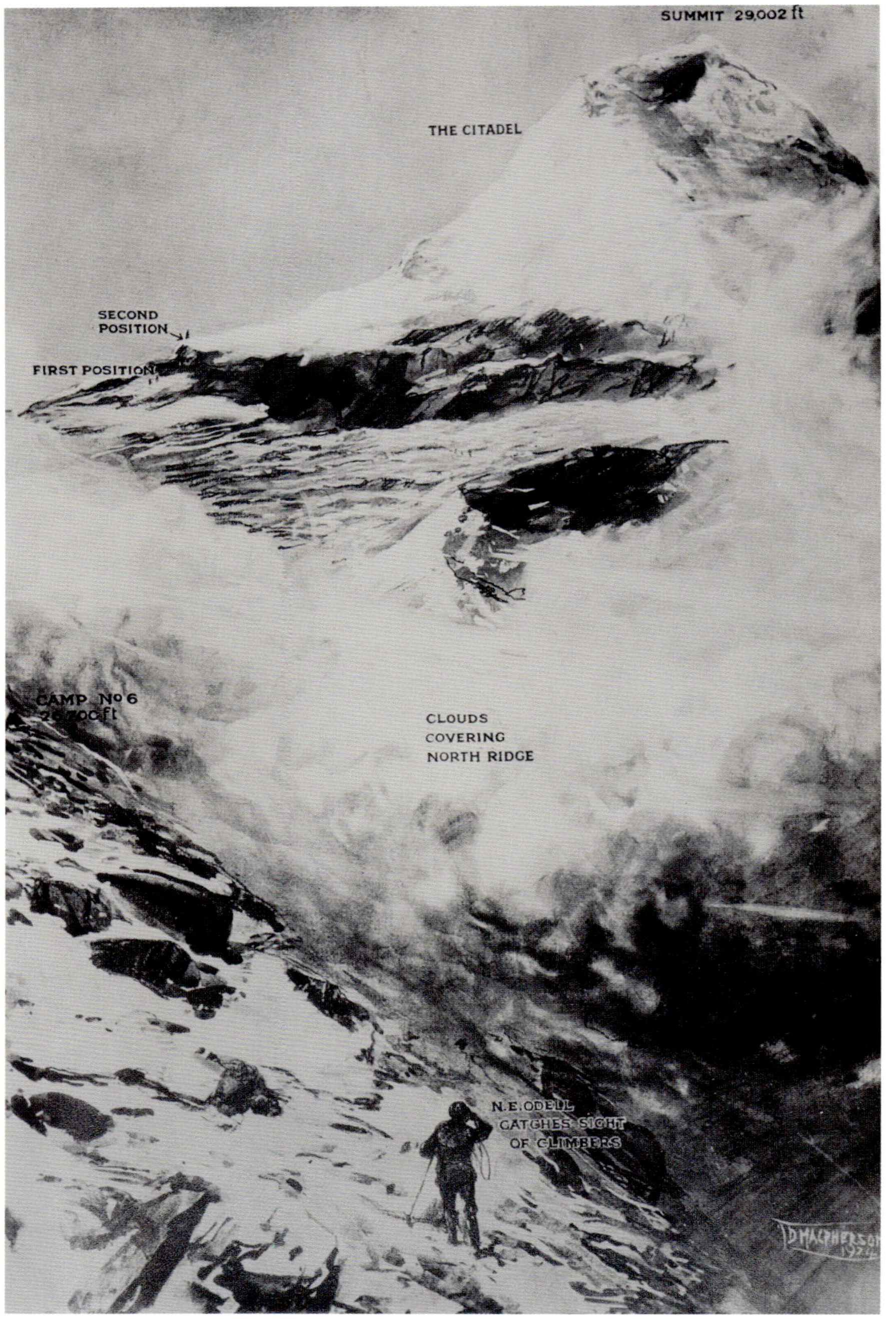

Odell watching for Mallory and Irvine.

Odell hält nach Mallory und Irvine Ausschau.

Odell kijkt uit naar Mallory en Irvine.

Odell pendiente de Mallory e Irvine.

Norton reaching his highest point without oxygen.

Norton bei seinem Höhenrekord ohne Sauerstoffgerät.

Norton op zijn hoogste punt zonder zuurstof.

Norton en su punto más alto sin oxígeno.

Photograph showing Norton and Somervell's progress on their ascent of Everest.

Fotografie mit einer Darstellung der einzelnen Etappen des Besteigungsversuchs von Norton und Somervell.

Foto met daarop de vorderingen van Norton en Somervell tijdens hun beklimming van de Everest.

Fotografía que muestra el progreso de Norton y Somervell en su ascenso al Everest.

Mallory and Irvine leaving the North Col for the last climb. This is the last known photo taken of the two of them together.

Mallory und Irvine verlassen den Nordsattel zu ihrem letzten Besteigungsversuch. Dies ist die letzte Fotografie, auf der beide Männer gemeinsam zu sehen sind.

Mallory en Irvine verlaten de noordelijke pas voor de eindklim. Dit is de laatste bekende foto waarop ze samen te zien zijn.

Mallory e Irvine dejando el Collado Norte para iniciar la última subida. Esta es la última fotografía tomada de ellos de la que se tiene conocimiento.

The attempted ascent of Everest by Mallory and Irvine.

Fotografie mit einer Darstellung der Stationen des Besteigungsversuchs von Mallory und Irvine.

De klimpoging op de Everest van Mallory en Irvine.

El intento de ascenso al Everest de Mallory e Irvine.

The coded telegram arrived in London on 19th June 1924. It stated: "Mallory Irvine Nove Remaincer Alcedo", which translated as "Mallory and Irvine killed in last engagement, arrived here, all in good order".

Das verschlüsselte Telegramm mit der Nachricht vom Verschwinden der Bergsteiger erreichte London am 19. Juni 1924. Die Worte: „Mallory Irvine Nove Remainder Alcedo", bedeuten „Mallory und Irvine bei letztem Auftrag getötet, hier angekommen, alles in Ordnung".

Het gecodeerde telegram arriveerde in London op 19 juni 1924. Het luidde: 'Mallory Irvine Nove Remainder Alcedo' (wat betekent: 'Mallory en Irvine omgekomen tijdens laatste poging, overigen afgedaald en maken het goed').

El telegrama codificado llegó a Londres el 19 de junio de 1924. Decía: "Mallory Irvine Nove Remainder Alcedo", que se traduce por "Mallory e Irvine muertos en el último intento, llegaron aquí, todos en buenas condiciones".

RECEIVED TELEGRAM

PLEASE SEND ANY REPLY TO THIS TELEGRAM Via Eastern

The first line of this Telegram contains the following particulars in the order named: Number of Message, Office of Origin, Number of Words, Date, Time handed in (in Letters, see Clock above), and Official instructions.

KA 429 S PHARIJONG 11 19 GX = 16.50

OBFERRAS LONDON ENGLAND =

MALLORY IRVINE NOVE REMAINDER ALCEDO =

all in good order

NORTON ROMGBUK

Sketch map of Mount Everest from surveys by Major Wheeler in 1921, with additions by the Expedition of 1924.

Kartenskizze des Mount Everest nach Aufnahmen von Major Wheeler aus dem Jahre 1921, mit von der Expedition des Jahres 1924 vorgenommenen Ergänzungen.

Kaart van de Everest geschetst op basis van inspecties van majoor Wheeler in 1921, aangevuld door de expeditie van 1924.

Boceto del mapa del Monte Everest de las mediciones realizadas por le mayor Wheeler en 1921, con añadidos de la Expedición de 1924.

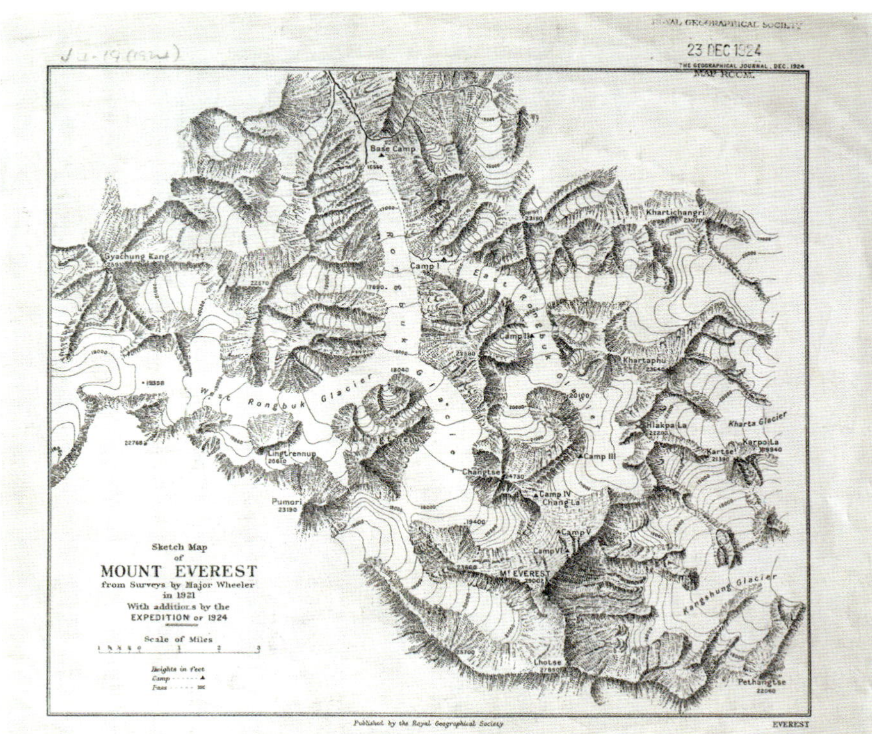

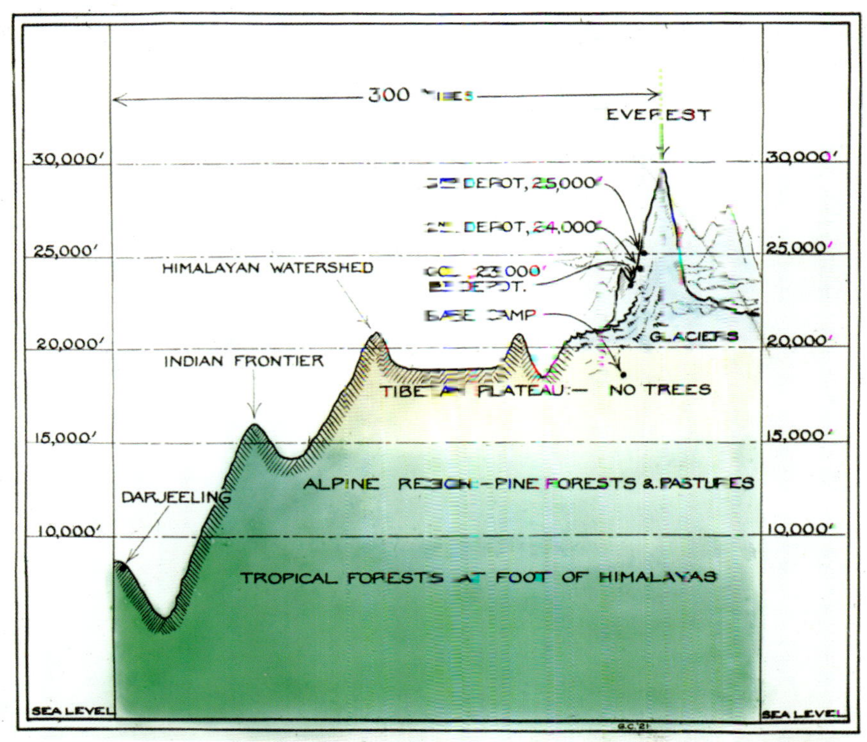

Diagram of the ascent to Everest with details of altitude.

Diagramm des Aufstiegs zum Gipfel des Mount Everest mit genauen Höhenangaben.

Diagram van de klim naar de Everest met hoogteaanduidingen.

Diagrama del ascenso al Everest con datos de altitud.

Mallory and Irvine, Legendary Heroes
Mallory und Irvine – legendäre Helden
Mallory en Irvine, legendarische helden
Mallory e Irvine, héroes de leyenda

Did George Mallory and Andrew Irvine, who both disappeared on 8 June 1924, reach the summit of Everest almost thirty years before Hillary and Tenzing Norgay? This question has fed the legend of these two British heroes ever since. Numerous expeditions have been launched to search for their bodies and solve the mystery. On 1 May 1999, Mallory's corpse was found at 8,170 metres. His camera, which could have provided evidence of his reaching the summit of Everest successfully, could not be found. From the sunglasses in his pocket, it could be concluded that Mallory died during the night, on the way back. Letters were found on him, but not the photo of his wife, which he had promised to leave at the summit should he succeed. So? The mystery remains intact today. Andrew Irvine's body was reportedly spotted by a Chinese Alpinist in 1960, but has never been seen again, despite numerous attempts to find it.

Hadden de op 8 juni 1924 verdwenen klimmers George Mallory en Andrew Irvine bijna dertig jaar vóór Hillary en Tenzing Norgay de top van de Everest al bereikt? Die vraag houdt de legende rond deze twee Britse helden levend. Diverse expedities zijn gelanceerd om hun lichamen op te sporen en het mysterie te ontrafelen. Op 1 mei 1999 werden de overblijfselen van Mallory gevonden op 8170 meter hoogte. Zijn fototoestel, dat zijn succes op de top van de Everest had kunnen aantonen, werd niet teruggevonden. Omdat zijn zonnebril in zijn zak zat, werd aangenomen dat Mallory 's nachts stierf, op de terugweg. Op zijn lichaam trof men brieven aan maar niet de foto van zijn vrouw, die hij beloofd had te zullen achterlaten op de top als hij die had bereikt. Dus? Tot op de dag van vandaag blijft het een mysterie. Het lichaam van Andrew Irvine werd in 1960 door een Chinese klimmer ontdekt, maar is daarna nooit meer teruggevonden ondanks vele pogingen.

George Mallory und Andrew Irvine sind am 8. Juni 1924 verschwunden. Ist Gelang ihnen bereits rund dreißig Jahren vor Hillary und Tenzing Norgay der Aufstieg zum Gipfel des Mount Everest gelungen? Diese Frage hat die Legende um diese beiden britischen Helden von jeher genährt. So wurden mehrere Expeditionen durchgeführt, um nach ihren Leichen zu suchen und das Rätsel rund um ihr Verschwinden zu lösen. Am 1. Mai 1999 wurde die Leiche Mallorys auf etwa 8150 Metern Höhe gefunden. Seine Kamera, die eine mögliche Erstbesteigung des Mount Everest hätte beweisen können, fehlte jedoch. Da Mallory seine Sonnenbrille in der Tasche hatte, wurde angenommen, dass er in der Nacht, auf dem Rückweg, gestorben ist. Man fand zwar Briefe bei ihm, jedoch nicht das Foto seiner Frau, das er im Falle eines Erfolgs auf dem Gipfel zurücklassen wollte. Somit bleibt das Rätsel bis heute ungelöst. Die Leiche Andrew Irvines wurde angeblich 1960 von einem chinesischen Bergsteiger gesehen, konnte allerdings trotz mehrfacher Suchaktionen nicht gefunden werden.

¿Alcanzaron George Mallory y Andrew Irvine, desaparecidos el 8 de junio de 1924, la cumbre del Everest casi treinta años antes que Hillary y Tenzing Norgay? Esta pregunta no ha dejado de alimentar la leyenda de estos dos héroes británicos. Son varias las expediciones que se han puesto en marcha para buscar sus cuerpos y desvelar el misterio. El 1 de mayo de 1999 se encontró el cadáver de Mallory a 8170 metros, aunque su cámera de fotos no, que habría podido servir de testimonio de su éxito en la cumbre del Everest. Con sus gafas de sol en un bolsillo, Mallory habría muerto durante la noche, en el camino de regreso. Sobre él se encontraron varias cartas, pero no la fotografía de su esposa, que había prometido dejar en la cumbre en caso de victoria. ¿Entonces qué ocurrió? Todavía hoy el misterio está por resolver. El cuerpo de Andrew Irvine habría sido localizado por un alpinista chino en 1960 pero nunca pudo ser hallado pese a haberlo intentado en varias ocasiones.

Andrew Irvine.

George Leigh Mallory.

Altimeter found on Mallory's body.

Hoogtemeter gevonden op Mallory's lichaam.

Höhenmesser, der bei der Leiche Mallorys gefunden wurde.

Altímetro encontrado en el cuerpo de Mallory.

Mallory's hobnail boot.

Mallorys mit Nägeln beschlagener Stiefel.

Mallory's bergschoenen met stijgijzers.

Bota con tachuelas de Mallory.

Goggles belonging to George Leigh Mallory.

Sneeuwbril van George Leigh Mallory.

Mallorys Schneebrille.

Gafas protectoras pertenecientes a George Leigh Mallory.

Wristwatch found on Mallory's body, which was eventually discovered at 8,170m on 1st May 1999 (75 years after his disappearance).

Armbanduhr, die bei der am 1. Mai 1999 auf 8170 m Höhe entdeckten Leiche Mallorys gefunden wurde (75 Jahre nach seinem Verschwinden).

Polshorloge gevonden op Mallory's lichaam dat pas op 1 mei 1999 (75 jaar na zijn verdwijning) werd ontdekt op 8170 meter hoogte.

Reloj de pulsera encontrado en el cuerpo de Mallory, descubierto a (8170 m) el 1 de mayo de 1999 (75 años después de su desaparición).

Climbing rope fragment found on Mallory's body.

Überrest eines Kletterseils, das bei der Leiche Mallorys gefunden wurde.

Stuk klimtouw gevonden op Mallory's lichaam.

Fragmento de una cuerda de escalar encontrado en el cuerpo de Mallory.

Open box of "Swan Vestas" matches (found on Mallory's body).

Offene Streichholzschachtel der Marke „Swan Vestas“ (bei Mallorys Leiche gefunden).

Open luciferdoosje van het merk *Swan Vestas* (gevonden op Mallory's lichaam).

Caja de cerillas abierta "Swan Vestas" (encontrada en el cuerpo de Mallory).

Tin of meat lozenges (found on Mallory's body).

Dose mit Brühwürfeln (bei Mallorys Leiche gefunden).

Blikje met vleesblokjes (gevonden op Mallory's lichaam).

Lata de carne en conserva (encontrada en el cuerpo de Mallory).

Pocketknife (found on Mallory's body).

Taschenmesser (bei Mallorys Leiche gefunden).

Zakmes (gevonden op Mallory's lichaam).

Pañuelo de bolsillo (encontrado en el cuerpo de Mallory).

Handkerchief bearing the monogram G.L.M. (George Leigh Mallory).

Taschentuch mit dem Monogramm G.L.M. (George Leigh Mallory).

Zakdoek met monogram G.L.M. (George Leigh Mallory).

Pañuelo con el monograma G.L.M. (George Leigh Mallory).

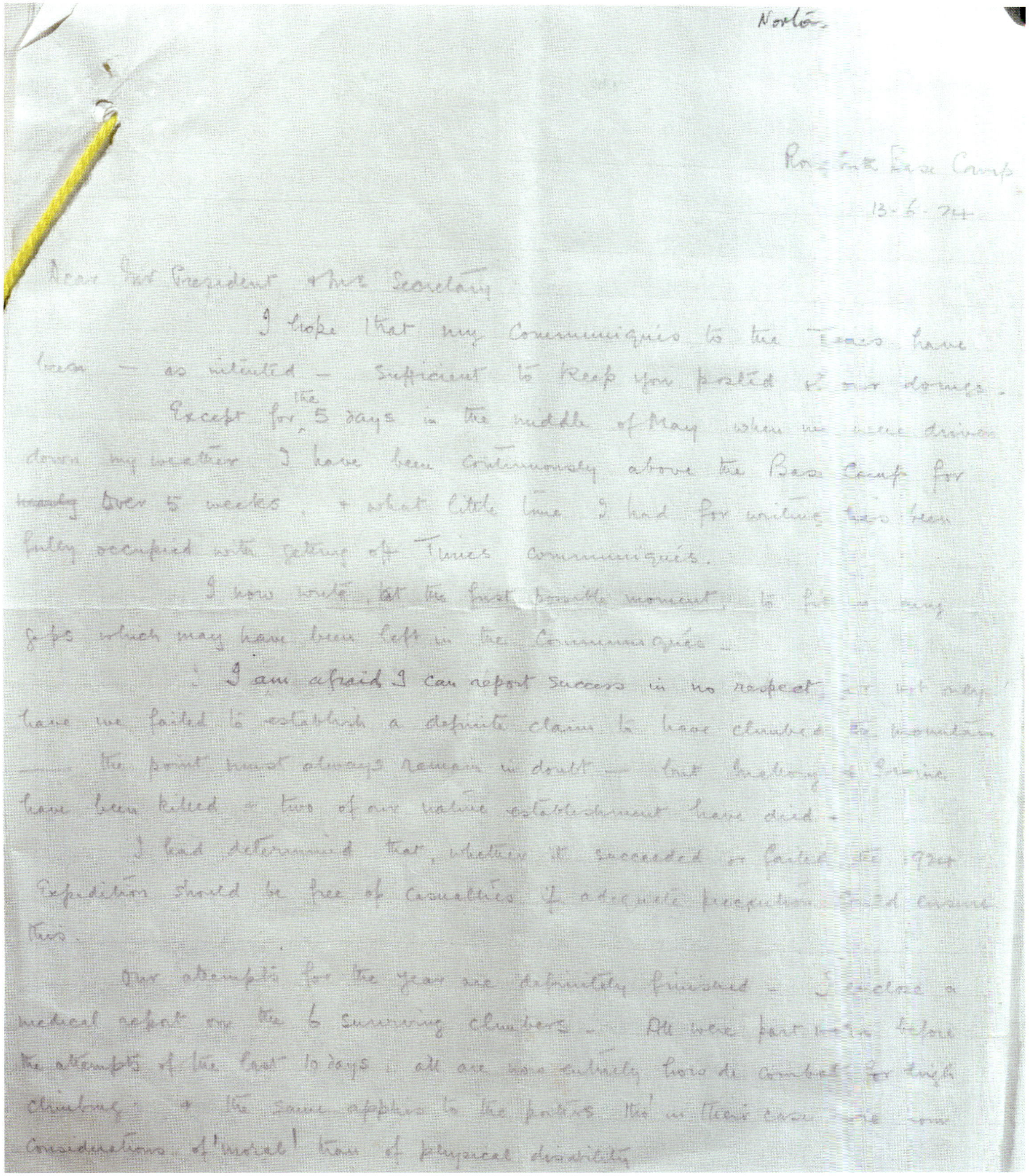

Norton.

Rongbuk Base Camp
13-6-24.

Dear Mr President & Mr Secretary

I hope that my Communiqués to the Times have been — as intended — sufficient to keep you posted of our doings.

Except for the 5 days in the middle of May when we were driven down by weather I have been continuously above the Base Camp for ~~nearly~~ over 5 weeks, & what little time I had for writing has been fully occupied with getting off Times communiqués.

I now write, at the first possible moment, to fill in any gaps which may have been left in the Communiqués.

I am afraid I can report success in no respect, for not only have we failed to establish a definite claim to have climbed the mountain — the point must always remain in doubt — but Mallory & Irvine have been killed & two of our native establishment have died.

I had determined that, whether it succeeded or failed, the 1924 Expedition should be free of casualties if adequate precaution could ensure this.

Our attempts for the year are definitely finished. I enclose a medical report on the 6 surviving climbers. All were past work before the attempts of the last 10 days: all are now entirely hors de combat for high climbing & the same applies to the porters tho' in their case more from considerations of 'moral' than of physical disability

Letter from Norton to the Royal Geographical Society informing the RGS of Mallory and Irvine's disappearance, 13rd June 1924.

Brief von Norton an die Royal Geographical Society, in dem er diese vom Verschwinden Mallorys und Irvines in Kenntnis setzt, 13. Juni 1924.

Brief van Norton aan de *Royal Geographical Society* waarin hij de verdwijning van Mallory en Irvine meldt (13 juni 1924).

Carta de Norton a la *Royal Geographical Society* en la que informa sobre la desaparición de Mallory e Irvine, 13 de junio de 1924.

Bhootiyas from Mustan
Province of Nari
Western Tibet

1933

Everest Puts Up a Fight
Der Mount Everest leistet Widerstand

After the tragic disappearance of George Mallory and Andrew Irvine the doors to Tibet remain sealed for many years. Authorisation is finally granted to the English to launch an expedition in 1933. A senior civil servant of the British administration in India, Hugh Ruttledge, 48 years old, will take charge of the group. Two of the thirteen Alpinists who make up the expedition party, Frank Smythe and Eric Shipton, are among the brightest stars of the age. For the first time, a chief radio operator is brought into the team. Thanks to the telephone line that he had been able to install in camp IV, at the top of the col, the climbers learn that the monsoon has already arrived in the Gulf of Bengal. There is no time to lose! It is already the end of May when the three Alpinists, Jack Longland, Percy Wyn-Harris and Lawrence Wager, are finally able to start their ascent towards the summit from camp V, established at 7,800 metres. They follow along the ridge, then turn off, crossing the walls of the north face, and finally stop at 8,350 metres, the planned altitude for the sixth and final camp. Longland has to go back down again with the Sherpas, but his group is caught in the storm. Visibility is reduced to a few metres. The men try to find the path and struggle for survival. The nightmare lasts for two hours, but it seems an eternity.
Meanwhile, Wyn-Harris and Wager are getting ready at camp VI. On 30 May 1933, a little before 6am, they start out and are soon warmed by the first rays of sunshine. Unroped, they are close to the "First Step", the towering projection on the path leading directly to the summit, when they discover an ice axe lying on a rock. The name of a Swiss manufacturer can be read clearly on the shining steel axe head: "Willisch de Täsch". This is the ice axe belonging to either Mallory or Irvine, the two heroes who disappeared in 1924!
Evidently it is difficult, if not downright impossible, to get across the two projections: the First and, critically, the Second "Steps" that block the climb. They decide to take the same path as Norton nine years earlier: a narrow gully. The location is formidable: under a rocky corridor lies a 3,000 metre abyss! The two men do not manage to climb any higher than Norton; his record is therefore preserved. It is 12.30pm on 30 May. It is too late to hope to reach the summit, which waits only 300 metres above them. They are forced to abandon. On the descent, Wyn-Harris will recover the historic ice axe and leave his own in its place. His teammate, in a last effort, climbs up the ridge to take a look at the South Face of Everest and at Nepal from the other side. It is the very first time that mankind will experience this view.
For their part, Smythe and Shipton will attempt a new attack. Due to the bad weather, they are forced to spend two nights in a row at 8,350 metres, without oxygen masks. The following day, at 6am, the wind finally drops and the two Alpinists leave camp. Two hours later, while climbing, Shipton lets out a cry. Exhausted by the sleepless nights spent at such high altitude, he is at the limit of his endurance and has to leave his teammate. Smythe continues on alone and clears the "First Step", but, on his own, he cannot advance any further and starts to become delirious. He realises that he can go no further. There will be no new attack. Norton's record remains unbroken. After several days of vain hope, the good weather does not return. Hugh Ruttledge gives the order to break camp.

Nach dem tragischen Verschwinden von George Mallory und Andrew Irvine werden die Tore Tibets auf Jahre hin verschlossen. Schließlich erhalten die Briten 1933 erneut die Genehmigung, eine Expedition durchzuführen. Die Leitung übernimmt ein hoher Beamter der britischen Verwaltungsbehörden in Indien, der 48-jährige Hugh Ruttledge. Zwei der dreizehn Bergsteiger der Gruppe, Frank Smythe und Eric Shipton, gehören zu den Besten ihrer Zeit. Zum ersten Mal nimmt auch ein Funker an der Expedition teil. Dank der Telefonverbindung, die auf der Passhöhe vom Lager IV eingerichtet wurde, erfahren die Bergsteiger, dass der Monsun schon den Golf von Bengalen erreicht hat. Jetzt dürfen sie keine Zeit mehr verlieren! Erst Ende Mai können die drei Bergsteiger, Jack Longland, Percy Wyn-Harris und Lawrence Wager, von dem auf 7.800 Metern Höhe angelegten Lager V aus, mit dem Aufstieg zum Gipfel beginnen. Sie gehen dem Grat entlang, steigen dann über die

De Everest geeft zich niet gewonnen
El Everest opone resistencia

Felsplatten der Nordseite und machen auf 8.350 Metern halt, wo das sechste und letzte Lager vorgesehenen war. Longland muss mit den Sherpas wieder absteigen, doch seine Gruppe gerät in einen Sturm. Die Sicht beträgt nur wenige Meter. Die Männer versuchen, den Weg wiederzufinden und müssen um ihr Überleben fürchten. Zwei Stunden dauert der Alptraum, der ihnen wie eine Ewigkeit erscheint.
Währenddessen bereiten sich Wyn-Harris und Wager in Lager VI vor. Am 30. Mai 1933 beginnen sie noch vor sechs Uhr mit dem Aufstieg. Bald werden sie von den ersten Sonnenstrahlen aufgewärmt. Ohne angeseilt zu sein, gelangen sie in die Nähe des „First Step" (Erste Stufe), des Vorsprungs, der sich auf dem direkten Weg zum Gipfel erhebt. Plötzlich entdecken sie einen Eispickel, der dort auf dem Felsen ruht. Auf dem glänzenden Stahl des Metallkopfs ist deutlich der Name des schweizerischen Herstellers zu erkennen: „Willisch aus Täsch". Es muss sich um den Eispickel von Mallory oder Irvine handeln, den verschwundenen Helden von 1924!
Ganz offensichtlich ist es schwierig, wenn nicht gar unmöglich, die beiden Felsstufen zu überqueren, die auf dem Weg zum Gipfel liegen: den „First Step" und vor allem den „Second Step". Wyn-Harris und Wager entschließen sich daher, denselben Weg wie Norton neun Jahre zuvor zu nehmen: durch eine enge Steilschlucht. Der Ort ist furchteinflößend: Unter der felsigen Schlucht ist nichts als ein gähnender Abgrund von 3.000 Metern! Den beiden Männern gelingt es nicht, höher zu kommen als Norton, dessen Rekord von 1924 infolgedessen intakt bleibt. Es ist der 30. Mai, die Uhr zeigt 12.30 Uhr. Es ist zu spät, um den Gipfel noch zu erreichen, der sich nur 300 Meter über ihnen befindet. Sie müssen den Aufstieg abbrechen. Beim Abstieg nimmt Wyn-Harris den geschichtsträchtigen Eispickel mit und lässt seinen eigenen zurück. Sein Gefährte unternimmt eine letzte Anstrengung und erklimmt den Grat, um auf der anderen Seite einen Blick auf die Südwand des Everest und auf Nepal zu werfen. Es ist das erste Mal, dass sich einem Menschen dieser Anblick bietet.
Smythe und Shipton ihrerseits nehmen den Berg erneut in Angriff. Aufgrund der schlechten Wetterlage sind sie gezwungen, ohne Sauerstoffmaske zwei Nächte nacheinander auf 8.350 Metern Höhe zu verbringen. Am nächsten Morgen um 6 Uhr lässt der Wind endlich nach und die beiden Bergsteiger können das Lager verlassen. Zwei Stunden später stößt Shipton beim Aufstieg einen Schrei aus. Übermüdet von den zwei schlaflosen Nächten auf dieser Höhe, steht er am Rande eines Schwächeanfalls und muss seinen Gefährten allein ziehen lassen. Smythe setzt den Aufstieg fort und überquert den „First Step", doch allein auf sich gestellt kommt er nicht weiter und beginnt zu delirieren. Er sieht ein, dass er nicht weitergehen kann. Es wird keinen neuen Aufstieg geben. Nortons Rekord bleibt weiterhin bestehen. Nach mehreren Tagen vergeblicher Hoffnung hat sich das Wetter immer noch nicht verbessert, und so gibt Hugh Ruttledge den Befehl, die Zelte abzubrechen.

Na de tragische verdwijning van George Mallory en Andrew Irvine bleven de poorten van Tibet jarenlang gesloten. Uiteindelijk krijgen de Britten toestemming voor een expeditie in 1933. De 48-jarige Hugh Ruttledge, een hoge Britse overheidsfunctionaris in India, neemt de leiding. Twee van de dertien deelnemende alpinisten, Frank Smythe en Eric Shipton, behoren tot de top in die tijd. En voor het eerst beschikt het team over een ervaren radio-operator. Dankzij de telefoonlijn, geïnstalleerd in kamp IV ter hoogte van de pas, vernemen de klimmers dat de moesson de Golf van Bengalen al heeft bereikt. Er is geen tijd meer te verliezen! Eind mei kunnen drie alpinisten, Jack Longland, Percy Wyn-Harris en Lawrence Wager, eindelijk beginnen aan hun klim naar de top vanuit kamp V, dat op 7800 meter hoogte is ingericht. Ze volgen de bergkam, steken vervolgens zwaar door over het gesteente van de noordelijke helling en houden uiteindelijk halt op 8350 meter, de hoogte waarop het zesde en laatste kamp is gepland. Longland ziet zich genoodzaakt af te dalen met de Sherpa's, maar zijn groep wordt verrast door een storm. Er is nauwelijks enkele meters zicht. De mannen proberen hun weg te vinden en vechten voor hun leven. Twee uur lang beleven zij een nachtmerrie waar geen einde aan lijkt te komen.

Ondertussen bereiden Wyn-Harris en Wager zich voor in kamp VI. Op 30 mei 1933, even voor 6.00 uur, zijn zij op weg, al snel opgewarmd door de eerste zonnestralen. Los van elkaar komen ze aan in de buurt van 'De eerste stap', de verheffing op de directe route naar de top, waar ze een ijsbijl vinden, die daar op een rots ligt. Op het glimmende staal van de metalen kop is de naam van de Zwitserse fabrikant te lezen: 'Willisch de Täsch'. De ijsbijl is van Mallory of van Irvine, de twee helden die in 1924 verdwenen.
Uiteindelijk blijkt het moeilijk, praktisch onmogelijk, om de top te bereiken via de verheffingen van 'De eerste stap' en vooral 'De tweede stap', die de doorgang blokkeren. Ze besluiten dezelfde route te kiezen als Norton negen jaar eerder: een nauwe doorgang. Deze plek is zeer indrukwekkend met onder de kleurrijke rotsen een gapende diepte van 3000 meter. De twee mannen slagen er niet in hoger te klimmen dan Norton, die daarmee zijn record behoudt. Het 30 mei, 12.30 uur en te laat om de top nog te bereiken, al bevindt die zich slechts 300 meter boven hen. Noodgedwongen geven ze op. Tijdens de afdaling zal Wyn-Harris de historisch belangrijke ijsbijl ophalen en zijn eigen werktuig achterlaten. Met een laatste inspanning gaat zijn klimmaat naar de andere zijde van de bergkam om de zuidkant van de Everest en Nepal te bekijken. Het is voor het eerst dat een mens dit spectaculaire panorama ziet.
Op hun beurt doen Smythe en Shipton eveneens een poging. Gedwongen door het slechte weer brengen ze twee opeenvolgende nachten zonder zuurstofmasker door op een hoogte van 8350 meter. Om zes uur in de ochtend daarna neemt de wind eindelijk in kracht af en verlaten de twee alpinisten het kamp. Twee uur later, tijdens de klim, schreeuwt Shipton het uit. Hondsmoe van de slapeloze nachten op deze grote hoogte is hij een flauwte nabij en hij moet zijn kameraad in de steek laten. Smythe gaat alleen verder en overwint 'De eerste stap', maar hij maakt vervolgens geen vorderingen en begint te ijlen. Hij beseft dat hij niet verder kan. Er zal geen nieuwe poging volgen en het record van Norton houdt stand. Na vele dagen van vergeefse hoop wil het weer maar niet opknappen. Hugh Ruttledge geeft opdracht de kampen af te breken.

Tras la trágica desaparición de George Mallory y Andrew Irvine, las puertas del Tíbet permanecen cerradas durante años. Finalmente se autoriza a los ingleses a montar una expedición en 1933. Un alto funcionario de la administración británica en India, Hugh Ruttledge, de 48 años, encabeza el grupo. Dos de los trece alpinistas que componen la expedición, Frank Smythe y Eric Shipton, se cuentan entre los más brillantes de esta época. Y por primera vez, integra el equipo un jefe operador de radio. Gracias a la línea telefónica que se ha podido instalar en el campamento IV en la parte superior del collado, los escaladores se enteran de que el monzón ya ha llegado al Golfo de Bengala. ¡No hay tiempo que perder! Ya estamos a finales del mes de mayo cuando tres alpinistas, Jack Longland, Percy Wyn-Harris y Lawrence Wager, pueden comenzar por fin el ascenso a la cumbre desde el campamento V, ubicado a 7800 metros. Bordean la cresta, después giran a través de las placas rocosas de la vertiente norte, y por último se detienen a 8350 metros, la altitud prevista para el sexto y último campamento. Longland debe descender con los *sherpas*, pero su grupo se ve atrapado por la tormenta. Solamente se ve a unos metros. Los hombres intentan encontrar el camino y luchan por sobrevivir. Durante dos horas, viven una pesadilla que dura toda una eternidad.
Entretanto, Wyn-Harris y Wager se preparan en el campamento VI. El 30 de mayo de 1933, poco antes de las 6:00 de la mañana, se ponen en marcha y pronto entran en calor gracias a los primeros rayos del sol. Desatados, llegan cerca del «primer paso», ese desnivel que se alza sobre el camino directo hacia la cumbre, cuando descubren un piolet que yace allí, sobre la roca. Sobre el acero brillante de su cabeza metálica se lee con claridad el nombre de un fabricante suizo: «Willisch de Täsch». Es el piolet de Mallory o de Irvine, ¡los dos héroes desaparecidos en 1924!
Definitivamente, es difícil, incluso imposible, atravesar los dos salientes, el «primer paso» y, especialmente el «segundo paso», que bloquean la subida. Deciden tomar el mismo camino que Norton tomaría nueve años antes: un paso estrecho. El lugar es impresionante: bajo el pasillo rocoso, ¡3000 metros de vacío! Ninguno de los dos hombres consigue subir más alto que Norton, que mantiene su récord. Son las 12:30 del día 30 de mayo. Es demasiado tarde para esperar coronar la cumbre, que no obstante solo se encuentra a 300 metros por encima de ellos. Se ven obligados a abandonar. En el descenso, Wyn-Harris recupera el piolet cargado de historia y deja el suyo en su lugar. Su compañero de equipo, en un último esfuerzo, escala la cresta para contemplar, por el otro lado, la cara sur del Everest y Nepal. Es la primera vez que un hombre puede contemplar este espectáculo.
A su vez, Smythe y Shipton emprenden un nuevo asalto. A causa del mal tiempo, se ven obligados a pasar dos noches consecutivas a 8.350 metros, sin máscara de oxígeno. Al día siguiente, a las 6:00 de la mañana, el viento se aplaca por fin y los dos escaladores abandonan el campamento. Dos horas más tarde, en la subida, ¡Shipton da un grito! Muy cansado a consecuencia de estas noches sin poder dormir a esta altitud, está a punto de desmayarse y debe dejar a su compañero. Smythe continúa solo y atraviesa el «primer paso», pero él solo no consigue avanzar y comienza a divagar. ¡Comprende que no podrá llegar mucho más lejos! No habrá un nuevo asalto. ¡El récord de Norton permanece intacto! Tras varios días de vana esperanza, el buen tiempo no hace acto de presencia. Hugh Ruttledge da la orden de plegar los campamentos.

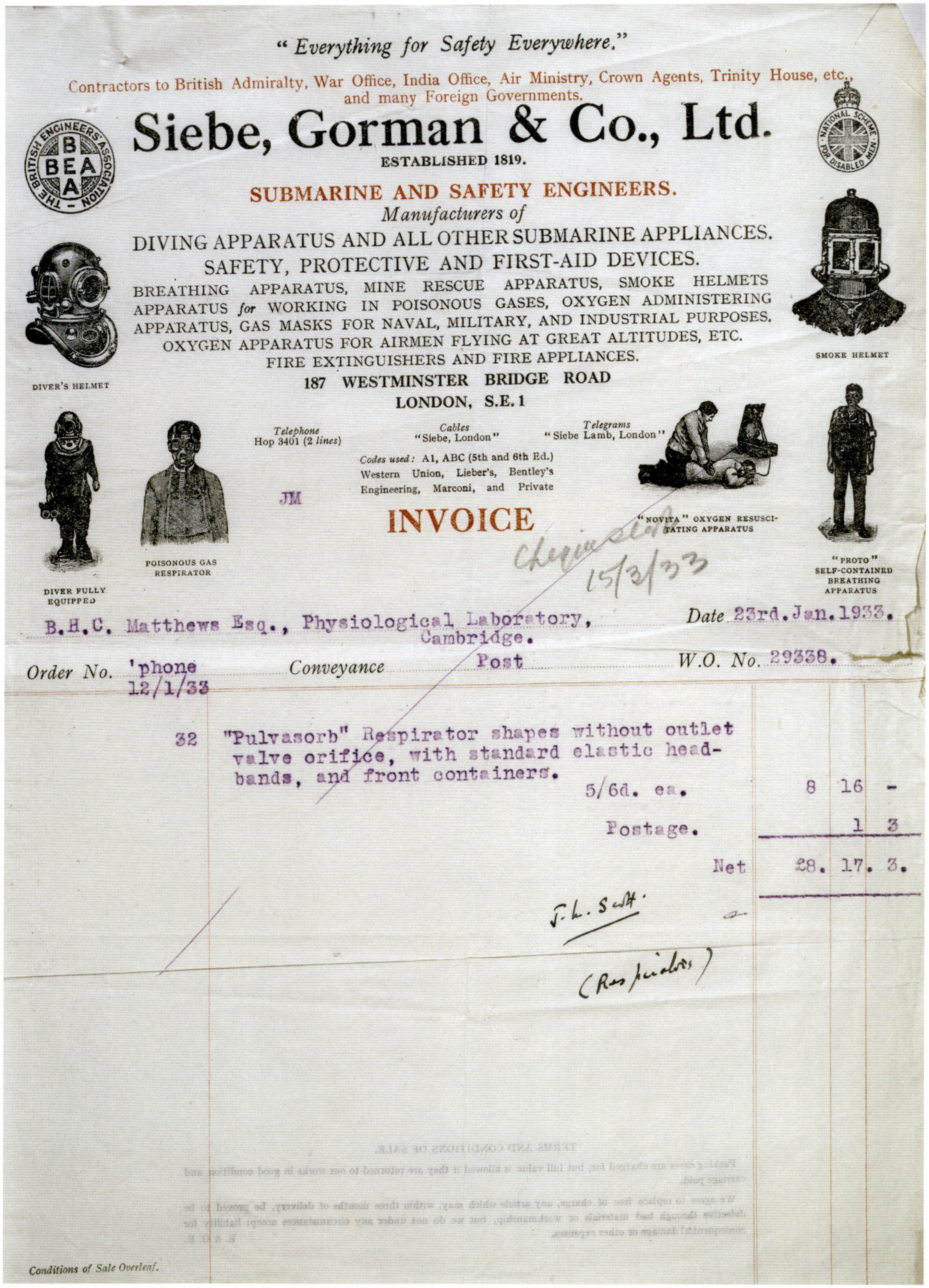
"Everything for Safety Everywhere."

Contractors to British Admiralty, War Office, India Office, Air Ministry, Crown Agents, Trinity House, etc., and many Foreign Governments.

Siebe, Gorman & Co., Ltd.

ESTABLISHED 1819.

SUBMARINE AND SAFETY ENGINEERS.

Manufacturers of

DIVING APPARATUS AND ALL OTHER SUBMARINE APPLIANCES.
SAFETY, PROTECTIVE AND FIRST-AID DEVICES.
BREATHING APPARATUS, MINE RESCUE APPARATUS, SMOKE HELMETS
APPARATUS for WORKING IN POISONOUS GASES, OXYGEN ADMINISTERING
APPARATUS, GAS MASKS FOR NAVAL, MILITARY, AND INDUSTRIAL PURPOSES.
OXYGEN APPARATUS FOR AIRMEN FLYING AT GREAT ALTITUDES, ETC.
FIRE EXTINGUISHERS AND FIRE APPLIANCES.

187 WESTMINSTER BRIDGE ROAD
LONDON, S.E.1

Telephone Hop 3401 (2 lines) | Cables "Siebe, London" | Telegrams "Siebe Lamb, London"

Codes used: A1, ABC (5th and 6th Ed.) Western Union, Lieber's, Bentley's Engineering, Marconi, and Private

JM

INVOICE

Cheque sent 15/3/33

B.H.C. Matthews Esq., Physiological Laboratory, Cambridge.

Date 23rd.Jan.1933.

Order No. 'phone 12/1/33 Conveyance Post W.O. No. 29338.

32	"Pulvasorb" Respirator shapes without outlet valve orifice, with standard elastic head-bands, and front containers. 5/6d. ea.	8	16	-
	Postage.		1	3
	Net	£8.	17.	3.

J. L. Scott.

(Respirators)

Conditions of Sale Overleaf.

Siebe Gorman & Co. Ltd. – Invoice for respiratory devices for the 1933 Everest Expedition.

Siebe Gorman & Co., Ltd – Rechnung über Atemgeräte für die Mount Everest-Expedition von 1933.

Factuur van Siebe Gorman & Co., Ltd voor zuurstofapparatuur voor de Everest-expeditie van 1933.

Siebe Gorman & Co., Ltd – Factura de dispositivos de oxígeno para la Expedición al Everest de 1933.

The interpreter Karma Paul (front left), who will take part in numerous British expeditions, and three Ghurkhas.

Der Dolmetscher Karma Paul (vorne links), der an zahlreichen britischen Expeditionen teilnahm, und drei Gurkhas.

De tolk Karma Paul (linksvoor), die aan verschillende Britse expedities deelnam, en drie Gurkha's.

El intérprete, Karma Paul (delante a la izquierda), que participará en varias expediciones británicas, y tres *gurkhas*.

Choosing porters, Darjeeling.

Auswahl von Trägern in Darjeeling.

Dragers worden geselecteerd in Darjeeling.

Selección de portadores, Darjeeling.

Marketplace in Darjeeling (Bengal).

Marktplatz von Darjeeling in Bengalen.

Markt in Darjeeling (Bengalen).

Mercado en Darjeeling (Bengala).

Sir John Laurence "Jack" Longland crossing a Tibetan river by rope bridge.

Sir John Laurence „Jack“ Longland bei der Überquerung eines Flusses in Tibet mithilfe einer Seilbrücke.

Sir John Laurence 'Jack' Longland steekt een Tibetaanse rivier over via een touwbrug.

Sir John Laurence "Jack" Longland cruzando un río tibetano a través de un puente de cuerda.

Tibetan children between Tashidzom and Shi.

Tibetische Kinder zwischen Tashi Dzom und Shi.

Tibetaanse kinderen tussen Tashidzom en Shi.

Niños tibetanos entre Tashidzom y Shi.

Listening to "Father William" on the gramophone at Kharta Shikar.

Bewohner von Kharta Shikar hören „Father William" auf dem Grammophon.

Luisteren naar 'Father William' op de grammofoon in Kharta Shikar.

Escuchando "Father William" en el gramófono en Kharta Shikar.

Doctor and climber Raymond Greene – the novelist Graham Greene's brother – with two porters.

Der Arzt und Bergsteiger Raymond Greene – Bruder des Schriftsteller Graham Greene – mit zwei Trägern.

De klimmende dokter Raymond Greene (broer van de schrijver Graham Greene) met twee dragers.

El doctor y escalador Raymond Greene, hermano del escritor Graham Greene, con dos portadores.

Jack Longland pole jumping at Tengkye Dzong.

Jack Longland beim Stabhochsprung in Tengkye Dzong.

Polsstokspringende Jack Longland in Tengkye Dzong.

Jack Longland practicando el salto con garrocha en Tengkye Dzong.

Porters boxing at Tengkye. The climber and boxing champion Hugh Boustead gave lessons to the porters.

Träger beim Boxen in Tengkye. Sie wurden von Bergsteiger und Box-Champion Hugh Boustead unterrichtet.

Boksende dragers in Tengkye. Klimmer en bokskampioen Hugh Boustead gaf de dragers les.

Portadores boxeando en Tengkye. El escalador y campeón de boxeo Hugh Boustead dio clases a los portadores.

Yaks fording the Yaru River near Mende.

Yaks bei der Durchquerung des Yaru bei Mende.

Jaks waden door de Yaru bij Mende.

Yaks vadeando el río Yaru cerca de Mende.

A porter fording a river and carrying a friend and a dog.

Träger bei der Durchquerung eines Flusses. Er trägt einen Freund und einen Hund.

Een drager brengt een vriend en een hond naar de overkant van een rivier.

Un portador vadea un río cargando a un amigo y un perro.

Edward Shebbeare with an umbrella.

Edward Shebbeare met paraplu.

Edward Shebbeare mit Schirm.

Edward Shebbeare con un paraguas.

Hugh Boustead at camp.

Hugh Boustead in het kamp.

Hugh Boustead im Lager.

Hugh Boustead en el campamento.

Sighting Mount Everest from the top of Shekar Dzong.

Sichtung des Mount Everest vom Shekar Dzong aus.

De Everest gezien vanaf de top van Shekar Dzong.

Divisando el Monte Everest desde la cumbre de Shekar Dzong.

Camp scene at dusk on the way to Everest.

Lagerszene in der Dämmerung auf dem Weg zum Mount Everest.

Kamptafereel bij schemering op de route naar de Everest.

Escena del campamento al anochecer en ruta hacia el Everest.

The great climber Jack Longland and Edward Shebbeare.

De grote klimmer Jack Longland en Edward Shebbeare.

Der große Bergsteiger Jack Longland und Edward Shebbeare.

El gran escalador Jack Longland y Edward Shebbeare.

Leiva, the Sirdar (chief of the Sherpas).

Leiva, de sirdar (leider van de Sherpa's).

Der Sirdar Leiva (Anführer der Sherpas)

Leiva, el Sirdar (jefe de los *sherpas*).

Members of the 1933 Expedition (from left to right): Smijth-Windham, Greene, Wood-Johnson, Brocklebank, Russel, Shipton, McLean, Smythe, Thomson and Harris (back row); Longland, Ruttledge, Birnie, Wager, Shebbeare, Crawford and Boustead (front row).

Die Teilnehmer der Expedition von 1933 (von links nach rechts): Smijth-Windham, Greene, Wood-Johnson, Brocklebank, Russel, Shipton, McLean, Smythe, Thomson und Harris (hintere Reihe), Longland, Ruttledge, Birnie, Wager, Shebbeare, Crawford und Boustead (vordere Reihe).

Deelnemers aan de expeditie in 1933 (v.l.n.r.): Smijth-Windham, Greene, Wood-Johnson, Brocklebank, Russel, Shipton, McLean, Smythe, Thomson en Harris (achter); Longland, Ruttledge, Birnie, Wager, Shebbeare, Crawford en Boustead (voor).

Miembros de la Expedición de 1933 (de izquierda a derecha): Smijth-Windham, Greene, Wood-Johnson, Brocklebank, Russel, Shipton, McLean, Smythe, Thomson y Harris (fila trasera); Longland, Ruttledge, Birnie, Wager, Shebbeare, Crawford y Boustead (fila delantera).

Blessing the expedition at Rongbuk.

Segnung der Expedition in Rongpu.

Zegening van de expeditie in Rongbuk.

Bendiciendo la expedición en Rongbuk.

Makalu, a summit over 8,000m, near Everest.

Makalu, ein Gipfel über 8000 m in der Nähe des Everest.

Makalu, een top van meer dan 8000 meter hoogte, nabij de Everest.

Makalu, una cumbre sobre 8000 m, cerca del Everest.

Raymond Greene shaving.

Raymond Greene beim Rasieren.

Raymond Greene scheert zich.

Raymond Greene afeitándose.

"The barbershop", Base Camp.

„Beim Barbier", Basislager.

'De kapper', basiskamp.

"La peluquería", campamento base.

For the first time an expedition boasts radio equipment.

Diese Mount Everest-Expedition verfügt erstmals über Funk.

Voor het eerst beschikt een expeditie over een radio.

Por primera vez, una expedición tiene un equipo de radio.

Sherpas taking a rest between Camps I and II.

Sherpas bei der Rast zwischen Lager I und II.

Sherpa's rusten uit tussen Kamp I en II.

Sherpas tomando un descanso entre los campamentos I y II.

Lawrence Wager in a trough.

Lawrence Wager im „Trog“.

Lawrence Wager in de ‘trog’.

Lawrence Wager en una depresión.

The North-East ridge of Mount Everest with notes added showing the point reached by Norton, Wyn-Harris, Wager and Smythe, the place at which Mallory and Irvine were last seen in 1924, the First and Second steps and the spot where Mallory's ice-axe was found.

Foto vom Nordostgrat des Mount Everest mit Darstellung der von Norton, Wyn-Harris, Wager und Smythe erreichten Stationen, des Orts, an dem Mallory und Irvine 1924 zuletzt gesehen wurden, des First und Second Step sowie des Fundorts von Mallorys Eispickel.

De noordoostelijke kam van de Everest met aantekeningen die laten zien welk punt werd bereikt door Norton, Wyn-Harris, Wager en Smythe, waar Mallory en Irvine voor het laatst werden gezien in 1924, waar de 'Eerste' en de 'Tweede stap' zich bevinden en waar Mallory's ijsbijl werd gevonden.

La cresta noreste del Monte Everest con notas añadidas que muestran el punto alcanzado por Norton, Wyn-Harris, Wager y Smythe, el último en el que fueron vistos Mallory e Irvine en 1924, el primer y segundo paso y el punto donde se encontró la piqueta de Mallory.

Eric Shipton in a trough of the Rongbuk glacier.

Eric Shipton in einem „Trog" auf dem Rongpu-Gletscher.

Eric Shipton in een trog van de Rongbuk-gletsjer.

Eric Shipton en una depresión del glaciar Rongbuk.

A glacier table, Lawrence Wager on the right.

Ein Gletschertisch, zur Rechten Lawrence Wager.

Een gletsjertafel, Lawrence Wager rechts ervan.

Una mesa de glaciar, con Lawrence Wager a la derecha.

The first assault party (Percy Wyn-Harris and Lawrence Wager).

Die erste Seilschaft: Percy Wyn-Harris und Lawrence Wager.

Het team van de eerste poging (Percy Wyn-Harris en Lawrence Wager).

El primer grupo de asalto (Percy Wyn-Harris y Lawrence Wager).

Mount Everest viewed from an altitude of 6,700m, from above Base Camp.

Der Mount Everest von einem Gipfel auf 6700 m Höhe über dem Basislager aus gesehen.

De Everest gezien vanaf een piek op 6700 meter hoogte, boven het basiskamp.

El Monte Everest desde un pico a 6700 m, sobre el campamento base.

 EVEREST PUTS UP A FIGHT 1933 – DER MOUNT EVEREST LEISTET WIDERSTAND 1933

Captain Eugene St. John Birnie being brought down by a Sherpa from Camp II.

Captain Eugene St. John Birnie wird von einem Sherpa aus Lager II zurückgebracht.

Kapitein Eugene St. John Birnie wordt door een Sherpa naar beneden gebracht vanuit Kamp II.

Un sherpa traslada al capitán Eugene St. John Birnie en el descenso desde el campamento II.

Team members ascending.

Mitglieder des Teams beim Aufstieg.

Klimmend team.

Los miembros del equipo en el ascenso.

1935

New Round of Observation
Neue Erkundungsversuche

Everest has now been putting up a fight for fifteen years! The question has to be asked: should these costly expeditions continue, expeditions that require hundreds of beasts of burden and cohorts of porters? In the spring of 1935 the Tibetan government authorises the English to launch a new attempt from Tibet by the summer of 1936. It is time to try a change of tactics and to attempt to mount not one but two expeditions within this time period, by organising the first, a very light one, during the monsoon, that is to say between June and September.

Eric Shipton, the brilliant Alpinist who participated in the previous expedition, takes charge of a small team of six mountaineers. To assist him, he has chosen one of his best friends, Bill Tilman, who is mountain-mad like himself. Within the party there is also a doctor, Dr Warren, a regular in the Alps, Edwin Kempson, a young medical student, Edmund Wigram and, for the first time, a New Zealand alpinist, Dan Bryant. Fifteen Sherpas have been selected, including a last-minute replacement, 19-year-old Tenzing Norgay. At the start of July, close to the former camp III on the Rongbuk glacier, Dr Warren finds the body of Maurice Wilson in the camp debris, an adventurer who the previous year had left in a desperate, single-handed attempt at Everest. This former British officer turned mystic imagined that he would be able to climb up to the summit using only the power of the spirit and by following a regime of asceticism!

From 12 July, Shipton, Kempson and Warren, accompanied by nine Sherpas, set up their camp close to the North Col. Nobody had ever climbed these slopes when the monsoon season was in full sway. For three days they explore the col's surroundings to study the quality of the snow. However the weather deteriorates and they are forced to leave the camp. The team begins the descent and discovers that an enormous avalanche has been triggered underneath the ridge that has swept away all trace of their climb. No-one had heard anything from up on the col! Conclusion: at more than 6,000 metres, during the monsoon season, the snow is too unstable and it is illusory to want to climb Everest!

For two months, the Alpinists will explore the whole region through multiple ascents and seeking out new ways of climbing the North Col. The expedition will scale twenty-six peaks! In order to observe the west flank of Everest, Tilman and the young Wigram climb up the western section of the gigantic Rongbuk glacier again, and ascend to 6,000 metres, to the Lho La Col, which marks the frontier with Nepal. As for Shipton and the New Zealander Bryant, they climb another col from where they have an unobstructed view of the South Face of Everest. The two alpinists examine the possibility of scaling the Himalayan giant by means of the Khumbu glacier, which tumbles down the length of this mountainside. An immense ice fall at the base of the glacier constitutes however a sizeable obstacle. To find out more it will be necessary to step out onto the glacier itself. Yet this is situated on the Nepalese side, and Nepal is completely sealed off to foreigners.

Seit fünfzehn Jahren leistet der Mount Everest nun bereits jedem Besteigungsversuch Widerstand. Es stellt sich die Frage, ob weitere kostspielige Expeditionen mit Hunderten von Lasttieren und Kohorten von Trägern noch organisiert werden müssen. Im Frühjahr 1935 erteilt die Regierung Tibets den Briten die Genehmigung bis zum Sommer 1936 einen weiteren Versuch zu unternehmen. Es ist an der Zeit, die Taktik zu ändern und in der kurzen Zeitspanne nicht nur eine, sondern zwei Expeditionen auf die Beine zu stellen. Die erste sehr kleine Expedition soll ihren Versuch während des Monsuns zwischen Juni und September wagen.

Eric Shipton, ein hervorragender Bergsteiger, der bereits an der letzten Expedition teilgenommen hat, übernimmt die Leitung einer kleinen Gruppe von sechs Bergsteigern. Zu seiner Unterstützung hat er einen seiner besten Freunde ausgewählt, Bill Tilman, der wie Shipton selbst in die Berge vernarrt ist. Zu den Teilnehmern gehören außerdem der Arzt Dr. Warren, der Alpen Kenner Edwin Kempson, der junge Medizinstudent Edmund Wigram und mit Dan Bryant zum ersten Mal auch ein Bergsteiger aus Neuseeland. Fünfzehn

Nieuwe observatieronde
Nueva ronda de observación

Sherpas werden ausgewählt, darunter auch der in letzter Minute als Ersatzmann ernannte 19-jährige Tenzing Norgay.
Anfang Juli findet Dr. Warren in der Nähe des Lagers III auf dem Rongpu-Gletscher die Leiche des Abenteurers Maurice Wilson. Er war im Vorjahr im Alleingang zur Besteigung des Mount Everest aufgebrochen, ein Versuch, der zum Scheitern verurteilt war. Der ehemalige britische Offizier, der zum Mystiker geworden war, glaubte den Gipfel allein durch seine Willenskraft und die Befolgung einer streng asketischen Lebensweise bezwingen zu können.
Am 12. Juli errichten Shipton, Kempson und Warren in Begleitung von neun Sherpas ihr Lager in der Nähe des Nordpasses. Noch nie zuvor hatten Bergsteiger versucht, die Hänge während des Monsuns zu erzwingen. Innerhalb von drei Tagen erkunden sie die Umgebung des Passes und untersuchen die Eigenschaften des Schnees. Doch die Wetterlage verschlechtert sich und zwingt sie zum Verlassen ihres Lagers. Als die Männer mit dem Abstieg beginnen, stellen sie fest, dass eine Lawine über dem Grat abgegangen ist und sämtliche Spuren ihres Aufstiegs unter sich begraben hat. Vom Grat aus hatte niemand etwas davon mitbekommen. Sie kommen zu dem Schluss, dass der Schnee auf einer Höhe von über 6.000 Metern während des Monsuns zu instabil und die Besteigung des Mount Everest während dieser Zeit daher illusorisch ist.
Im Laufe der nächsten zwei Monate erkunden die Bergsteiger die gesamte Region, nehmen einen Besteigungsversuch nach dem anderen vor und suchen nach neuen Möglichkeiten, um den Nordpass zu bezwingen. Insgesamt besteigen die Teilnehmer der Expedition 26 Gipfel! Tilman und der junge Wigram beschließen, die Westflanke des Everest zu erkunden. Sie besteigen dazu den westlichen Teil des gigantischen Rongpu-Gletschers bis zum Lho La-Pass in 6.000 Metern Höhe, der die Grenze zu Nepal darstellt. Shipton und der Neuseeländer Bryant erklimmen unterdessen einen anderen Pass, von dem aus sie eine ungehinderte Aussicht auf die Südseite des Everest genießen. Die beiden Bergsteiger untersuchen die Möglichkeit, den Mount Everest über den Khumbu-Gletscher zu besteigen, der sich über die Südflanke des Berges ergießt. Der gewaltige Eisbruch am Fuße des Gletschers stellt jedoch ein enormes Hindernis dar. Zur weiteren Erkundung müssten sie den Gletscher selbst besteigen. Doch dieser liegt im Hoheitsgebiet Nepals, und der Zugang bleibt Ausländern weiterhin verwehrt.

Intussen biedt de Everest al veertig jaar verzet en de vraag dringt zich op of er wel moet worden doorgegaan met het organiseren van dure expedities met honderden dieren en grote aantallen dragers. In de lente van 1935 geven de Tibetaanse autoriteiten de Britten toestemming voor een nieuwe klimpoging die zal plaatshebben in de zomer van 1936. Het moment is aangebroken voor een andere tactiek. Binnen de beschikbare tijd zal de beklimming door twee expedities in plaats van één worden uitgevoerd. De eerste, zeer lichte expeditie zal plaatsvinden in de moessontijd, dus tussen juni en september.
Eric Shipton, een geweldige alpinist die aan de vorige expeditie heeft deelgenomen, neemt de leiding over een kleine ploeg van zes klimmers. Als steun en toeverlaat kiest hij een van zijn beste vrienden, Bill Tilman, die even bezeten is van bergbeklimmen als hij. Tot de groep behoort ook dokter Warren, de Alpen-kenner Edwin Kempson, de jonge medicijnenstudent Edmund Wigram en voor het eerst een Nieuw-Zeelandse alpinist, Dan Bryant. Veertig Sherpa's worden geselecteerd, waaronder de 19-jarige Tenzing Norgay, die op het allerlaatste moment als vervanger meegaat.
Begin juli vindt dokter Warren in de restanten van het oude kamp III op de gletsjer van Rongbuk het lichaam van Maurice Wilson, een avonturier die een jaar eerder een hopeloze individuele poging deed om de Everest te beklimmen. Deze Britse oud-officier en mysticus had verwacht de top te kunnen bereiken op louter geesteskracht, levend als een asceet.
Vanaf 12 juli richten Shipton, Kempson en Warren, vergezeld van negen Sherpa's, dicht bij de noordelijke pas hun kamp in. Nooit eerder had iemand midden in het moessonseizoen deze berghelling betreden. Gedurende drie dagen verkennen zij de omgeving van de

pas om de sneeuwkwaliteit te testen. Maar het weer verslechtert en ze moeten het kamp verlaten. Het team daalt af en ontdekt dat een enorme lawine die onder de bergkam naar beneden is geraasd, alle sporen van hun klim heeft uitgewist. Vanuit de pas had niemand iets gehoord. Conclusie: tijdens de moesson is de sneeuw op een hoogte van meer dan 6000 meter te rul, waardoor het onverantwoord is om de Everest te beklimmen.
Twee maanden lang zullen de alpinisten de hele omgeving van de noordelijke pas onderzoeken, de klimplaatsen voorzien van zekeringen en zoeken naar nieuwe klimroutes. De expeditie zal zesentwintig pieken beklimmen. Om de westflank van de Everest te observeren, klimmen Tilman en de jonge Wigram via het oostelijke deel van de enorme gletsjer van Rombuk naar de bergpas Lho La, die op 6000 meter hoogte de grens met Nepal markeert. Shipton en de Nieuw-Zeelander Bryant banen zich ondertussen een weg door een andere pas, waar zij een onvoorstelbaar uitzicht hebben op de zuidzijde van de Everest. Deze twee alpinisten onderzoeken de mogelijkheid om de reus van de Himalaya te beklimmen via de Khumbu-gletsjer die zijn weg naar beneden zoekt via deze zijde. Een gigantische ijsval aan de voet van de gletsjer vormt echter een flink obstakel. Een gedetailleerde observatie maakt het evenwel noodzakelijk zich op de gletsjer zelf te begeven, maar die bevindt zich in Nepal en dat land laat geen buitenlanders toe.

¡Ya hace quince años que el Everest se resiste! Y la cuestión que se plantea es la siguiente: ¿es necesario continuar organizando expediciones costosas, con cientos de bestias de carga y cohortes de portadores? En la primavera de 1935, el gobierno del Tíbet autoriza a los ingleses a volver a intentar un nuevo asalto hasta el verano de 1936. Es el momento de cambiar de táctica e intentar organizar no una, sino dos expediciones en este lapso de tiempo, montando la primera, más ligera, durante el monzón, es decir, entre junio y septiembre.
Eric Shipton, este brillante alpinista que ha participado en la expedición anterior, encabeza un pequeño equipo de seis montañeros. Para respaldarle, elige a uno de sus mejores amigos, un apasionado de la montaña como él, Bill Tilman. En este grupo también hay un médico, el Dr. Warren, acostumbrado a escalar los Alpes, Edwin Kempson, un joven estudiante de medicina, Edmund Wigram y, por primera vez, un alpinista neozelandés, Dan Bryant. Se han escogido quince sherpas, entre los que figura un sustituto de última hora, de 19 años, Tenzing Norgay.
A primeros de julio, cerca del antiguo campamento III en el glaciar de Rongbuk, el Dr. Warren encuentra entre los restos del campamento, el cuerpo de un aventurero, Maurice Wilson, que había partido el año anterior en una expedición en solitario, desesperado por coronar el Everest. Este antiguo oficial británico, convertido a místico, pensaba que podía subir a la cumbre gracias a la fuerza única del espíritu, ¡siguiendo un régimen de ascesis!

A partir del 12 de julio, Shipton, Kempson y Warren, acompañados por nueve sherpas, establecen su campamento cerca del Collado Norte. Nunca antes nadie había escalado estas pendientes en pleno monzón. Durante tres días, exploran los alrededores del collado para estudiar la calidad de la nieve. Pero el tiempo se estropea y hay que abandonar el campamento. El equipo inicia el descenso y descubre que una enorme avalancha ha caído bajo la cresta y ha barrido todo rastro del ascenso. Desde el collado, ¡nadie ha oído nada! Conclusión: a más de 6000 metros, durante el monzón, la nieve es demasiado inestable y resulta ilusorio querer escalar el Everest.
Durante dos meses, los alpinistas exploran toda la región, encadenando los ascensos y buscando nuevas vías para subir al Collado Norte. ¡La expedición escala veintiséis picos! Para observar el flanco oeste del Everest, Tilman y el joven Wigram suben por la parte occidental del gigantesco glaciar de Rongbuk y escalan hasta 6000 metros, en el collado de Lho La, que marca la frontera con Nepal. En cuanto a Shipton y al neozelandés Bryant, escalan otro collado desde el que tienen una vista inexpugnable de la cara sur del Everest. Los dos alpinistas estudian la posibilidad de escalar el Gigante Himalaya por el glaciar de Khumbu que baja a lo largo de esta vertiente. Sin embargo, una inmensa cascada de hielo en la parte inferior del glaciar constituye un obstáculo importante. Para obtener más información, habría que alcanzar el glaciar mismo. Ahora bien, se encuentra en el lado de Nepal y este país está completamente cerrado a los extranjeros.

Eric Shipton recruiting Sherpas in Darjeeling. Tenzing Norgay stands 4th from the left.

Eric Shipton bei der Rekrutierung von Sherpas in Darjeeling, Tenzing Norgay ist der Vierte von links.

Eric Shipton recruteert Sherpa's in Darjeeling. Tenzing Norgay is de vierde van links.

Eric Shipton seleccionando *sherpas* en Darjeeling. Tenzing Norgay de pie el 4º por la izquierda.

Tibetan women at the village of Changmu.

Tibeterinnen im Dorf Changmu.

Tibetaanse vrouwen in Changmu.

Mujeres tibetanas en el pueblo de Changmu.

The Dodang Peak between Tibet and Sikkim, seen from the north.

Der Dodang Peak zwischen Tibet und Sikkim, von Norden aus gesehen.

De piek van de Dodang tussen Tibet en Sikkim, gezien vanuit het noorden.

El Pico Dodang entre El Tibet y Sikkim, visto desde el norte.

Tibetan woman weaving.

Tibeterin beim Weben.

Wevende Tibetaanse vrouw.

Mujer tibetana tejiendo.

Tibetan encampment.

Tibetisches Lager.

Tibetaans kampement.

Campamento tibetano.

Team members gather by a camp on the Tibetan Plateau to read and write.

Expeditionsteilnehmer versammeln sich im Lager auf der tibetanischen Hochebene zum Lesen und Schreiben.

Deelnemers verzamelen zich bij een kamp op het Tibetaanse plateau om te lezen en schrijven.

Los miembros del equipo se reúnen en un campamento para leer y escribir en la meseta tibetana.

Team members at a camp near Everest.

Expeditionsmitglieder in einem Lager in der Nähe des Mount Everest.

Deelnemers in een kamp nabij de Everest.

Los miembros del equipo en un campamento cerca del Everest.

Karma Paul holds a fish that has been caught. This faithful interpreter will accompany numerous expeditions.

Karma Paul met een gevangen vis. Deze betrouwbare tolk neemt deel aan verschillende expedities.

Karma Paul hält einen gefangenen Fisch. Der treue Dolmetscher war bei zahlreichen Expeditionen dabei.

Karma Paul sujeta un pez capturado. Este intérprete fiel acompañará a numerosas expediciones.

A Tibetan porter carrying a large load.

Een Tibetaanse drager met een zware last.

Ein tibetischer Träger beim Transport einer schweren Last.

Un culi tibetano llevando una carga pesada.

The monastery and village of Rongbuk.

Das Kloster und Dorf Rongpu.

Het klooster en het dorp Rongbuk.

El monasterio y el pueblo de Rongbuk.

A team member sits on a horse, while another team member consults with a Tibetan.

Ein Teammitglied sitzt auf einem Pferd, während ein weiteres mit einer Tibeterin spricht.

Een deelnemer te paard en een tweede overlegt met een Tibetaan.

Un miembro del equipo sentado en un caballo mientras que otro miembro del equipo consulta con un tibetano.

The Dzongpen of Sar and his family.

Der Dzongpen von Sar und seine Familie.

De Dzong Pen van Sar met zijn gezin.

El Dzongpen de Sar y su familia.

Edwin Garnett Hone Kempson.

Edmund Wigram.

Eric Shipton.

Sherpa porters.

Sherpa-Träger.

Sherpadragers.

Portadores *sherpas*.

1935 Party at Rongbuk. From left to right: Bryant, Wigram, Warren and Spender (back row); Tilman, Shipton and Kempson (front row).

Bergsteiger in Rongpu, 1935, von links nach rechts: Bryant, Wigram, Warren und Spender (hintere Reihe), Tilman, Shipton und Kempson (vordere Reihe).

Deelnemers van 1935 in Rongbuk (v.l.n.r.): Bryant, Wigram, Warren en Spender (achter); Tilman, Shipton en Kempson (voor).

El grupo en Rongbuk, 1935. De izquierda a derecha: Bryant, Wigram, Warren y Spender (fila trasera); Tilman, Shipton y Kempson (fila delantera).

Michael Spender.

L.V. „Dan“ Bryant.

Pinnacles on the East Rongbuk glacier, with Tilman in the foreground.

Eistürme auf dem östlichen Rongpu-Gletscher, mit Tilman im Vordergrund.

IJspieken op de oostelijke Rongbuk-gletsjer met Tilman op de voorgrond.

Cumbres en el lado este del glaciar Rongbuk, con Tilman en primer plano.

Eric Shipton on top of a mountain peak at 6,435m.

Eric Shipton auf einem Gipfel (6435 m).

Eric Shipton op de top van een 6435 meter hoge piek.

Eric Shipton en la cima de un pico a 6435 m.

Lake on the main Rongbuk Glacier.

See auf dem Rongpu-Hauptgletscher.

Een meer op de hoofdgletsjer van Rongbuk.

Lago en el glaciar Rongbuk principal.

A peak at 6,435m, near Everest.

Ein Gipfel in 6435 m Höhe in der Nähe des Mount Everest.

Een piek van 6435 meter hoogte nabij de Everest.

Un pico a 6435 m, cerca del Everest.

A mountaineer from the expedition on a peak at an altitude of 6,325m.

Ein Expeditionsteilnehmer auf einem Gipfel (6325 m).

Een klimmer van de expeditie op een 6325 meter hoge piek.

Un montañero de la expedición en un pico a 6325 m.

Area of the Kharta and Khartachangri glaciers.

Das Gebiet um die Kharta- und Khartachangri-Gletscher.

Indruk van de Kharta en de Khartachangri-gletsjers.

Área de glaciares de Kharta y Khartachangri.

Mount Everest from the north-east.

Der Mount Everest von Nordosten aus gesehen.

De Everest gezien vanuit het noordoosten.

El Monte Everest desde el noreste.

Everest and Nuptse viewed from a peak at 6,435m, above Rongbuk.

Der Mount Everest und der Nuptse von einem Gipfel auf 6435 m über Rongpu.

De Everest en de Nuptse vanaf een 6435 meter hoge piek, boven Rongbuk.

Everest y Nuptse desde un pico a 6435 m, sobre Rongbuk.

View from a peak above Kharta Chu showing Lhotse, the South Col and the summit of Everest.

Blick von einem Gipfel über Kharta Chu auf den Lhotse, den Südsattel und den Gipfel des Mount Everest.

Uitzicht vanaf een piek boven Kharta Chu met de Lhotse, de zuidelijke pas en de top van de Everest.

Vista desde un pico sobre Kharta Chu mostrando Lhotse, el Collado Sur y la Cumbre del Everest.

Charles Warren at the foot of a peak at 6,930m.

Charles Warren am Fuß eines Gipfels (6930 m).

Charles Warren aan de voet van een 6930 meter hoge piek.

Charles Warren al pie de un pico a 6930 m.

Shipton rock-climbing in the Lhonah Valley.

Shipton beim Klettern im Lhonah-Tal.

Shipton beklimt een rots in de Lhonah-vallei.

Shipton escalando en roca en el valle Lhonah.

Gyachung Kung (7,952m) in the distance.

Gyachung Kung (7952 m) im Hintergrund.

Gyachung Kung (7952 m) op de achtergrond.

Gyachung Kung (7952 m) a lo lejos.

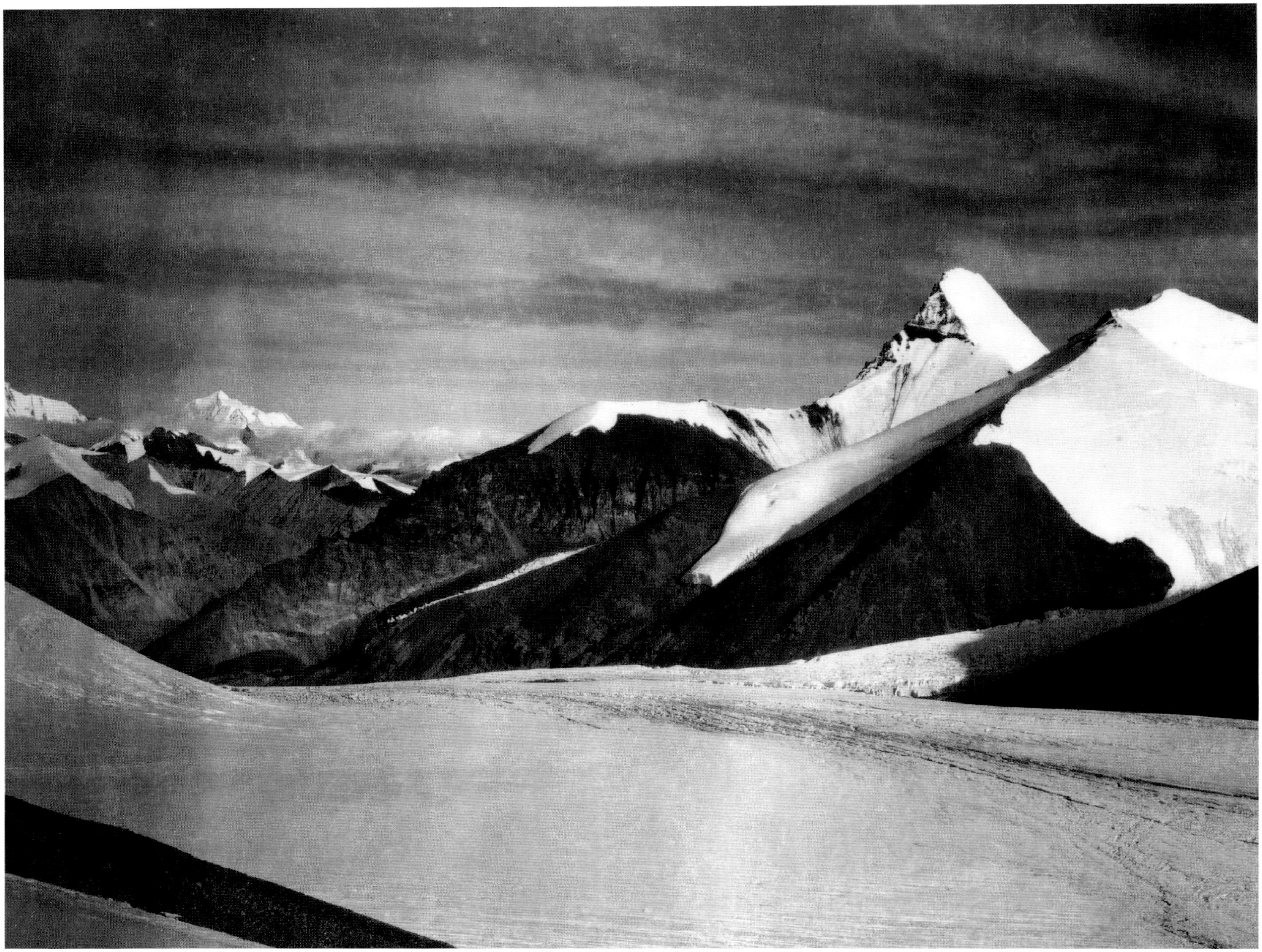

Kellas Dark Rock Peak at 7,065m.

Kellas Dark Rock Peak auf 7065 m Höhe.

Donkere rots van de Kellas op 7065 meter hoogte.

Kellas Dark Rock Peak a 7065 m.

Team members ascending a snowy ridge.

Mitglieder des Teams bei der Besteigung eines verschneiten Grats.

Een team beklimt een besneeuwde kam.

Miembros del equipo ascendiendo una cresta nevada.

Lingtren (Tibet-Nepal watershed) viewed from the West Rongbuk glacier.

Der Lingtren (Einzugsgebiet von Tibet/Nepal) vom westlichen Rongpu-Gletscher aus gesehen.

De Lingtren (waterscheiding tussen Tibet en Nepal) gezien vanaf de westelijke Rongbuk-gletsjer.

Lingtren (línea divisoria de aguas El Tíbet-Nepal) desde el oeste del glaciar Rongbuk.

Crossing the East Rongbuk glacier.

Überquerung des östlichen Rongpu-Gletschers

Over de oostelijke Rongbuk-gletsjer.

Cruzando el lado este del glaciar Rongbuk.

Camp II on the Rongbuk glacier.

Lager II auf dem Rongpu-Gletscher.

Kamp II op de Rongbuk-gletsjer.

El campamento II en el glaciar de Rongbuk.

The East Rongbuk glacier.

Der östliche Rongpu-Gletscher.

De oostelijke Rongbuk-gletsjer.

El lado este del glaciar Rongbuk.

Camp II on the East Rongbuk glacier.

Lager II auf dem östlichen Rongpu-Gletscher.

Kamp II op de oostelijke Rongbuk-gletsjer.

El campamento II en el lado este del glaciar de Rongbuk.

The West Rongbuk glacier.

Der westliche Rongpu-Gletscher.

De westelijke Rongbuk-gletsjer.

El lado oeste del glaciar Rongbuk.

Looking down the West Rongbuk glacier from Lingtren Nup.

Blick vom Lingtren Nup auf den westlichen Rongpu-Gletscher.

Neerkijkend op de westelijke Rongbuk-gletsjer vanaf de Lingtren Nup.

Mirando hacia abajo en el lado oeste del glaciar Rongbuk desde Lingtren Nup.

Mount Everest and Lhotse seen from Lingtren Nup.

Der Mount Everest und der Lhotse vom Lingtren Nup aus gesehen.

De Everest en de Lhotse gezien vanaf de Lingtren Nup.

El Monte Everest y Lhotse vistos desde Lingtren Nup.

Lhotse (left, behind) and Pumori seen from Lingtren Nup.

Der Lhotse (links, hinten) und der Pumori vom Lingtren Nup aus gesehen.

De Lhotse (linksachter) en de Pumori gezien vanaf de Lingtren Nup.

Lhotse (detrás a la izquierda) y Pumori visto desde Lingtren Nup.

Mount Everest seen from a peak at 6,930m.

Der Mount Everest von einem Gipfel (6930m) aus gesehen.

De Everest gezien vanaf een 6930 meter hoge piek.

El Monte Everest visto desde un pico a 6930 m.

Team members crossing the main Rongbuk glacier.

Deelnemers gaan de hoofdgletsjer van Rongbuk over.

Mitglieder des Teams bei der Überquerung des Rongpu-Hauptgletschers.

Los miembros del equipo cruzando el glaciar Rongbuk principal.

Charles Warren taking a photograph while smoking a pipe.

Charles Warren maakt pijprokend een foto.

Ein pfeiferauchender Charles Warren beim Fotografieren.

Charles Warren tomando una fotografía mientras fuma en pipa.

Mount Everest and Lhotse.

Der Mount Everest und der Lhotse.

De Everest en de Lhotse.

El Monte Everest y Lhotse.

Summits near Everest.

Gipfel um den Mount Everest.

Toppen in de omgeving van de Everest.

Cumbres cerca del Everest.

Chomolonzo and Makalu rising above the clouds.

Der Chomolonzo und der Makalu erheben sich über den Wolken.

De Chomolonzo en de Makalu rijzen boven de wolken uit.

Chomolonzo y Makalu surgiendo entre las nubes.

The summit of Kellas Rock Peak.

Der Gipfel des Kellas Rock Peak.

De top van de Kellas-rots.

La cumbre de Kellas Rock Peak.

Camp on the East Rongbuk glacier with Mount Kellas behind.

Lager auf dem östlichen Rongpu-Gletscher mit dem Mount Kellas im Hintergrund.

Kamp op de oostelijke Rongbuk-gletsjer met de Kellas op de achtergrond.

Campamento en el lado este del glaciar Rongbuk con el Monte Kellas detrás.

Shipton and the Sherpas including Tenzing Norgay, on the North Col

Shipton und die Sherpas, einschließlich Tenzing Norgay, auf dem Nordsattel.

Shipton en de Sherpa's, waaronder Tenzing Norgay, op de noordelijke pas.

Shipton y los *sherpas*, incluyendo a Tenzing Norgay, en el Collado Norte.

Porters descending an ice pinnacle on the East Rongbuk glacier.

Träger beim Abstieg über einen Eisturm im östlichen Rongpu-Gletscher.

Dragers dalen af langs een ijspiek op de oostelijke Rongbuk-gletsjer.

Portadores descendiendo una cumbre helada en el lado este del glaciar Rongbuk.

Kharta Changri in the background.

Der Kharta Changri im Hintergrund.

De Kharta Changri op de achtergrond.

Kharta Changri al fondo.

"The Sherpa Tigers" of 1935 gather to have a group photograph taken.

„Die Sherpa-Tiger“ von 1935 versammeln sich für ein Gruppenfoto.

'De Sherpa-tijgers' van 1935 verzamelen zich voor een groepsfoto.

"Los tigres *sherpas*" de 1935 se reúnen para una fotografía de grupo.

1936

Defeated by the Monsoon

Bezwungen vom Monsun

As planned, after the round of observations in 1935 the second expedition is arranged for the following spring. Once more, it will entail significant resources and have the same leader as in 1933, Hugh Ruttledge. The strong team is composed of alpinists who, for the most part, have tested their mettle on Everest, in particular Smythe, Shipton and Wyn-Harris.

Sixty of the best Sherpas are chosen to set up the camps on the Rongbuk glacier as from 25 April 1936. Among them are the renowned Ang Tharkay and his young protégé, 19-year-old Tenzing Norgay. This expedition, however, is struck by misfortune from the outset. From 30 April, thanks to radio links, Ruttledge learns that the weather is already on the turn. It is unusually warm. On 10 May heavy snowfall transforms the landscape. It is nothing too serious despite everything, so, on 15 May, Smythe and Shipton take their camp up onto the North Col with fifty Sherpas. Fourteen of them go back down again straight away. Morale is high among the others, who are ready to take camps V and VI up to an altitude of 8,470 metres. Unfortunately, the thick layer of snow prohibits all advances for the moment and the alpinists wait dejectedly in their tents for three whole days. On 19 May Shipton decides to evacuate the camp and to descend from the col.

Ruttledge, the leader of the expedition, has gathered his men at the base camp when an alarming message reaches them on 22 May: the monsoon is already beating down on the Darjeeling hills! No-one in living memory has experienced the monsoon starting so early, especially this early in the year! The following day large flakes of snow cover the slopes of Everest and it quickly turns stormy.

Shipton is champing at the bit. He knows that, should his men not reach the North Col as soon as the next lull appears, it will be too late. Along with Wyn-Harris he decides to carry out a reconnaissance mission on the slopes of the North Col. To start with the snow seems to hold. The two men rope up at the approach to a difficult crossing. Wyn-Harris holds on at the edge of a crevasse and Shipton moves slowly forward. His crampons bite deeply into the hard surface. He has moved forward fifteen metres and Wyn-Harris is about to follow him, when the muffled rumble of an avalanche sounds from the top of the slope. The slab of snow carries Shipton towards a wall of ice 120 metres high and smashes into pieces. In a desperate effort, Wyn-Harris leaps onto the edge of the crevasse and clings on with his ice axe that he has hurled into the snow. Shipton stops sliding, but the snowy mass is so strong that the ice axe cannot hold his teammate. Miraculously, the avalanche suddenly stops. For several minutes Eric Shipton, panting, attempts to catch his breath, while his teammate comes to rejoin him, relieved. Ruttledge and Smythe have followed the scene from a distance with deep anxiety. The missions ends with a certain bitterness.

Im Frühling wird, nach der Erkundungsexpedition von 1935, wie vorgesehen unter Aufwendung gewaltiger Mittel eine zweite Expedition auf die Beine gestellt, die wie bereits 1933, von Hugh Ruttledge geleitet wird. Auch diesmal zählen zu den Teilnehmern der Gruppe Bergsteiger, die sich auf dem Mount Everest bereits ihre ersten Sporen verdient haben, darunter Smythe, Shipton und Wyn-Harris.

Sechzig der besten Sherpas werden ausgewählt, um vom 25. April 1936 an die Lager auf dem Rongpu-Gletscher zu errichten, unter ihnen auch der berühmte Ang Tharkay und sein junger Protegé Tenzing Norgay. Doch die Expedition scheint von Anfang an vom Unglück verfolgt zu sein. Am 30. April erfährt Ruttledge über Funk, dass die Wetterverhältnisse sich bereits ändern. Es ist ungewöhnlich warm für die Jahreszeit. Am 10. Mai wird die Landschaft durch Schneefälle vollkommen verwandelt. Dies ist trotz allem noch kein Grund zu Sorge, und am 15. Mai errichten Smythe und Shipton mit fünfzig Sherpas ihr Lager auf dem Nordpass. Vierzehn Sherpas treten unmittelbar danach den Abstieg an. Die Stimmung unter den übrigen Teilnehmern ist ausgezeichnet, und sie sind bereit, Lager V und VI auf einer Höhe von 8470 Metern aufzuschlagen. Unglücklicherweise verhindert die dicke Schneedecke jedes weitere Vorankommen, und die Bergsteiger blasen drei Tage lang in ihren Zelten

Verslagen door de moesson

Vencidos por el monzón

Trübsal. Am 19. Mai beschließt Shipton, das Lager zu räumen und mit dem Abstieg vom Nordpass zu beginnen.
Der Expeditionsleiter Ruttledge hat seine Männer im Basislager versammelt, als sie am 22. Mai die besorgniserregende Nachricht erreicht: Der Monsunregen ergießt sich bereits über die Hügel von Darjeeling. Seit Menschengedenken hatte noch nie jemand ein so schnelles Vordringen des Monsuns erlebt, und vor allem nicht so früh im Jahr! Am nächsten Morgen fallen auf den Hängen des Everest bereits dichte Schneeflocken, und bald bricht der Sturm los.
Shipton kann seine Ungeduld nur mühsam beherrschen. Er weiß, dass es zu spät sein wird, wenn seine Männer erst zum Nordpass aufbrechen, nachdem sich der Sturm gelegt hat. Mit Wyn-Harris beschließt er, die Hänge des Nordpasses zu erkunden. Zunächst scheint der Schnee zu halten. Kurz vor einer schwierigen Traverse seilen sich die beiden Männer an. Wyn-Harris hält sich am Rand einer Gletscherspalte fest und Shipton bewegt sich langsam vorwärts. Seine Steigeisen dringen tief in die harte Oberfläche ein. Als er fünfzehn Meter zurückgelegt hat und Wyn-Harris sich bereit macht, ihm zu folgen, vernehmen sie vom oberen Teil des Hangs das dumpfe Grollen einer Lawine. Das Schneebrett reißt Shipton bis zu einer 120 Meter hohen Eismauer mit, die in tausend Stücke zerbricht. In dieser aussichtslos scheinenden Situation springt Wyn-Harris zum Rand der Gletscherspalte und klammert sich an seinen, in den Schnee geschlagenen Eispickel. Shipton rutscht nicht mehr weiter, aber die Schneemassen sind so schwer, dass der Pickel seinen Gefährten nicht mehr halten kann. Wie durch ein Wunder kommt die Lawine in diesem Augenblick zum Stillstand. Eric Shipton ringt mehrere Minuten nach Luft und versucht, wieder zu Atem zu kommen, während sein Begleiter ihn erleichtert erreicht. Von weitem haben Ruttledge und Smythe die Szene angstvoll verfolgt. Die Mission endet mit einem bitteren Nachgeschmack.

Na de observatieronde van 1935 gaat, zoals gepland, de tweede expeditie plaatsvinden in de volgende lente. Opnieuw gebeurt dat met een enorme hoeveelheid hulpmiddelen en met Hugh Ruttledge, die ook in 1933 de expeditie leidde. De sterke ploeg bestaat uit alpinisten die zich op de Everest al ruimschoots hebben bewezen, onder wie Smythe, Shipton en Wyn-Harris.
De beste zestig Sherpa's zijn gekozen om vanaf 25 april 1936 de kampen op de gletsjer van Rongbuk op te zetten. De gerenommeerde Ang Tharkay en zijn 19 jaar jonge beschermeling Tenzing Norgay zijn van de partij. Maar deze expeditie heeft vanaf het begin te kampen met tegenslag. Al op 30 april verneemt Ruttledge via de radioverbinding dat het weer gaat omslaan. Het is ongewoon warm. En op 10 mei veranderen fikse sneeuwbuien het landschap. Al met al zijn er geen ernstige bezwaren en dus verplaatsen Smythe en Shipton met vijftig Sherpa's hun kampement op 15 mei naar de noordelijke pas. Veertig van hen dalen direct weer af. De overige deelnemers hebben een uitstekende moraal en zijn er klaar voor om via de kampen V en VI naar een hoogte van 8470 meter te gaan. Helaas belemmert het dikke pak sneeuw elke voortgang en brengen de alpinisten drie lange dagen ongeduldig door in hun tent. Op 19 mei besluit Shipton het kamp te verlaten en af te dalen vanuit de pas.
Ruttledge, de expeditieleider, heeft zijn manschappen verzameld in het basiskamp als hen op 22 mei een alarmerend bericht bereikt: de moessonregen valt al in de heuvels van Darjeeling. Sinds mensenheugenis is er nog nooit een moesson geweest die zich zo snel verplaatst. De volgende dag vallen er grote sneeuwvlokken op de hellingen van de Everest en al snel onweert het.
Shipton negeert dit stopteken. Hij weet dat zijn mannen de noordelijke pas moeten bereiken na de volgende korte rust omdat anders de kans is verkeken. Met Wyn-Harris besluit hij een verkenningstocht te maken op de hellingen van de noordelijke pas. Aanvankelijk lijkt de sneeuw hen te kunnen dragen. Bij het naderen van een lastige oversteek binden de mannen de touwen om. Wyn-Harris houdt halt bij de rand van een kloof en Shipton gaat langzaam vooruit. Zijn stijgijzers dringen goed in het harde oppervlak. Hij is dertig meter gevorderd en Wyn-Harris maakt zich gereed om te volgen wanneer het rommelende geluid van een lawine neerdaalt vanaf de helling. De sneeuwmassa sleurt Shipton naar een 120 meter hoge ijswal en spat daar uiteen. Wanhopig springt Wyn-Harris over de rand van de kloof en klampt zich vast aan zijn ijsbijl die hij in de sneeuw heeft geslagen. Shipton glijdt niet weg maar de sneeuwmassa is niet zo compact dat de ijsbijl zijn kameraad lang kan tegenhouden. Als door een wonder stopt de lawine op dat moment. Minutenlang snakt Eric Shipton naar adem tot zijn maat zich tot zijn opluchting weer bij hem voegt. Vanuit de verte hebben Ruttledge en Smythe het gebeuren met grote bezorgdheid gadegeslagen. Een expeditie met een wrang einde.

Tal y como estaba previsto, después de la ronda de observación de 1935, la segunda expedición se pone en marcha la primavera siguiente. Una vez más, con unos medios impresionantes y con el mismo jefe que en 1933, Hugh Ruttledge. Encontramos en este fuerte equipo a alpinistas que ya han hecho muchas pruebas en el Everest, en concreto, Smythe, Shipton y Wyn-Harris.
Se eligen sesenta de los mejores sherpas para instalar los campamentos en el glaciar de Rongbuk a partir del 25 de abril de 1936. Entre ellos, el prestigioso Ang Tharkay y su joven protegido de 19 años, Tenzing Norgay. Pero esta expedición se ve golpeada de entrada por la mala suerte. El 30 de abril, gracias a las conexiones de radio, Ruttledge se entera de que el tiempo ya está cambiando. Hace un calor poco habitual. Y el 10 de mayo, las fuertes caídas de nieve transforman el paisaje. Nada demasiado grave a pesar de todo. El 15 de mayo, Smythe y Shipton ascienden con cincuenta sherpas a su campamento en el Collado Norte. De ellos, catorce descienden tan pronto como ascienden. Los demás tienen la moral muy alta y están preparados para subir a los campamentos V y VI hasta una altitud de 8470 metros. Lamentablemente, el espesor de la capa de nieve prohíbe momentáneamente seguir avanzando y los alpinistas se mueren de aburrimiento durante tres días en su tienda de campaña. El 19 de mayo, Shipton decide evacuar el campamento y descender del collado.
El 22 de mayo, Ruttledge, el jefe de la expedición, reúne a sus hombres en el campamento base y en ese momento recibe un mensaje alarmante: ¡el monzón ya está arrasando las colinas de Darjeeling! En la historia del hombre, nadie había conocido un avance tan rápido del monzón, y sobre todo en una época tan temprana del año. Al día siguiente, caen copos grandes de nieve sobre las pendientes del Everest y, rápidamente, comienza la tormenta.
Shipton se consume de impaciencia. Sabe que si sus hombres no llegan al Collado Norte antes de la próxima tregua será demasiado tarde. Con Wyn-Harris, decide hacer un reconocimiento de las pendientes del Collado Norte. Al principio, la nieve parece contenerse. Al acercarse a una travesía difícil, los dos hombres se atan. Wyn-Harris se mantiene en el borde de una grieta y Shipton avanza lentamente. Sus ganchos muerden bien la superficie dura. Ha progresado quince metros y Wyn-Harris se dispone a seguirlo cuando el ruido sordo de una avalancha se propaga desde lo alto de la pendiente. La placa de nieve arrastra a Shipton hacia una pared de hielo de 120 metros de altura y se rompe en pedazos. En un esfuerzo desesperado, Wyn-Harris salta sobre el borde de la grieta y se agarra a su piolet que ha clavado en la nieve. Shipton deja de resbalar, pero la masa de nieve es tan grande que el piolet no puede sujetar a su compañero. Milagrosamente, la avalancha se detiene en ese instante. Durante varios minutos, Eric Shipton, jadeante, intenta recuperar el aliento mientras que su compañero de equipo se reúne con él, aliviado. De lejos, Ruttledge y Smythe han seguido la escena con angustia. Fin de la misión con cierta amargura.

Preparing to recruit porters in Darjeeling (Bengal).

Vorbereitungen für die Rekrutierung von Trägern in Darjeeling (Bengalen).

De rekrutering van dragers wordt voorbereid in Darjeeling (Bengalen).

Preparando la selección de portadores en Darjeeling (Bengala).

The Darjeeling vaccinator B. Suraj Ram is seen here vaccinating Everest porters.

Der Impfarzt B. Suraj Ram aus Darjeeling bei der Impfung von Trägern der Mount Everest-Expedition.

B. Suraj Ram uit Darjeeling dient de dragers vaccins toe.

Aquí vemos a B. Suraj Ram, vacunador de Darjeeling, vacunando a los portadores del Everest.

Every porter is issued with an identity disc.

Jeder Träger erhält eine Erkennungsmarke.

Elke drager krijgt een identiteitsbewijs.

Se entrega un disco de identificación a cada portador.

Page from the 1936 Everest album showing portraits of Sherpas who took part in the expedition, including Tenzing Norgay (first, 4th row down).

Seite aus einem Album über die Mount Everest-Expedition von 1936 mit Porträts aller Sherpas, die an der Expedition teilnahmen, einschließlich Tenzing Norgay (erster, 4. Reihe von unten).

Pagina uit het Everest-album van 1936 met portretten van Sherpa's die deelnamen aan de expeditie, waaronder Tenzing Norgay (eerste in rij vier).

Página del álbum del Everest de 1936 mostrando los retratos de *sherpas* que participaron en la expedición, incluyendo a Tenzing Norgay (primero, 4ª fila por abajo).

1936 Mount Everest Expedition team (from left to right). Front row: Gavin, Shipton, Smijth-Windham; middle row: Oliver, Smythe, Ruttledge, Morris, Humphreys; back row: Wigram, Kempson, Warren and Harris.

Die Teilnehmer der Mount Everest-Expedition von 1936 (von links nach rechts): Gavin, Shipton, Smijth-Windham (vordere Reihe), Oliver, Smythe, Ruttledge, Morris, Humphreys (mittlere Reihe), Wigram, Kempson, Warren und Harris (hintere Reihe).

De deelnemers aan de expeditie van 1936 (v.l.n.r.): Gavin, Shipton, Smijth-Windham (voor); Oliver, Smythe, Ruttledge, Morris, Humphreys (midden); Wigram, Kempson, Warren en Harris (achter).

1936, el equipo de Expedición al Monte Everest (de izquierda a derecha). Fila delantera: Gavin, Shipton, Smijth-Windham; fila del medio: Oliver, Smythe, Ruttledge, Morris, Humphreys; fila trasera: Wigram, Kempson, Warren y Harris.

A group of Tibetans in Sikkim.

Eine Gruppe Tibeter in Sikkim.

Een groep Tibetanen in Sikkim.

Un grupo de tibetanos en Sikkim.

Members of the expedition having a meal in the camp.

Mitglieder der Expedition bei einer Mahlzeit im Lager.

Deelnemers van de expeditie aan de maaltijd in het kamp.

Miembros de la expedición comiendo en el campamento.

John Morris at the 1936 Base Camp dining table, surrounded by familiar British brands including Huntley & Palmers ginger nut biscuits, Heinz tomato ketchup and sardines from Sainsbury's.

John Morris am Esstisch der Expedition von 1936 im Basislager, umgeben von bekannten britischen Marken der damaligen Zeit wie Ingwerplätzchen von Huntley & Palmers, Tomatenketchup von Heinz und Sardinen von Sainsbury's.

John Morris aan het diner in het basiskamp van 1936, te midden van bekende Britse merkproducten zoals koekjes met noot en gember van Huntley & Palmers, tomatenketchup van Heinz en sardientjes van Sainsbury's.

John Morris cenando en el campamento base en 1936, rodeador por marcas británicas conocidas, incluyendo las galletas de frutos secos de jengibre Huntley & Palmers, ketchup Heinz y sardinas Sainsbury's.

Al fresco lunch near the Rongbuk monastery.

Lunch im Freien in der Nähe des Rongpu-Klosters.

Al fresco lunch bij het Rongbuk-klooster.

Almuerzo al fresco cerca del monasterio Rongbuk.

Porters enjoying the late afternoon sunshine at Camp II on the East Rongbuk glacier, while Oliver practices his step-cutting on one of the glacier's spectacular pinnacles.

Träger genießen die Nachmittagssonne in Lager II auf dem östlichen Rongpu-Gletscher, während Oliver sich im Einschlagen von Kerben in einen der spektakulären Eistürme übt.

Dragers genieten van de namiddagzon in kamp II op de oostelijke Rongbuk-gletsjer, terwijl Oliver oefent in treden uithakken op een van de spectaculaire ijspieken.

Los portadores disfrutando de los últimos rayos de sol de la tarde en el campamento II en el lado este del glaciar Rongbuk, mientras que Oliver practica la escalada en diagonal en una de las espectaculares cumbres del glaciar.

Wyn-Harris wearing oxygen equipment (15.8 kilos).

Wyn-Harris mit Sauerstoffgerät (15,8 kg).

Wyn-Harris draagt een zuurstofapparaat (15,8 kg).

Wyn-Harris llevando el equipo de oxígeno (15,8 kilos).

Crossing a small crevasse using an ice-axe for balance.

Überquerung einer kleinen Gletscherspalte mithilfe eines Eispickels, um das Gleichgewicht zu halten.

Het oversteken van een kleine kloof met een ijsbijl als steun.

Cruzando una grieta pequeña utilizando una piqueta para mantener el equilibrio.

A column of more than 30 porters carrying supplies up a slope leading to the North Col on Mount Everest.

Een colonne van meer dan dertig dragers brengt voorraden via een helling naar de noordelijke pas van de Everest.

Eine Kolonne von mehr als 30 Trägern transportiert Vorräte über einen Abhang, der hinauf zum Mount Everest führt.

Una columna de más de 30 portadores llevando suministros cuesta arriba en dirección al Collado Norte en el Monte Everest.

Sherpas resting.

Rustende Sherpa's.

Sherpas bei der Rast.

Sherpas descansando.

Afternoon clouds build up, signalling the start of the monsoon.

Am Nachmittag bilden sich Wolken, die den Beginn des Monsun ankündigen.

Een groeiend wolkendek in de middag kondigt de moesson aan.

Formación de nubes por la tarde como preludio del monzón.

H.W. Tilman, who was not considered for the 1936 expedition, conquered Nanda Devi (7,435m) at the same time. As a result of this performance, he will be leader of the next expedition to Mount Everest.

H.W. Tilman wurde bei der Expedition von 1936 nicht berücksichtigt und bezwang zum gleichen Zeitpunkt stattdessen den Nanda Devi (7435 m). Aufgrund dieser Leistung wird er zum Leiter der nächsten Expedition ernannt.

Niet in aanmerking gekomen voor de expeditie van 1936, trotseert H.W. Tilman de Nanda Devi (7435 m) in dat jaar. Op grond van deze prestatie zou hij de volgende Everest-expeditie leiden.

Aunque no fue incluido en la expedición de 1936, H.W. Tilman superó el Nanda Devi (7435 m) al mismo tiempo. En consecuencia de este logro, será jefe de la siguiente expedición al Monte Everest.

1938

Repeated Failed Attempts
Wiederholte Fehlschläge

Bill Tilman had not been retained for the 1936 expedition because he had had trouble acclimatising to the very high altitude. He will take his revenge two years later. Meanwhile, along with Noel Odell, who was the last to have seen the 1924 heroes Mallory and Irvine alive, he has conquered the highest mountain in the Indies, the legendary Nanda Devi ("the happy goddess"), without using oxygen. This time, spring 1938, he is to lead the expedition and he has chosen a scaled down team of seven people. The group is very close-knit. Surrounding the close partnership of Bill Tilman and Eric Shipton are the greatest names in British alpinism: the veteran Noel Odell, Frank Smythe, Charles Warren and two young Himalaya regulars, Captain Peter Oliver and Peter Lloyd. Despite his reluctance regarding oxygen masks, Bill Tilman agrees to take two models of breathing apparatus along: the latest design, weighing 15 kilograms and delivering pure oxygen via a full face mask, and the other, lighter design, which leaves the nose free and allows the wearer to breathe air at the same time as oxygen.

The expedition arrives on the Rongbuk glacier from 7 April 1938. However, just as two years previously, the monsoon arrives in the region exceptionally early. Regardless, at the end of May, while Oliver descends again, Odell, Warren and Tilman attempt a sortie on Everest's north ridge, following the trail broken by the energetic and enthusiastic Sherpa Tenzing Norgay. They reach 7,470 metres before they cannot advance any further. During the ascent, Warren tests both models of oxygen breathing apparatus in turn. When he tries the new, closed circuit model that covers his whole face he starts to suffocate. The open circuit apparatus, which leaves the nose free, works much better.

The North Col is henceforth inaccessible from its eastern side, which is too exposed to the monsoon and potential avalanches. The Sherpas transport supplies and materials over the central section of the Rongbuk glacier, in order to climb the North Col from another side on 3 June. The very next day, Tilman, Lloyd, Smythe and Shipton attack the north ridge of Everest with Ang Tharkay and six other Sherpas, among whom the young Tenzing is the most adept of all. Braving the storm, they pitch camp V at 7,860 metres of altitude, then, the day afterwards, they pitch the following camp at 8,300 metres. On 8 June the two most hardened alpinists, Smythe and Shipton, leave early in the morning, but the glacial cold numbs their limbs and, along with the effect of the snow, into which they sink up to their thighs, prevents them from climbing very high. The frozen slabs hidden by the powdery top layer are extremely dangerous. It is then the turn of Tilman and Lloyd to make a fresh attempt, which is equally fruitless. At this new failure the mission is concluded.

This is the summer of 1938 and London has other things to worry about. War is approaching and Everest will be forgotten for many years.

Bill Tilman war für die Expedition von 1936 nicht in Betracht gezogen worden, weil er Schwierigkeiten hatte, sich in sehr großen Höhen zu akklimatisieren. Zwei Jahre später bekam er seine Revanche. In der Zwischenzeit hatte er gemeinsam mit Noel Odell, der Mallory und Irvine 1924 als letzter gesehen hatte, ohne Sauerstoff den höchsten Berg Indiens bezwungen, den legendären Nanda Devi („Göttin der Freude"). Im Frühling 1938 wird er zum Leiter der Expedition ernannt und stellt eine kleine Gruppe von sieben Bergsteigern zusammen. Unter den Teilnehmern der Gruppe herrscht eine gute Kamaradschaft. Neben dem Duo Bill Tilman und Eric Shipton sind die ganz großen Namen unter den britischen Bergsteigern vertreten: der Veteran Noel Odell, Frank Smythe, Charles Warren und zwei junge, jedoch erfahrene Himalaya-Bergsteiger, Captain Peter Oliver und Peter Lloyd. Trotz seiner Skepsis gegenüber Sauerstoffmasken, erklärt sich Bill Tilman bereit, zwei verschiedene Atemgeräte mitzunehmen: das neueste Modell mit einem Gewicht von 15 Kilogramm, bei dem die Sauerstoffzufuhr über eine Maske erfolgt, die das ganze Gesicht bedeckt, und ein leichteres Gerät, das die Nase frei lässt, sodass der Träger gleichzeitig Luft und Sauerstoff einatmen kann.

Opnieuw mislukkingen
Fracasos repetidos

Am 7. April 1938 erreicht die Expedition den Rongpu-Gletscher. Doch wie schon zwei Jahre zuvor sucht der Monsun die Region außergewöhnlich früh heim. Während Oliver wieder ins Tal zurückkehrt, wagen sich Odell, Warren und Tilman Ende Mai dennoch hinter dem dynamischen und begeisterungsfähigen Sherpa Tenzing Norgay, der die Spur anlegt, an die Besteigung über den Nordgrat des Mount Everest. Auf 7470 Meter Höhe kommt der weitere Aufstieg ins Stocken. Unterwegs hat Warren nacheinander beide Sauerstoffgeräte getestet. Bei dem neuen Modell, das über einen geschlossenen Kreislauf verfügt und das gesamte Gesicht bedeckt, fehlt ihm die Luft zum Atmen. Das Atemgerät mit dem offenen Kreislauf, bei dem die Nase frei bleibt, funktioniert weitaus besser.
Der Zugang zum Nordpass über die Ostseite ist nicht passabar, weil er dem Monsun zu stark ausgesetzt und die Lawinengefahr zu groß ist. Die Sherpas transportieren die Verpflegung und das Material über den mittleren Teil des Rongpu-Gletschers und erreichen den Nordpass am 3. Juni schließlich via eine andere Seite. Am nächsten Morgen nehmen Tilman, Lloyd, Smythe und Shipton mit Ang Tharkay und sechs weiteren Trägern den Nordgrat des Everest in Angriff. Darunter ist auch Tenzing Norgay, der beste unter den Sherpas. Inmitten des tosenden Sturms errichten sie auf 7860 Metern Höhe Lager V und am übernächsten Tag auf 8300 Metern Höhe Lager VI. Am frühen Morgen des 8. Juni brechen die beiden abgehärtetsten Bergsteiger, Smythe und Shipton, auf, doch wegen der eisigen Kälte, die ihre Glieder gefühllos werden lässt, und des Schnees, in den sie bis zu ihren Oberschenkeln einbrechen, wird der weitere Aufstieg unmöglich. Die vereisten, von Pulverschnee bedeckten Felsplatten sind zu gefährlich. Anschließend unternehmen Tilman und Lloyd einen neuen, ebenso unfruchtbaren Versuch. Die Mission endet mit einem erneuten Fehlschlag.
Im Sommer des Jahres 1938 hat London andere Sorgen. Der Krieg steht bevor, und so gerät der Mount Everest für viele Jahre in Vergessenheit.

Bill Tilman was niet teruggekeerd voor de expeditie van 1936 omdat hij problemen had met acclimatiseren op zeer grote hoogte. Twee jaar later neemt hij revanche. Ondertussen heeft hij zonder zuurstof de hoogste berg van de Andes, de legendarische Nanda Devi (de Godin van de Vreugde), bedwongen samen met Noel Odell, die als laatste de helden van 1924, Mallory en Irvine, in leven had gezien. Ditmaal, in de lente van 1938, is hij de leider van de expeditie. Hij stelt een klein, maar hecht team van zeven personen samen. Naast de bevriende Bill Tilman en Eric Shipton maken de bekende Britse alpinisten Noel Odell (de veteraan), Frank Smythe en Charles Warren en de twee jonge Himalaya-kenners kapitein Peter Oliver en Peter Lloyd deel uit van het team. Hoewel hij bedenkingen heeft bij zuurstofapparaten, staat Bill Tilman toe dat er twee modellen worden meegenomen: het nieuwste model met een gewicht van 15 kilo dat zuivere zuurstof levert en een masker heeft dat het gehele gezicht bedekt, en een lichter model waarvan het masker de neus vrijlaat en het mogelijk maakt zowel buitenlucht als zuivere zuurstof in te ademen.
De expeditie komt op 7 april 1938 aan bij de gletsjer van Rongbuk. Maar net als twee jaar eerder arriveert de moesson uitzonderlijk vroeg in het gebied. Desondanks wagen Odell, Warren en Tilman, terwijl Oliver afdaalt, een poging via de noordelijke bergkam van de Everest, waarbij de dynamische en enthousiaste Sherpa Tenzing Norgay de route uitzet. Ze bereiken zonder problemen een hoogte van 7470 meter. Tijdens de klim test Warren de twee zuurstofmaskermodellen. Met het nieuwste model dat een gesloten circuit heeft en het hele gezicht bedekt, snakt hij naar adem. Het zuurstofmasker met een open circuit, dat de neus vrijlaat, werkt veel beter.
De noordelijke pas is vervolgens onbereikbaar via de oostzijde vanwege de hevige moesson en het lawinegevaar. De Sherpa's transporteren de levende have en het materiaal over het centrale deel van de Rongbuk-gletsjer, zodat de noordelijke pas op 3 juni vanaf de andere kant kan worden beklommen. Een dag later zetten Tilman, Lloyd, Smythe en Shipton de aanval in op de noordelijke bergkam van de Everest. Ze doen dat samen met Ang Tharkay en

zes andere Sherpa's, van wie de jonge Tenzing de meeste indruk maakt. De storm trotserend zetten ze op een hoogte van 7860 meter kamp V op en een dag later het volgende kamp op 8300 meter. De twee meest geharde alpinisten, Smythe en Shipton, vertrekken op 8 juni vroeg in de ochtend, maar heel hoog komen zij niet door de vrieskou die hun ledematen gevoelloos maakt, en de conditie van de sneeuw waarin zij tot hun dijen wegzakken. De ijslaag op het gesteente is bedekt met stuifsneeuw en dat is een te groot risico. Vervolgens zijn Tilman en Lloyd aan de beurt om een nieuwe, volstrekt vruchteloze poging te doen. De expeditie eindigt na deze mislukking. In de zomer van 1938 heeft Londen het te druk met andere dingen. Er komt oorlog en de Everest zal jarenlang worden vergeten.

Bill Tilman no había estado disponible para la expedición de 1936, porque tenía dificultades para aclimatarse a una altitud tan elevada. Dos años después, se toma la revancha. Mientras tanto, conquista sin oxígeno la montaña más alta de las Indias, la legendaria Nanda Devi («la diosa de la felicidad») junto con Noel Odell, el último que vio vivos a los héroes de 1924, Mallory e Irvine. Esta vez, en la primavera de 1938, es el jefe de la expedición y elige un equipo reducido de siete personas. Todos están muy unidos. Alrededor del dúo de amigos Bill Tilman y Eric Shipton están los nombres más grandes del alpinismo británico: Noel Odell, el veterano, Frank Smythe, Charles Warren y dos jóvenes acostumbrados al Himalaya, el capitán Peter Oliver y Peter Lloyd. A pesar de sus reticencias respecto a las máscaras de oxígeno, Bill Tilman acepta llevar dos modelos de respiradores: el más reciente pesa 15 kilogramos y libera oxígeno puro con una máscara sobre el conjunto del rostro, y el otro, más ligero, deja la nariz libre y permite respirar aire al mismo tiempo que oxígeno.

La expedición llega al glaciar de Rongbuk el 7 de abril de 1938. Pero al igual que dos años antes, el monzón hace acto de presencia excepcionalmente pronto en la región. Pese a todo, a finales de mayo, mientras que Oliver desciende, Odell, Warren y Tilman prueban una salida por la arista norte del Everest detrás del *sherpa* dinámico y entusiasta Tenzing Norgay, que abre el camino. Ya han alcanzado 7470 metros cuando no pueden seguir avanzando. Durante el ascenso, Warren prueba sucesivamente los dos modelos de aparatos de oxígeno. Con el nuevo modelo de circuito cerrado, que recubre por completo el rostro, se ahoga. El respirador de circuito abierto, que deja la nariz libre, funciona mucho mejor.

En adelante, el Collado Norte queda inaccesible por su vertiente este, demasiado expuesta al monzón y a los riesgos de avalanchas. Los *sherpas* transportan víveres y material a la parte central del glaciar de Rongbuk para escalar el Collado Norte por otro lado el 3 de junio. A partir del día siguiente, Tilman, Lloyd, Smythe y Shipton atacan la arista norte del Everest con Ang Tharkay y otros seis *sherpas*, entre los que se encuentra el mejor de todos, el joven Tenzing. Desafiando la tormenta, montan el campamento V a 7860 metros de altitud, y a los dos días el campamento siguiente a 8300 metros. El 8 de junio, los dos alpinistas más aguerridos, Smythe y Shipton, parten a primera hora de la mañana, pero el frío glaciar, que les entumece los miembros, y el estado de la nieve, en la que se hunden hasta los muslos, les impiden subir demasiado alto. Las placas rocosas heladas escondidas por la nieve en polvo son terriblemente peligrosas. A continuación, les toca a Tilman y a Lloyd intentarlo de nuevo, aunque de forma infructuosa. La misión termina con este nuevo fracaso.

En el verano de 1938, Londres tiene otras preocupaciones. La guerra se acerca, el Everest caerá en el olvido durante años.

A group of Lepchas in Sikkim.

Eine Gruppe Lepcha in Sikkim.

Een groep Lepcha's in Sikkim.

Un grupo de *lepchas* en Sikkim.

A woman in a garden with her children, Sikkim.

Mutter mit Kindern in einem Garten, Sikkim.

Een vrouw met kinderen in een tuin in Sikkim.

Una mujer con sus hijos en un jardín, Sikkim.

Tibetan man with his horse, Sikkim.

Ein Tibeter mit seinem Pferd, Sikkim.

Tibetaanse man met zijn paard in Sikkim.

Un hombre tibetano con su caballo, Sikkim.

A mountain landscape in Sikkim.

Berglandschaft in Sikkim.

Berglandschap in Sikkim.

Un paisaje de montaña en Sikkim.

Campsite beside a mountain range, Sikkim.

Lager neben einer Bergkette, Sikkim.

Kampement naast bergketen in Sikkim.

Emplazamiento del campamento al lado de una cadena montañesa, Sikkim.

Members of the 1938 Everest Expedition en route from Sikkim to Tibet.

Mitglieder der Mount Everest-Expedition von 1938 auf dem Weg von Sikkim nach Tibet.

Deelnemers van de Everest-expeditie in 1938 op weg van Sikkim naar Tibet.

Miembros de la Expedición al Everest de 1938 en ruta desde Sikkim a El Tíbet.

In the heights of Sikkim.

In den Höhen von Sikkim.

Op grote hoogte in Sikkim.

En las alturas de Sikkim.

A mountain pass in Sikkim on the border with Tibet.

Ein Bergpass an der Grenze zwischen Tibet und Sikkim.

Een bergpas in Sikkim op de grens met Tibet.

Un paso montañoso en Sikkim, en la frontera con El Tibet.

A cane bridge in Sikkim.

Eine Brücke aus Schilfrohr in Sikkim.

Een loopbrug van touw in Sikkim.

Un puente de caña en Sikkim.

Clearing snow in Upper Sikkim.

Schneeschaufeln im Norden von Sikkim.

Sneeuwruimen in Noord-Sikkim.

Retirando nieve en el Alto Sikkim.

A team member sleeping on an area of bare rock.

Ein Mitglied des Teams beim Schlafen auf dem schroffen Felsgestein.

Een teamlid slaapt op ruige rotsgrond.

Un miembro del equipo durmiendo en una roca desigual.

A team member bathing in a local hot spring.

Ein Mitglied des Teams beim Baden in einer heißen Quelle.

Een teamlid neemt een bad in een warmwaterbron.

Un miembro del equipo bañándose en un manantial local de agua caliente.

Ang Tharkay, one of the best Sherpas and an excellent cook, and a young brother.

Ang Tharkay, einer der besten Sherpas und ein ausgezeichneter Koch, mit seinem jüngeren Bruder.

Ang Tharkay, een van de beste Sherpa's en een uitmuntend kok, met een jongere broer.

Ang Tharkay, uno de los mejores *sherpas* y excelente cocinero, y un hermano más pequeño.

Base Camp with Mount Everest in the distance.

Basislager mit dem Mount Everest im Hintergrund.

Basiskamp met de Everest op de achtergrond.

El campamento base con el Monte Everest a lo lejos.

Harold William "Bill" Tilman, the leader of the expedition.

Der Expeditionsleiter Harold William „Bill“ Tilman.

Harold William ‘Bill’ Tilman, de expeditieleider.

Harold William "Bill" Tilman, el líder de la expedición.

A column of porters on the march from Base Camp to Camp I.

Eine Kolonne von Trägern auf dem Fußmarsch vom Basislager zu Lager I.

Colonne-dragers op weg van het basiskamp naar kamp I.

Una columna de portadores en marcha desde el campamento base al campamento I.

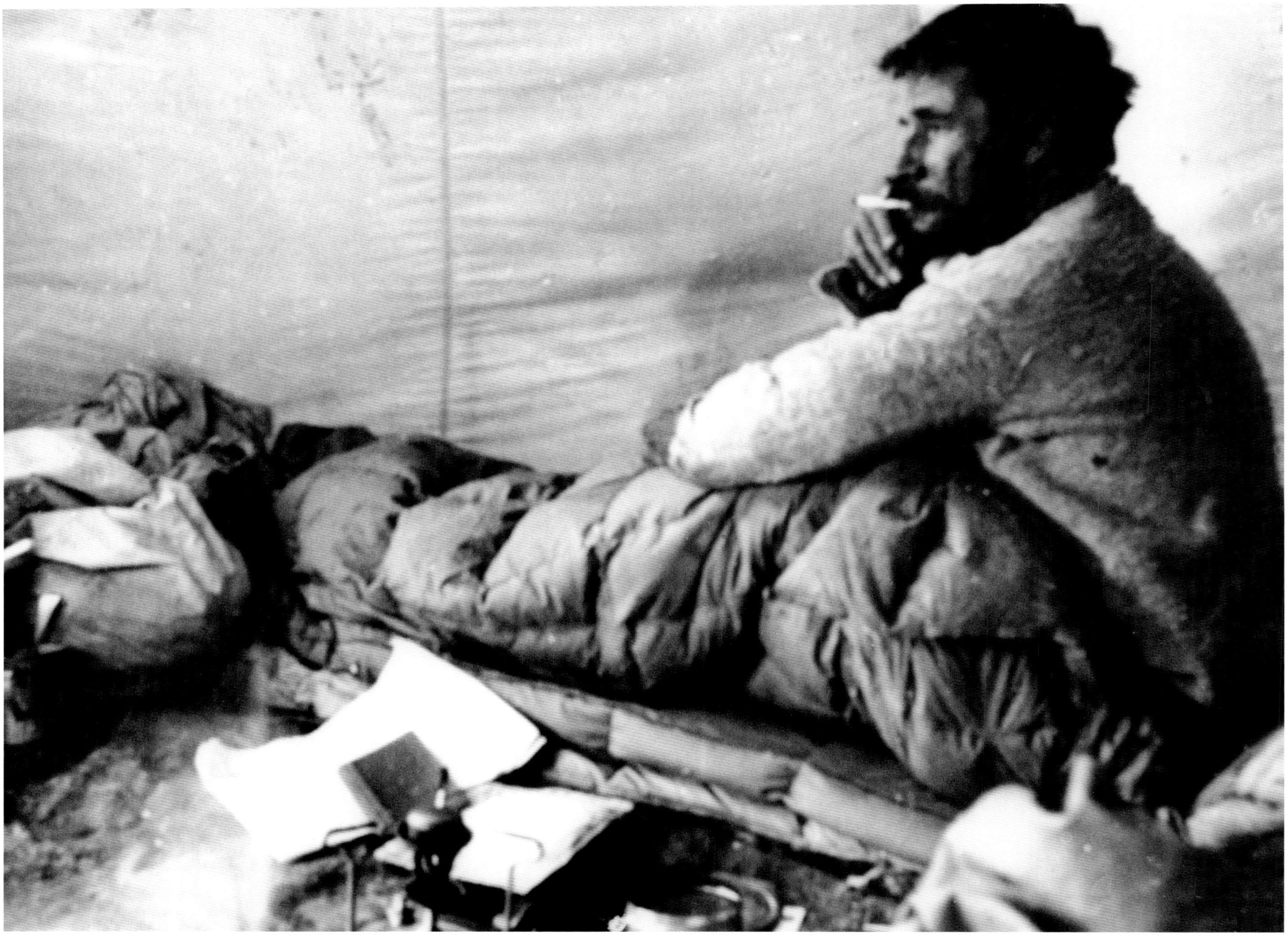

Bill Tilman smoking a cigarette in a sleeping bag, in his tent.

Bill Tilman beim Rauchen im Schlafsack in seinem Zelt.

Bill Tilman rookt een sigaret in een slaapzak in een tent.

Bill Tilman fumando un cigarro en un saco de dormir en una tienda de campaña.

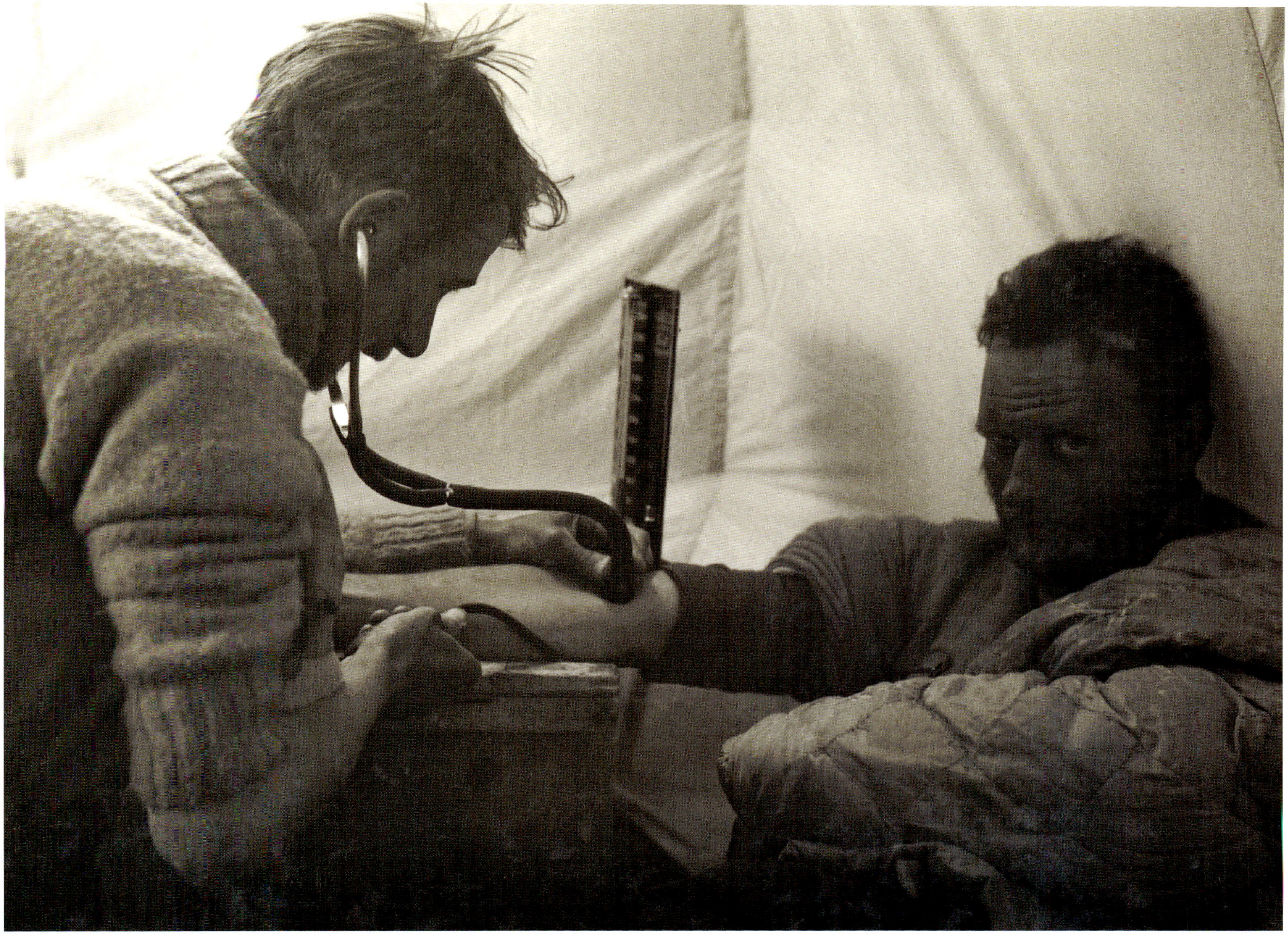

Charles Warren taking Eric Shipton's blood pressure.

Charles Warren beim Blutdruckmessen mit Eric Shipton.

Charles Warren meet de bloeddruk van Eric Shipton.

Charles Warren tomando la tensión arterial a Eric Shipton.

Eastern descent from Lhakpa La. Peter Oliver and Sherpas with Everest hidden by cloud.

Abstieg vom Lhakpa La über die Ostroute, Peter Oliver und Sherpas vor dem wolkenverhangenen Mount Everest.

Oostelijke afdaling van de Lhakpa La. Peter Oliver en Sherpa's, de Everest in bewolking.

Descenso este desde Lhakpa La. Peter Oliver y algunos *sherpas* con el Everest visto entre una nube.

Tents pitched and team members looking across at the peak.

Zelte und Mitglieder des Teams, die über einen Gipfel schauen.

Tenten en teamleden ernaast, kijkend naar een piek.

Las tiendas de campaña y los miembros del equipo mirando por un pico.

Climbers crossing a snowfield.

Bergsteiger bei der Überquerung eines Schneefelds.

Klimmers op besneeuwd terrein.

Los escaladores cruzando un campo de nieve.

Members of the 1938 expedition at Rongbuk (from left to right): Warren, Lloyd, Tilman, Oliver, Smythe, Odell and Shipton.

Mitglieder der Expedition von 1938 bei Rongpu (von links nach rechts): Warren, Lloyd, Tilman, Oliver, Smythe, Odell und Shipton.

Deelnemers aan de expeditie van 1938 in Rongbuk (v.l.n.r.): Warren, Lloyd, Tilman, Oliver, Smythe, Odell en Shipton.

Miembros de la Expedición de 1938 en Rongbuk (de izquierda a derecha): Warren, Lloyd, Tilman, Oliver, Smythe, Odell y Shipton.

A team member holding a rope in a snow field.

Ein Mitglied des Teams hält ein Seil auf einem Schneefeld.

Een teamlid houdt een touw vast op besneeuwd terrein.

Un miembro del equipo sujetando una cuerda en un campo de nieve.

Noel Odell is a veteran of British Everest expeditions.

Noel Odell, ein Veteran der britische Mount Everest-Expeditionen.

Noel Odell is een Britse expeditie-veteraan.

Noel Odell es un veterano de las expediciones británicas al Everest.

Sherpas on the north ridge of Everest.

Sherpas auf dem Nordgrat des Mount Everest.

Sherpa's op de noordelijke kam van de Everest.

Sherpas en la cresta norte del Everest.

A party heads up the trail from Camp III to the start of the slope leading to the North Col.

Eine Gruppe von Bergsteigern beim Weg von Lager III zum Beginn des Abhangs, der zum Nordsattel führt.

Een team vertrokken uit kamp III liet een spoor na dat doorloopt tot het begin van de helling naar de noordelijke pas.

Un grupo sigue el rastro desde el campamento III hasta el inicio de la pendiente que conduce al Collado Norte.

Camp V, at an altitude of 7,865m.

Lager V in 7865 m Höhe.

Kamp V op 7865 meter hoogte.

El campamento V a 7865 m.

1951

The Hidden Face of Everest
Das verborgene Gesicht des Mount Everest

The war is over and Everest is still there, nettling British pride once more. In 1947 the Himalayan Committee (the ex-Everest Committee), intends to relaunch the adventure. Off his own bat and all alone, an eccentric Englishman of Canadian origin, Earl Denman, enters Tibet illegally the same year and hires two Sherpas at cut-price rates, one of which is the remarkable Tenzing Norgay. He arrives on the Rongbuk glacier, the Tibetan army patrols hot on his heels. Exceedingly poorly equipped, wearing inappropriate footwear, suffering from hunger and cold and with relatively little mountaineering experience, Denman manages to reach the foot of the North Col, however, he is forced to retreat due to the wind. Earl Denman nonetheless successfully accomplishes a return journey between Darjeeling and Everest of more than 1,000 kilometres on foot, without shoes for part of the journey and in less than five weeks.
Subsequently, two events will completely reshuffle the cards. October 1950: Chinese communists invade Tibet. The country is closed off to foreigners for a long period of time. At the same time, however, Nepal opens its borders. From this point on Everest can be approached from the South Face, the Nepalese side. For the British, this means going back to square one.
The expedition is planned for the autumn of 1951. It is the Everest veteran, Eric Shipton, who leads the expedition. The small team also includes two talented alpinists practiced at climbing in the Alps: Michael Ward and one of his friends, the Scot William Murray. A young British mountaineering star, Tom Bourdillon, is also in the group. In Nepal Edmund Hillary and Harold Riddiford, two young Alpinists from New Zealand who have just climbed a Himalayan peak, are permitted to join the expedition. The small party reaches the Khumbu glacier on 25 September 1951 just as the last rains of the monsoon are passing over. At the end of the month, Bourdillon, Ward and Riddiford start to explore the great ice fall. For their part, Hillary and Shipton climb the slopes of neighbouring Pumori in order to obtain a detailed view of the highest section of Everest. As they subsequently compare points of view, the alpinists arrive at the following conclusion: to reach the summit they will need to clear the ice flow, then a hemmed-in passage – the West comb – and rejoin the South Col before attacking the south-eastern ridge of Everest. It is the start of the route that will be the most technically demanding. The ice fall is particularly formidable. Composed of unstable blocks of ice, seracs and gigantic pinnacles, the ice fall is 600 metres high.
On 4 October Bourdillon, Shipton and the two New Zealanders, Hillary and Riddiford, start out accompanied by three Sherpas, including an old travelling companion, Ang Tharkay. For hours they look for ways of opening up a path between the gigantic ice concretions. At regular intervals, the sound of something like the rumbling of a train through a tunnel can be heard at a distance: an avalanche is hurtling down the slopes of Everest. Arriving nearby the West comb, they avoid first the start of an avalanche then falling blocks of ice; it is already late and imperative for the team to return to the camp set up at the foot of the ice fall before nightfall. It is only on 28 October, after several days of observing the state of the snow and awaiting the auspicious moment, that the real attempt is launched. The group of alpinists, together with the three Sherpas, clears the ice fall, following the route that has been marked out previously. They arrive, exhausted, on the upper edge of the West comb. An enormous crevasse blocks the glacier that occupies the narrow valley and is impossible to bypass. Sirdar Ang Tharkay recommends retracing their steps, it is becoming dangerous at this time of year. The alpinists' mission is therefore at an end. They have the feeling that the most difficult challenge has been overcome. The pathway towards the summit is open and the next time they will succeed. Of that much they are certain.

Der Krieg ist vorbei, der Mount Everest ist noch immer nicht bezwungen und stellt eine Herausforderung für den Stolz der Briten dar. 1947 ist das Himalayan Committee – das ehemalige Mount Everest Committee – bereit, sich dieser Herausforderung erneut zu stellen. Im selben Jahr reist der exzentrische Engländer kanadischer Herkunft, Earl Denman, auf eigene Faust illegal nach Tibet und heuert zu niedrigen Preisen zwei Sherpas an, darunter den bemerkenswerten Tenzing Norgay. Denman erreicht den Rongpu-Gletscher, wobei ihm Patrouillen der tibetanischen Armee dicht auf den Fersen sind. Sehr schlecht ausgerüstet, mit mangelhaftem Schuhwerk und unter Hunger und Kälte leidend gelangt der im Bergsteigen unerfahrene Mann bis zum Fuß des Nordpass, doch wegen des Windes muss er umkehren. Dennoch gelingt ihm eine Meisterleistung, nämlich die Strecke zwischen Darjeeling und

De verborgen kant van de Everest
La cara oculta del Everest

dem Mount Everest in weniger als fünf Wochen zu Fuß zurückzulegen: hin und zurück mehr als 1.000 Kilometer, zum Teil ohne Schuhe.
In den folgenden Jahren werden die Karten infolge zweier Ereignisse vollkommen neu gemischt: Im Oktober 1950 marschieren die chinesischen Kommunisten in Tibet ein. Das Land wird Ausländern für lange Zeit verschlossen bleiben. Doch gleichzeitig öffnet Nepal seine Grenzen. Somit ist der Mount Everest von der Südseite, aus Nepal, zugänglich. Für die Briten heißt es, von vorn anzufangen.
Die neue Expedition ist für den Herbst 1951 vorgesehen. Eric Shipton als Veteran des Mount Everest übernimmt die Leitung. In seiner kleinen Gruppe befinden sich zwei große, äußerst erfahrene Bergsteiger: Michael Ward und einer seiner Freunde, der Schotte William Murray. Der hochbegabte junge Brite Tom Bourdillon, der sich unter den Bergsteigern bereits einen Namen gemacht hat, nimmt ebenfalls an der Expedition teil. In Nepal erhalten Edmund Hillary und Harold Riddiford, zwei junge Bergsteiger aus Neuseeland, die Genehmigung, zur Expedition zu stoßen, nachdem sie bereits einen der Gipfel des Himalaya erklommen haben. Die kleine Gruppe kommt mit den letzten Regenfällen des Monsun am 25. September 1951 am Khumbu-Gletscher an. Noch am Ende des Monats beginnen Bourdillon, Ward und Riddiford mit der Erkundung des Khumbu-Eisbruchs. Hillary und Shipton besteigen ihrerseits die Hänge des benachbarten Pumori, um sich ein genaues Bild vom obersten Teil des Everest zu machen. Nach einem Austausch ihrer Erkenntnisse gelangen die Bergsteiger zu folgender Schlussfolgerung: Zur Besteigung des Gipfels müssen sie zunächst den Eisbruch überqueren, dann eine von Bergen umschlossene Passage, das Tal des Schweigens oder auf Englisch *Western Cwm* genannt, und wieder zum Südpass zurückkehren, bevor der Südostgrat des Everest in Angriff genommen werden kann. Dies ist der Anfang der Route, die technisch als die schwierigste gilt. Insbesondere der Eisbruch ist imponierend. Er besteht aus instabilen Eisblöcken und gewaltigen, eisigen Zacken und Spitzen und erreicht eine Höhe von 600 Metern.
Am 4. Oktober beginnen Bourdillon, Shipton und die beiden Neuseeländer Hillary und Riddiford, begleitet von drei Sherpas, mit dem Aufstieg, einschließlich ihres alten Weggenossen Ang Tharkay. Stundenlang versuchen sie, sich zwischen den gigantischen Formen aus Eis einen Weg zu bahnen. In der Ferne ist regelmäßig ein dumpfes Grollen zu hören, ähnlich eines Zuges der durch einen Tunnel fährt, aber es ist der Abgang einer Lawine über den Hängen des Mount Everest. Beim näher kommen zum Tal des Schweigens, werden sie fast von einer beginnenden Lawine, dann von herabfallenden Eisblöcken mitgerissen. Es ist spät geworden, und die Gruppe ist gezwungen, vor Sonnenuntergang zum Lager, am Fuße des Eisbruchs, zurückzukehren.
Erst am 28. Oktober, nach tagelanger Beobachtung der Schneelage und einen günstigen Moment abwartend, wird ein ernsthafter Besteigungsversuch unternommen. Sämtliche Bergsteiger sowie drei Sherpas übersteigen den Eisbruch und folgen der Spur, die sie beim letzten Mal hinterlassen haben. Erschöpft erreichen sie den oberen Rand des Tals des Schweigens. Eine gewaltige Gletscherspalte versperrt ihnen den Weg zum Gletscher, der sich in dem engen Tal befindet, und es ist unmöglich, sie zu umgehen. Der Sirdar Ang Tharkay vertritt die Auffassung, die Gruppe solle kehrtmachen. In dieser Jahreszeit wird der Berg langsam gefährlich. Die Mission der Bergsteiger ist damit zu Ende, doch sie haben das Gefühl, die größten Schwierigkeiten überwunden zu haben. Der Weg zum Gipfel steht Bergsteigern jetzt offen und wird beim nächsten Mal der Richtige sein – davon sind sie überzeugt.

De oorlog is ten einde en de Everest tart nog altijd de Britse trots. In 1947 wil het Himalaya-comité (voormalig Everest-comité) de avontuurlijke uitdaging opnieuw aangaan. Op eigen initiatief gaat Earl Denman, een excentrieke Engelsman van Canadese afkomst, datzelfde jaar illegaal de Tibetaanse grens over en huurt tegen een zachte prijs twee Sherpa's in, onder wie de opvallende Tenzing Norgay. Hij komt op de gletsjer van Rongbuk aan met Tibetaanse legerpatrouilles op zijn hielen. Zonder goede uitrusting, slecht geschoeid en honger en dorst lijdend, bereikt deze onervaren bergbeklimmer de voet van de noordelijke pas. Daar ziet hij zich gedwongen terug te keren vanwege de wind. Earl Denman heeft in elk geval blijk gegeven van zijn wilskracht door de duizend kilometer heen en terug tussen Darjeeling en de Everest te voet af te leggen. Dat deed hij voor een groot deel van de route zonder schoenen en in minder dan vijf weken.
Vervolgens zorgen twee gebeurtenissen ervoor dat de kaarten opnieuw worden geschud. In oktober 1950 vallen de Chinese communisten Tibet

binnen. Het land wordt voor lange tijd afgegrendeld van de buitenwereld. Maar in diezelfde periode opent Nepal zijn grenzen. De Everest is voortaan toegankelijk via de zuidzijde, de Nepalese kant. De Britten moeten helemaal opnieuw beginnen.
De expeditie wordt gepland voor het najaar van 1951. De Everest-veteraan Eric Shipton neemt de leiding. In zijn kleine ploeg heeft hij met Michael Ward en een van diens vrienden, de Schot William Murray, twee geweldige klimmers die gehard zijn in het bergmassief van de Alpen. De veelbelovende, jonge Britse alpinist Tom Bourdillon is ook van de partij. In Nepal krijgen Edmund Hillary en Harold Riddiford, twee jonge alpinisten uit Nieuw-Zeeland die samen een bergtop in de Himalaya willen beklimmen, toestemming zich bij de expeditie te voegen. De kleine groep begeeft zich op 25 september 1951 in de laatste moessonregen op de Khumbu-gletsjer. Eind september zullen Bourdillon, Ward en Riddiford de grote ijsval onderzoeken. Hillary en Shipton beklimmen ondertussen de hellingen van de naburige Pumori om een beter beeld te krijgen van het hoogste gedeelte van de Everest. Als de alpinisten vervolgens hun indrukken bespreken, komen ze tot de volgende conclusie: om de top te bereiken, moeten ze eerst de enorme ijsval overwinnen, daarna de westelijke kam over en de zuidelijke pas weer in, voordat ze aan de beklimming van de Everest kunnen beginnen vanaf de zuidoostkant. Het is klimtechnisch het zwaarste parcours. Vooral de ijsval zorgt voor twijfels. Bestaande uit instabiele ijsblokken en gigantische sleuven en verheffingen, heeft die een hoogte van 600 meter.
Op 4 oktober gaan Bourdillon, Shipton en de twee Nieuw-Zeelanders, Hillary en Redford, op weg. Ze worden vergezeld door drie Sherpa's, onder wie een oude bekende, Ang Tharkay. Urenlang proberen ze zich een weg te banen door de enorme ijsmassa's. Regelmatig horen ze een ver gedender als van een trein in een tunnel: een lawine die van de Everest-hellingen rolt. Bij de westelijke kam aangekomen, weten de klimmers maar net een beginnende lawine en vallende ijsblokken te ontwijken. Het is al laat en de ploeg moet voor de nacht terugkeren naar het kamp dat aan de voet van de gletsjer is opgezet.
Pas op 28 oktober, na dagenlange observatie van de sneeuwconditie en in afwachting van het juiste moment, gaat de echte recordpoging van start. Alle alpinisten en de drie Sherpa's trotseren de ijsval via de route die eerder is uitgestippeld. Ze komen afgemat aan op het hoogste punt van de westelijke bergkam. Daar stuiten ze op een enorme gletsjerspleet in een kloof waar geen weg omheen is. Sirdar Ang Tharkay is van mening dat een nieuwe poging in hetzelfde seizoen te gevaarlijk wordt. Daarmee zit de opdracht van de alpinisten erop. Ze hebben de indruk dat het zwaarste werk is verricht. De weg naar de top is uitgestippeld en de volgende expeditie zal succesvol zijn, daarvan zijn ze overtuigd.

La guerra ha terminado y el Everest sigue estando ahí, lo que comienza de nuevo a tocar el orgullo británico. En 1947, el comité del Himalaya (excomité del Everest) pretende volver a lanzar la aventura. Un inglés excéntrico de origen canadiense, Earl Denman, entra solo ilegalmente en el Tíbet ese mismo año, y contrata a bajo precio a dos sherpas, entre ellos el prestigioso Tenzing Norgay. Llega al glaciar de Rongbuk y se encuentra con las patrullas del ejército tibetano en sus puestos. El hombre, muy mal equipado, mal calzado, hambriento y muerto de frío, tiene bastante poca experiencia en la montaña, llega hasta el pie del Collado Norte, pero se ve obligado a recular a causa del viento. Aun así Earl Denman conseguirá la proeza de caminar más de 1.000 kilómetros de ida y vuelta entre Darjeeling y el Everest. Sin zapatos de viaje. Y en menos de cinco semanas.
Seguidamente, tendrán lugar dos acontecimientos que cambiarán por completo los mapas. Octubre de 1950: los comunistas chinos invaden el Tíbet. El país se cierra a los extranjeros durante mucho tiempo. Pero en la misma época, Nepal abre sus fronteras. En lo sucesivo, se podrá acceder al Everest por la cara sur, la vertiente nepalesa. Pero para los británicos, es como volver a empezar.
La expedición está programada para el otoño de 1951. La encabeza un veterano del Everest, Eric Shipton. Con él en el pequeño equipo dos grandes escaladores habituados a los macizos alpinos: Michael Ward y uno de sus amigos, el escocés William Murray. Una joven gloria del alpinismo británico, Tom Bourdillon, también está en el grupo. En Nepal, Edmund Hillary y Harold Riddiford, dos jóvenes alpinistas neozelandeses que acaban de escalar una cumbre del Himalaya, reciben autorización para incorporarse a la expedición. La pequeña tropa llega al glaciar de Khumbu el 25 de septiembre de 1951 con las últimas lluvias del monzón. A finales de mes, Bourdillon, Ward y Riddiford empiezan a explorar la gran cascada de hielo. Por su parte, Hillary y Shipton escalan las pendientes del Pumori vecino para tener una visión precisa de la parte más elevada del Everest. Confrontando a continuación sus puntos de vista, los alpinistas llegan a la conclusión siguiente: para coronar la cima, hay que salvar la caída de hielo, después un paso encajado - la hondonada oeste - y llegar al Collado Sur antes de tomar la arista sureste del Everest. Es el inicio del recorrido, que es técnicamente lo más difícil. En especial, la cascada es temible. Formada por bloques de hielo inestables, seracs y pináculos gigantescos, tiene una altura de 600 metros.
El 4 de octubre, Bourdillon, Shipton y los dos neozelandeses, Hillary y Riddiford, se ponen en marcha, acompañados por tres *sherpas* entre los que se encuentra un viejo compañero de ruta, Ang Tharkay. Durante horas, intentan trazar un camino entre las gigantescas concreciones de hielo. Con cierta regularidad, en la lejanía, se oye como el rodamiento de un tren al entrar en un túnel: una avalancha baja rodando a lo largo de la pendiente del Everest. Una vez que llegan cerca de la hondonada oeste, un inicio de avalancha, después una caída de bloques de hielo, a punto están de llevárselos por delante; ya es tarde, el equipo debe regresar al campamento instalado al pie de la cascada de hielo antes de que se haga de noche.
No es hasta el 28 de octubre, después de días de observación del estado de la nieve y en espera del momento propicio, cuando se pone en marcha el verdadero intento. El grupo de alpinistas, así como tres sherpas, atraviesan la cascada de hielo siguiendo el itinerario trazado previamente. Llegan agotados al borde superior de la hondonada oeste. Una enorme grieta corta el glaciar que ocupa el estrecho valle y es imposible rodearlo. El sirdar, Ang Tharkay, opina que es mejor deshacer el camino, ya que es peligroso en esta estación. La misión de los alpinistas termina aquí. Tienen la sensación de haber hecho la parte más dura. La vía hacia la cumbre está abierta y la próxima vez será la definitiva. No les cabe duda de ello.

The 1951 expedition team. From left to right: Shipton, Murray, Bourdillon and Riddiford (back row); Ward and Hillary (front row).

Das Expeditionsteam von 1951, von links nach rechts: Shipton, Murray, Bourdillon und Riddiford (hintere Reihe), Ward und Hillary (vordere Reihe).

Het expeditieteam van 1951 (v.l.n.r.): Shipton, Murray, Bourdillon en Riddiford (achter); Ward en Hillary (voor).

El equipo de la expedición de 1951. De izquierda a derecha: Shipton, Murray, Bourdillon y Riddiford (fila trasera); Ward y Hillary (fila delantera).

Tibetans in the landscape.

Tibetanen in landschap.

Tibeter in der Landschaft.

Tibetanos en un paisaje.

Portrait of Sirdar Ang Tharkay,
one of the best Sherpas.

Portret van sirdar Ang Tharkay,
een van de beste Sherpa's.

Sirdar Ang Tharkay,
einer der besten Sherpas.

Retrato del Sirdar Ang Tharkay,
uno de los mejores *sherpas*.

A school in Namche Bazar (Nepal).

Schule in Namche Bazar (Nepal).

Een school in Namche Bazar (Nepal).

Una escuela en Namche Bazar (Nepal).

Bathing in the Arun. Under umbrellas (from left to right): Eric Shipton, Michael Ward and Bill Murray

Baden im Arun, unter Schirmen (von links nach rechts): Eric Shipton, Michael Ward und Bill Murray.

Baden in de Arun. Onder paraplu's (v.l.n.r.) : Eric Shipton, Michael Ward en Bill Murray.

Baño en el Arun. Bajo paraguas (de izquierda a derecha): Eric Shipton, Michael Ward y Bill Murray.

Road flanking mountain lake.

Weg entlang eines Bergsees.

Pad langs bergmeer.

Carretera que flanquea el lago de la montaña.

Khumjung village (Nepal)
near Mount Everest.

Das Dorf Khumjung (Nepal)
in der Nähe des Mount Everest.

Het dorp Khumjung (Nepal),
in de omgeving van de Everest.

Pueblo de Khumjung (Nepal),
cerca del Monte Everest.

Thyangboche monastery in its wonderful setting.

Das Kloster von Tengboche in seiner atemberaubenden landschaftlichen Umgebung.

Het Thyangboche-klooster met zijn prachtige omgeving.

El monasterio de Thyangboche en su maravilloso entorno.

An oxygen cylinder hanging in Thyangboche monastery, used as a gong.

Ein Sauerstoffzylinder im Kloster von Tengboche, der als Gong verwendet wird.

Een opgehangen zuurstoffles functioneert in het Thyangboche-klooster als gong.

Un cilindro de oxígeno suspendido en el monasterio Thyangboche, utilizado como gong.

Ama Dablam from Thyangboche.

Die Ama Dablam von Tengboche ausgesehen.

De Ama Dablam gezien vanuit Thyangboche.

Ama Dablam desde Thyangboche.

Twilight on the mountains.

Dämmerung in den Bergen.

Avondrood op de bergtop.

Crepúsculo en las montañas.

Ama Dablam from Imja Khola,
near Thyangboche.

Die Ama Dablam vom Imja Khola in der Nähe von Tengboche aus gesehen.

De Ama Dablam vanaf de Imja Khola,
bij Thyangboche.

Ama Dablam desde Imja Khola,
cerca de Thyangboche.

Landscape image of Mount Everest with clouds.

Landschaft um den wolkenverhangenen Mount Everest.

Panoramafoto van de Everest met wolken.

Imagen de un paisaje del Monte Everest con nubes.

Tom Bourdillon.

Yeti footprint with an
ice axe head.

Yeti-Fußspur und der Kopf
eines Eispickels.

Yeti-voetafdruk met ernaast
de kop van een ijsbijl.

Pisada de yeti con cabeza
de piqueta.

Yeti footprint leading off into the mountains with rucksack and ice axe.

Yeti-Fußspur, die in die Berge führt, mit Rucksack und Eispickel.

Yeti-voetafdrukken in de richting van de bergen met ernaast een rugzak en een ijsbijl.

Pisada de yeti que conduce a las montañas con mochila y piqueta.

Resting on the moraines. Edmund Hillary wears a check shirt and is facing away from the camera.

Rast in den Moränen. Edmund Hillary, mit dem Rücken zum Betrachter, trägt ein kariertes Hemd.

Uitrusten tussen morenes. Edmund Hillary, hier op de rug gezien, draagt een geblokt shirt.

Descansando en las morrenas. Edmund Hillary, de espaldas, viste una camisa a cuadros.

Edmund Hillary on a summit in the foreground of Everest.

Edmund Hillary auf einem Gipfel vor dem Mount Everest.

Edmund Hillary op een top voor de Everest.

Edmund Hillary en una cumbre delante del Everest.

Hillary on Pumori's 6,096m ridge, looking across the Khumbu Glacier to Nuptse.

Auf dem Grat des Pumori in 6096 m Höhe blickt Hillary über den Khumbu-Gletscher auf den Nuptse.

Hillary op de 6096 meter hoge kam van de Pumori, uitkijkend over de Khumbu-gletsjer in de richting van de Nuptse.

Hillary en la cresta de 6096 m del Pumori mirando por el glaciar de hacia Nuptse.

The Nup La Icefall.

Der Nup La-Eisbruch.

De Nup La-ijsval.

La cascada de hielo Nup La.

North Peak, Lho La and Everest.

Der Nordgipfel, der Lho La-Pass
und der Mount Everest.

De noordelijke piek, de Lho La en de Everest.

Pico Norte, Lho La y Everest.

In the Icefall.

Im Khumbu-Eisbruch.

In de ijsval.

En la cascada de hielo.

Everest (left), Lhotse (right) and the Khumbu glacier and Icefall in the middle.

Der Mount Everest (links), der Lhotse (rechts) sowie der Khumbu-Gletscher und der Eisbruch in der Mitte.

De Everest (links), de Lhotse (rechts) en de Khumbu-gletsjer en -ijsval in het midden.

Everest (a la izquierda), Lhotse (a la derecha) y el glaciar Khumbu y la cascada de hielo en el medio.

The Khumbu Glacier.

Der Khumbu-Gletscher.

De Khumbu-gletsjer.

El glaciar Khumbu.

1952

The Swiss Try Their Luck

Die Schweizer versuchen ihr Glück

The Nepalese government grants authorisation to climb Everest only very sparingly. Yet the English are not the only ones, each country will have its chance in turn. First in line, Switzerland now has the right to attempt the ascent throughout 1952. Great Britain will need to wait until 1953.
The team that will be brought together under the leadership of doctor and explorer Edouard Wyss-Dunant is very close-knit. All the alpinists on the expedition belong to a very exclusive circle of Genevan mountaineers, the *Androsace*. A climber made of strong stuff, René Dittert will be in charge of the attack ropes. Tenzing Norgay who, at 38 years old, has already participated in four attempts on Everest, is the undisputed leader of the Sherpas.
On 30 April 1952 the Swiss clear the ice fall and come out onto the famous West comb. A 5 metre wide crevasse blocks their path. Jean-Jacques Asper, the youngest of the party, but also the most agile of them all, tries twice to cross the crevasse at the end of a rope 18 metres long, but with no success. On the third attempt, he manages to sidestep the chasm and heaves himself up onto the tiny footholds that he has cut out along the rock face. With his teammates he then establishes a bridge of four ropes that will allow the porters to transport all the equipment onto the upper glacier. They still need to clear a rocky projection, henceforth known as the "Geneva Spur", when the oxygen breathing apparatus start to show signs of weakening. On 24 May Dittert gives the order to advance to a team of three alpinists, Lambert, Flory and Aubert, who will accompany six Sherpas led by Tenzing. The tents are somehow pitched on a tiny platform. The men squeeze on without unroping, watching out for their crampons. It is impossible to unroll the sleeping bags. Only Tenzing is brave enough to heat water and to distribute beakers of tea and little biscuits to all. On 26 May they are finally on the South Col. The wind is so violent that they cannot stand upright and are forced to crawl as they pitch the tent! The Sherpas are exhausted and descend back down the mountain. Only Tenzing will remain with the Swiss and, early in the morning, the four men attack the south-east ridge of Everest. They will bivouac at 8,400 metres and must take on oxygen to strengthen themselves. There is only one tent and two of the Alpinists, Flory and Aubert, have to abandon the exploit, heavy hearted, in order to let their teammates continue the adventure. Lambert and Tenzing settle down for the night, without a sleeping bag, stove, nor anything to drink save for snow melted by the flame of a candle. It is bitingly cold and they slap each other to keep their circulation going. The following day they attack the summit, hampered by the snow and fog. Stopping every three steps, they arrive above the final pyramid, at the record altitude of 8,573 metres. They are having difficulty breathing and cannot advance any further, even though they are only 260 metres from their goal. They are at the limits of their endurance and when they return to camp VI the brave Tenzing is at the point of blacking out.
A new expedition is set up in the autumn. Some new Alpinists will take part alongside Raymond Lambert and Dr Gabriel Chevalley, promoted to expedition leader. On location they meet the indispensable Tenzing Norgay. The Alpinists designated to make the ascent are equipped with new oxygen masks, ones that work well. This expedition is nonetheless marked by drama. On 3 October 1952 a block of ice breaks free and falls into the path of the advancing Alpinists. A young Sherpa is killed immediately. This fatal accident, combined with the unbearable cold and the hellish wind, will quickly terminate this latest attempt. Everest has escaped the Swiss.

Die nepalesische Regierung verteilt die Genehmigungen zur Besteigung des Everest nur tropfenweise. Da die Briten nicht mehr die einzigen sind, die eine Expedition durchführen möchten, darf ein Land nach dem anderen, der Reihe nach, sein Glück versuchen. Die Schweiz erhält als erstes Land für das gesamte Jahr 1952 das Recht, Besteigungsversuche am Mount Everest zu unternehmen. Großbritannien muss bis 1953 warten.
Unter den Teilnehmern der Gruppe, die für die Expedition unter Leitung des Arztes und Forschungsreisenden Edouard Wyss-Dunant zusammengestellt wird, herrscht eine gute Kameradschaft. Alle Teilnehmer der Expedition gehören zu einem exklusiven Klub Genfer Bergsteiger, dem „L'Androsace". René Dittert, ein erfahrener Bergsteiger mit einem eisernen Willen, wird zum Leiter der Seilschaften ernannt. Tenzing Norgay, der mit nunmehr 38 Jahren be-

Een Zwitserse poging
Los suizos prueban suerte

reits an vier Besteigungsversuchen teilgenommen hat, ist der unangefochtene Anführer der Sherpas.
Am 30. April 1952 überqueren die Schweizer den Eisbruch und gelangen zum berühmten Tal des Schweigens. Eine fünf Meter breite Gletscherspalte versperrt ihnen den Weg. Jean-Jacques Asper, das jüngste, aber beweglichste Mitglied der Gruppe versucht zwei Mal vergeblich, sie zu überqueren, indem er am Ende eines 18 Meter langen Seils hinüber pendelt. Beim dritten Versuch steigt er in den eisigen Abgrund hinab, und es gelingt ihm, die Kluft zu überspreizen und die winzigen Stufen hinaufzusteigen, die er in die Eiswand kerbt. Mit seinen Gefährten errichtet er daraufhin eine Brücke aus vier Seilen, über die die Träger die gesamte Ausrüstung auf den höher gelegenen Gletscher transportieren können. Nun muss nur noch ein Felsvorsprung erklommen werden, der „Éperon des Genevois" getauft wird. Doch die Sauerstoffgeräte zeigen erste Anzeichen von Schwäche. Am 24. Mai erteilt Dittert einer Gruppe von drei Bergsteigern – Lambert, Flory und Aubert – die Anweisung, den Anstieg in Begleitung von sechs, von Tenzing Norgay angeführten Sherpas, zu beginnen. Die Zelte werden mehr schlecht als recht auf einer winzigen Plattform aufgeschlagen. Die Männer harren dort eng zusammengepfercht aus, ohne ihre Seile oder Steigeisen abzunehmen. Die Schlafsäcke auszu- rollen ist ein Ding der Unmöglichkeit. Nur Tenzing Norgay bringt den Mut auf, Wasser zu kochen und Becher mit Tee und kleine Kekse an die Runde zu verteilen. Am 26. Mai gelangen die Bergsteiger endlich auf den Südpass. Der Wind bläst so heftig, dass sie nicht aufrecht stehen bleiben können und ihr Zelt kriechend errichten müssen. Die Sherpas sind erschöpft und steigen ab. Nur Tenzing Norgay bleibt bei den Schweizern, und früh am Morgen nehmen die vier Männer den südöstlichen Grat des Everest in Angriff. Sie biwakieren auf 8.400 Metern Höhe und müssen sich mit Sauerstoff versorgen. Es ist nur mehr ein Zelt vorhanden, und zwei der Bergsteiger, Flory und Aubert, müssen schweren Herzens aufgeben, um ihren Kameraden die Fortsetzung des Abenteuers zu ermöglichen.
Lambert und Tenzing Norgay schlagen ihr Nachtlager auf, ohne Schlafsack, ohne Kocher und ohne etwas anderes zu trinken, als über einer Kerzenflamme geschmolzener Schnee. In der beißenden Kälte versetzen sie sich Schläge, um ihre Blutzirkulation aufrechtzuerhalten. Am nächsten Morgen nehmen sie den Gipfel in Angriff, wenngleich behindert durch Schnee und Nebel. Alle drei Schritte müssen sie anhalten und gelangen doch schließlich bis zum Fuß der Gipfelpyramide, bis zum Höhenrekord von 8.573 Metern. Sie können kaum mehr atmen und kommen nicht weiter vorwärts, obwohl sie nur noch 260 Meter vom Ziel entfernt sind. Beide sind am Ende ihrer Kräfte, und als sie Lager VI wieder erreichen, ist der tapfere Tenzing Norgay am Rande der Bewusstlosigkeit.
Im Herbst wird eine neue Expedition auf die Beine gestellt. Diesmal nehmen neue Bergsteiger an der Seite Raymond Lamberts und Dr. Gabriel Chevalleys teil, der zum Leiter der Expedition ernannt wird. Vor Ort finden sie den unermüdlichen Tenzing Norgay. Die am Aufstieg beteiligten Bergsteiger sind mit neuen, gut funktionierenden Sauerstoffgeräten ausgestattet. Doch diese Expedition endet mit einer Tragödie. Am 3. Oktober 1952 löst sich ein Eisblock und fällt in die enge Schlucht, in der sich die Bergsteiger befinden. Ein junger Sherpa ist auf der Stelle tot. Der tödliche Unfall, die unerträgliche Kälte und der höllische Wind bereiten diesem neuen Versuch schnell ein Ende. Die Schweizer müssen sich am Mount Everest geschlagen geben.

De Nepalese overheid verstrekt spaarzaam toestemming om de Everest te beklimmen. Maar omdat de Engelsen niet langer de enige gegadigden zijn, zal elk land beurtelings de kans krijgen. Zwitserland staat bovenaan op de wachtlijst en krijgt het hele jaar 1952 om de beklimming te proberen. Groot-Brittannië zal moeten wachten tot 1953.
Onder leiding van de medische onderzoeker Edouard Wyss-Dunant wordt er een doorgewinterde expeditieploeg samengesteld. Alle alpinisten behoren tot de Androsace, een besloten kring van Geneefse klimmers. De zachtaardige René Ditter zal de opeenvolgende beklimmingen leiden. Onbetwiste aanvoerder van de Sherpa's is de 38-jarige Tenzing Norgay, die al aan vier Everest-expedities deelnam.
Op 30 april 1952 overwinnen de Zwitsers de ijsval en gaan op de beroemde westelijke bergkam uit de touwen. Een scheur van vijf meter breed blokkeert de doorgang. Jean-Jacques Asper, de jongste maar ook de lenigste van allemaal, probeert tweemaal vergeefs naar de overkant te slingeren aan een 18 meter lang koord. Bij de derde po-

ging lukt het hem de andere kant van de spleet te bereiken en zich omhoog te werken via minuscule treden die hij in de ijswand hakt. Samen met zijn ploeggenoten maakt hij vervolgens een brug van vier touwen waarover de dragers al het materiaal naar de hoofdgletsjer kunnen brengen. Ze moeten alleen nog over een rotsachtige uitsteeksel die 'Het Geneefse spoor' is gedoopt, als de zuurstofapparaten gaan haperen. Een team van drie alpinisten, Lambert, Flory en Aubert, begeleid door zes Sherpa's onder leiding van Tenzing, krijgt op 24 mei van Ditter opdracht voor de klim. De tenten worden zo goed en kwaad als het gaat opgezet op het kleine platform. Gezekerd en met hun stijgijzers nog ondergebonden proppen de mannen zich samen. Het is niet mogelijk de slaapzakken uit te rollen. Alleen Tenzing heeft de moed om water te koken en bekers thee met kleine biscuits rond te delen. Op 26 mei zijn ze eindelijk op de zuidelijke pas. De wind is zo sterk dat ze amper op de been kunnen blijven en ze zetten al glijdend de tent op. De Sherpa's zijn uitgeput en dalen weer af. Alleen Tenzing blijft bij de Zwitsers en deze vier mannen gaan vroeg in de ochtend de zuidoostelijke bergkam van de Everest te lijf. Ze zullen op 8400 meter hoogte bivakkeren en zuurstof nodig hebben. Er is maar één tent en twee alpinisten, Flory en Aubert, vertrekken met pijn in het hart om hun kameraden in staat te stellen het avontuur voort te zetten.
Lambert en Tenzing installeren zich voor de nacht, zonder slaapzak, zonder verwarming en met niets anders te drinken dan sneeuw die met een kaarsvlam is gesmolten. De kou is moordend en ze slaan zichzelf om hun bloedcirculatie op gang te houden. De volgende dag bestormen ze de top, gehinderd door sneeuw en mist. Na telkens drie stappen halt houdend, lukt het hen tot onder aan de hoogste piek te komen, op een recordhoogte van 8573 meter. Als ze nog maar 260 meter van het doel verwijderd zijn, krijgen ze ademhalingsproblemen en komen ze niet meer vooruit. De mannen hebben al hun kracht gegeven en nadat ze kamp VI weer hebben bereikt, bezwijkt de bijzonder gewaardeerde Sherpa Tenzing bijna.
In het najaar wordt opnieuw een expeditieploeg op de been gebracht. Nieuwe alpinisten vergezellen Raymond Lambert en dokter Gabriel Chevalley, die de leiding krijgt. Ter plaatse treffen ze uiteraard Tenzing Norgay aan. De alpinisten die de klim gaan uitvoeren, worden uitgerust met nieuwe zuurstofmaskers, die goed blijken te werken. Maar deze expeditie zal in het teken staan van een drama. Op 3 oktober 1952 laat een ijsblok los en komt neer in de corridor waar de alpinisten op dat moment doorheen trekken. Een jonge Sherpa is op slag gedood. Dit dodelijke ongeval maakt samen met de ondraaglijke kou en de helse wind een abrupt einde aan deze nieuwe poging. De Everest is de Zwitsers ontglipt.

El gobierno nepalés concede las autorizaciones para escalar el Everest con cuentagotas. Pero como los ingleses ya no son los únicos, cada país tendrá su oportunidad por turnos. Suiza, primera de la fila, tiene derecho a intentar el ascenso durante todo el año 1952. Gran Bretaña deberá esperar hasta 1953.
Es un equipo muy curtido el que se pondrá en marcha bajo la dirección de un médico explorador, Edouard Wyss-Dunant. Todos los alpinistas de la expedición pertenecen a un círculo muy cerrado de montañeros de Ginebra, el Androsace. René Dittert, escalador de carácter enérgico, será el jefe de las cordadas de asalto. Tenzing Norgay, con 38 años, que ya ha participado en cuatro intentos de escalar el Everest, es el jefe indiscutible de los sherpas.
El 30 de abril de 1952, los suizos atraviesan la cascada de hielo y desembocan en la famosa hondonada oeste. Una grieta de 5 metros de ancho corta el paso. Jean-Jacques Asper, el más joven, pero también el más ágil de todos, intenta atravesarla en dos ocasiones haciendo péndulo con una cuerda de 18 metros, sin conseguirlo. Al tercer intento, consigue pasar por encima del precipicio y subir por unos peldaños minúsculos que ha cavado a lo largo de la pared. Con sus compañeros de equipo, fabrica un puente de cuatro cuerdas que permitirá que los portadores transporten todo el equipo al glaciar superior. Aún habrá que atravesar un saliente rocoso, bautizado con el nombre de «Espolón de Ginebra», cuando los aparatos de oxígeno comienzan a dar signos de debilidad. El 24 de mayo, Dittert da la orden de asalto a un equipo de tres alpinistas, Lambert, Flory y Aubert, que acompañarán a seis sherpas conducidos por Tenzing. Las tiendas se montan mal que bien sobre una plataforma minúscula. Los hombres se apiñan sin desencordarse y guardan sus ganchos. No es posible desenrollar los sacos de dormir. Solo Tenzing tiene la valentía de calentar agua y repartir a la redonda vasos de té y galletitas. El 26 de mayo, por fin llegan al Collado Sur. El viento tiene tal fuerza que no pueden permanecer de pie y montan la tienda tumbados en el suelo. Los sherpas están agotados y descienden. Solamente Tenzing se queda con los suizos, y los cuatro hombres atacan la arista sureste del Everest por la mañana temprano. Acampan a 8.400 metros y deben repostar oxígeno. Solo queda una tienda y dos alpinistas, Flory y Aubert, deben abandonar, con el corazón en un puño, para permitir que sus compañeros prosigan con la aventura. Lambert y Tenzing se instalan por la noche, sin saco de dormir, sin hornillo y sin nada que beber aparte de la nieve que se funde con la llama de una vela. El frío es cortante y se dan golpes para mantener la circulación. Al día siguiente, atacan la cumbre, molestos con la nieve y la bruma. Parándose cada tres pasos, terminan por alcanzar la zona inferior de la pirámide final, a una altitud récord de 8.573 metros. Tienen dificultades para respirar y no pueden seguir avanzando cuando solo les quedan 260 metros para llegar a la meta. Están al límite de sus fuerzas y cuando encuentran el campamento VI, el valiente Tenzing está a punto de desfallecer.
Una nueva expedición se pone en marcha en otoño. En ella participan nuevos alpinistas al lado de Raymond Lambert y del Dr. Gabriel Chevalley, ascendido a jefe de misión. Sobre el terreno, se encontrarán con el ineludible Tenzing Norgay. Los alpinistas designados para el ascenso están provistos de nuevas máscaras de oxígeno que funcionan bien. Pero esta expedición está marcada por un drama. El 3 de octubre de 1952, un bloque de hielo se desprende y cae sobre el corredor por el que avanzan los alpinistas. Un joven sherpa muere inmediatamente. Este accidente mortal, conjugado con un frío insoportable y un viento infernal, pone fin rápidamente a este nuevo intento. El Everest queda fuera del alcance de los suizos.

The expedition of spring 1952. From left to right: Jean-Jacques Asper, René Dittert, Ernst Hofstetter, Gabriel Chevalley and André Roch. Raymond Lambert, Léon Flory and the head of the expedition, Edouard Wyss-Dunant, are not present.

Die Expedition vom Frühjahr 1952, von links nach rechts: Jean-Jacques Asper, René Dittert, Ernst Hofstetter, Gabriel Chevalley und André Roch. Es fehlen Raymond Lambert, Léon Flory und Expeditionsleiter Edouard Wyss-Dunant.

Deelnemers van de voorjaarsexpeditie in 1952 (v.l.n.r.): Jean-Jacques Asper, René Dittert, Ernst Hofstetter, Gabriel Chevalley en André Roch. Degenen die ontbreken zijn: Raymond Lambert, Léon Flory en de expeditieleider, Edouard Wyss-Dunant.

La expedición de la primavera de 1952. De izquierda a derecha: Jean-Jacques Asper, René Dittert, Ernst Hofstetter, Gabriel Chevalley y André Roch. Faltan Raymond Lambert, Léon Flory y el jefe de la expedición, Edouard Wyss-Dunant.

Gabriel Chevalley, Tenzing Norgay.

Lingtren (6,714 m) in the clouds.

Der wolkenumhangene Lingtren (6714 m).

De Lingtren (6714 m) met wolken rondom.

El Lingtren (6714 m) entre las nubes.

Everest, Lhotse and Nuptse with the ice fall and the West Comb in the foreground.

Der Mount Everest, der Lhotse und der Nuptse mit dem Eisbruch und Tal des Schweigens im Vordergrund.

De Everest, de Lhotse en de Nuptse met daarvoor de ijsval en de westelijke bergkam.

El Everest, el Lhotse y el Nuptse con la caída de hielo, en primer plano, y la hondonada oeste.

The Sherpas set off for Camp I.

Sherpas machen sich in Lager I auf den Weg.

De Sherpa's gaan op weg naar kamp I.

Los *sherpas* se ponen en camina hacia el campamento I.

Camp II, in the midst of the ice fall, with Pumori above.

Lager II inmitten des Eisbruchs, im Hintergrund der Pumori.

Kamp II op de ijsval met daarachter de Pumori.

El campamento II, en mitad de la caída de hielo, con el Pumori encima.

The threshold of the West Comb.

Der Eingang zum Tal des Schweigens.

De toegang van de westelijke kam.

El umbral de la hondonada oeste.

Surrounded by enormous seracs and pinnacles of ice, the Alpinists seem tiny as they stand at the entrance to the comb.

Am Eingang der Schlucht wirken die Bergsteiger inmitten der riesigen Zacken und Türme aus Eis und des Büßereises winzig.

Bij de toegang tot de kam lijken de alpinisten heel klein ten opzichte van de gigantische blokken en pieken van ijs.

A la entrada de la hondonada, los alpinistas parecen minúsculos en mitad de gigantescos seracs, penitentes y cumbres de hielo.

Following Jean-Jacques Asper's achievement, it is now possible to cross the large crevasse of the West Comb.

Die große Gletscherspalte im Tal des Schweigens kann dank der Bemühungen Jean-Jacques Aspers überquert werden.

De grote kloof van de westelijke kam kon worden overwonnen dankzij het onderzoek van Jean-Jacques Asper.

La gran grieta de la hondonada oeste ha podido ser atravesada gracias a una proeza de Jean-Jacques Asper.

The expedition column climbs up the circle of ice that protects Camp II.

Eine Kolonne der Expedition erklimmt den Eisvorhang, in dessen Schutz Lager III aufgeschlagen wurde.

Een kolonne van de expeditie beklimt de ijsheuvel die kamp III afschermt.

Una columna de la expedición escala el mirador de hielo que protege el campamento III.

After each snowfall the route must be determined afresh, then marked out.

Nach jedem Schneefall muss die Route erneut gespurt und anschließend markiert werden.

Na elke sneeuwval moet de route opnieuw worden bepaald en gemarkeerd.

Después de cada caída de nieve, el itinerario debe trazarse de nuevo y después balizarse.

Both men and equipment cross the crevasse thanks to a winch system.

Männer und Material überqueren die Gletscherspalte mithilfe einer Seilwinde.

Mannen en materieel gaan naar de andere kant van de kloof via een katrolsysteem.

Los hombres y el material atraviesan la grieta gracias a un sistema de torno elevador.

Camp IV in the middle of the West Comb.

Camp IV in der Mitte des Tals des Schweigens.

Kamp IV nabij de westelijke kam.

El campamento IV en mitad de la hondona oeste.

At the start of autumn the sun swiftly disappears into the West Comb and the temperature falls sharply.

Anfang Herbst geht die Sonne im Tal des Schweigens schnell unter und die Temperaturen fallen rapide ab.

Begin herfst verdwijnt de zon al vroeg achter de westelijke kam en daalt de temperatuur pijlsnel.

Al inicio del otoño, el sol desaparece pronto en la hondonada oeste y las temperaturas caen bruscamente.

The heavily loaded Sherpas are sometimes forced to use tree trunks in order to cross the crevasses.

Die schwer beladenen Sherpas müssen zuweilen Baumstämme zur Überquerung der Gletscherspalten verwenden.

Een zwaarbepakte Sherpa schuifelt over een boomstam naar de overkant van de kloof.

Los *sherpas* cargados con bultos pesados deben utilizar en ocasiones troncos de árboles para atravesar las grietas.

The upper part of the West Comb with Lhotse in the background.

Der obere Teil des Tals des Schweigens mit dem Lhotse im Hintergrund.

Het hoogste gedeelte van de westelijke kam met de Lhotse op de achtergrond.

La parte superior de la hondona oeste con el Lhotse al fondo.

The camp is buried under snow after the storm.

Das Camp ist nach dem Sturm von Schnee begraben.

Het kamp is ondergesneeuwd na de storm.

El campamento sepultado bajo la nieve después de la tormenta.

Resting on the Geneva Spur with a view over Cho Oyu.

Rast auf dem Éperon des Genevois mit Blick auf den Cho Oyu.

Rustpauze op het Geneefse spoor met uitzicht op de Cho Oyu.

Descanso en el Espolón de Ginebra, con la vista del Cho Oyu.

Pausing on the south ridge with the oxygen equipment used by the spring expedition.

Rast auf dem Südgrat mit dem Sauerstoffgerät, das die Expedition im Frühling verwendete.

Pauze op de zuidelijke kam bij zuurstofapparatuur die is gebruikt door de voorjaarsexpeditie.

Pausa en la arista sur, con el aparato de oxígeno utilizado por la expedición de primavera.

Some of the members of the expedition of autumn 1952. From left to right: Ernst Reiss, Tenzing Norgay, Gustave Gross, Norman Dyhrenfurth, Arthur Spöhel and Gabriel Chevalley.

Ein Teil der Mitglieder der Herbstexpedition von 1952, von links nach rechts: Ernst Reiss, Tenzing Norgay, Gustave Gross, Norman Dyhrenfurth, Arthur Spöhel und Gabriel Chevalley.

Deelnemers van de herfstexpeditie in 1952 (v.l.n.r.): Ernst Reiss, Tenzing Norgay, Gustave Gross, Norman Dyhrenfurth, Arthur Spöhel en Gabriel Chevalley.

Una parte de la expedición del otoño de 1952. De izquierda a derecha: Ernst Reiss, Tenzing Norgay, Gustave Gross, Norman Dyhrenfurth, Arthur Spöhel y Gabriel Chevalley.

On the schist rock face of the south-east ridge.

An der Schieferwand des Südostgrats.

Op het schistgesteente van de oostelijke kam.

En la pared de esquistos de la arista sureste.

René Aubert climbing the south ridge at around 8,400 metres.

René Aubert beim Aufstieg auf den Südgrat in etwa 8400 m Höhe.

René Aubert tijdens de beklimming van de zuidelijke kam, op ongeveer 8400 meter hoogte.

René Aubert en el ascenso de la arista sur, a unos 8400 metros.

Camp I, set up on a moraine on the Khumbu glacier.

Lager I auf einer Moräne des Khumbu-Gletschers.

Kamp I op morenes van de Khumbu-gletsjer.

El campo I instalado en una morrena del glaciar de Khumbu.

1953

The Union Jack Flies from the Roof of the World

Der Union Jack auf dem Dach der Welt

This time, the British do not want to miss their chance. We are in 1953 and next year it will be the turn of the French to climb Everest. Then it will be the turn of the Swiss again. The responsibility for this expedition is entrusted to a military man, Colonel John Hunt, a proven Alpinist and, moreover, an outstanding organiser. Some of the men were selected during an expedition in the spring of 1952 to Cho Oyu in the Himalayas, which was designed to test their ability at high altitude and to try out two types of oxygen breathing apparatus. On the one hand, these are the New Zealander Edmund Hillary and the Britons Thomas Bourdillon and Michael Ward who were already part of the 1951 Everest reconnaissance mission; on the other hand, another New Zealander, George Lowe and the Englishman Alfred Gregory. Other talented climbers such as Charles Evans, Michael Westmacott, Wilfrid Noyce, Charles Wylie and George Band come to join this core of seasoned Alpinists. A journalist from *The Times*, James Morris, will join the expedition later on.

At the start of March 1953, the convoys of three hundred and fifty porters move off from Kathmandu with 7 tonnes of material. Among the dozens of Sherpas chosen for the ascent, twenty-eight will be responsible for carrying up the heavy loads to the different camps based at altitude. Their leader is Tenzing Norgay, the most extraordinary "Tiger" of his generation, who is now on his fifth attempt at Everest! For the first time, the English have decided to include him in the attack party.

Upon arriving at the base camp, Colonel Hunt gives the Alpinists and Sherpas three weeks to acclimatise to the altitude by organising numerous ascents of neighbouring summits. Then, from mid-April, with the help of ropes, beams and metal ladders, they carry out reconnaissance missions to the ice fall and formidable West comb. The camps are then set up, in extremely dangerous and exhausting conditions. Camp VI is established at 7,010 metres on the face of the Lhotse, which adjoins the slopes of Everest. On 7 May the leader of the expedition reunites his troops and unveils his battle plan: the first attempt will be led by the Bourdillon-Evans roped party, the second by Tenzing and Hillary. Support teams will back up the attacking parties and help them to climb up to the camps nearest the summit.

Assisted by his teammates, over the next ten days the New Zealander George Lowe will begin the long ascent towards the Southern Col, cutting step after step and installing fixed ropes and handrails. Camp VII, at 7,315 metres, is resupplied from 17 May and, four days later, the South Col below the summit is finally reached. The support teams set up camp VIII there. 26 May is the date of the first attack, by the Bourdillon-Evans roped party as planned. At 1pm the next day, despite the breathing apparatus not working very well, the two Britons reach the South Peak of Everest at 8,760m. The second attack is launched on 28 May. Hillary and Tenzing, assisted by a small support team, climb up to 8,500 metres. The New Zealander and his brave Sherpa remain alone on a tiny platform battered by gusts of wind. They fortify themselves by inhaling some of the oxygen, eating frugally and drinking hot lemon juice. The next morning they leave at 6.30am and less than three hours later they are on the South Peak of Everest. After an hour of slow progress the two Alpinists encounter a last trial: a rocky projection 12 metres high. A simple exercise in the Alps, but almost unthinkable at more than 8,700 metres! Hillary, followed by Tenzing, squeezes his body between the rocks, using the slightest hold to get to the top of the overhang. There remain only some snowdrift mounds to get across before finally reaching the summit. The two men are standing on Everest, at an altitude of 8,848 metres! It is 11.30am on 29 May 1953. Hillary and Tenzing shake hands, the Sherpa then puts his arms round his friend's shoulders. The two conquerors of Everest will stay on the summit for a few minutes; they look in vain for any potential tracks made by Mallory and Irvine, the heroes who disappeared in 1924; kneeling in the snow, the Sherpa prepares offerings for the *Chomolungma* gods: a bar of chocolate, biscuits and sweets. For his part, Hillary makes a hole in the snow and places in it a small crucifix that was entrusted to him by Colonel Hunt. He takes a photo of his friend, who has slowly unrolled the four flags attached to his ice axe, which bear the colours of Great Britain, Nepal, India and the United Nations.

The oxygen reserves are running low, they need to come down from the summit without delay. George Lowe, who is on guard close to the South Col, sees them and goes to meet them with Wilfrid Noyce. They

Union Jack op het dak van de wereld

La Union Jack en el techo del mundo

congratulate them noisily and give the two men some hot soup. The two heroes, exhausted, are barely able to show their delight. Struggling for breath, Hillary leans across to his compatriot: “Well George, we knocked the bastard off!”. A coded message announcing the victory arrives three days later in London, where *The Times* prepares a special edition for the next day, 2 June 1953. By an extraordinary coincidence, on that very day England is jubilantly celebrating the coronation of Queen Elisabeth II. The speakers installed the length of the route of the royal carriage announce the British victory on Everest to the millions of English people gathered in the streets of London.

Wir schreiben das Jahr 1953. Diesmal wollen die Briten ihre Chance nicht ungenutzt lassen, denn im folgenden Jahr haben die Franzosen das Recht zur Besteigung des Mount Everest. Danach sind erneut die Schweizer an der Reihe. Die Leitung dieser Expedition wird Colonel John Hunt anvertraut, einem Soldaten, erfahrenen Bergsteiger und unübertroffenen Organisationstalent. Einige der Männer werden im Frühjahr bei einer Expedition auf den Cho Oyu im Himalaya ausgewählt. Hier stellen sie ihre Ausdauer in großer Höhe unter Beweis und testen zwei verschiedene Sauerstoffgeräte. Zu dieser Gruppe gehören auf der einen Seite der Neuseeländer Edmund Hillary und die Briten Thomas Bourdillon und Michael Ward, die bereits 1951 bei der Erkundungsmission am Mount Everest beteiligt waren, auf der anderen Seite ein weiterer Neuseeländer, George Lowe und der Engländer Alfred Gregory. Diesem Kern aus erfahrenen Bergsteigern schließen sich weitere talentierte Alpinisten wie Charles Evans, Michael Westmacott, Wilfrid Noyce, Charles Wylie und George Band an. Ein Journalist der *Times*, James Morris, schließt sich später der Expedition an

Anfang März 1953 setzt sich ein Konvoi von 350 Trägern von Katmandu, mit sieben Tonnen Material, in Bewegung. Unter den Dutzenden Sherpas, die für die Expedition ausgewählt wurden, haben 28 die Aufgabe, schwere Lasten in die, in großer Höhe angelegten Lager, zu tragen. Der Trupp wird von Tenzing Norgay angeführt, dem „Tiger vom Everest“ und außergewöhnlichsten Sherpa seiner Generation, der unterdessen bereits am fünften Besteigungsversuch teilnimmt. Zum ersten Mal haben die Engländer beschlossen, ihn in die Seilschaften, die zum Gipfel aufsteigen, mit aufzunehmen.

Nach der Ankunft im Basislager gibt Colonel Hunt seinen Bergsteigern und Sherpas drei Wochen Zeit, um sich in dieser Höhe zu akklimatisieren, und lässt sie zur Vorbereitung zahlreiche benachbarte Gipfel besteigen. Ab Mitte April erkunden die Männer schließlich mit Hilfe von Seilen, Holzbalken und Metallleitern den Eisbruch und das ehrfurchtgebietende Tal des Schweigens. Anschließend werden unter äußerst gefährlichen und ermüdenden Bedingungen die Lager errichtet. Lager VI wird in 7.010 Metern Höhe an der Fassade des Lhotse, der seitlich an den Mount Everest angrenzt, errichtet. Am 7. Mai versammelt Expeditionsleiter Hunt seine Männer und enthüllt ihnen seinen Schlachtplan: Der erste Versuch soll von der Seilschaft Bourdillon-Evans und der zweite von Tenzing Norgay und Hillary durchgeführt werden. Hilfstruppen sollen die Seilschaften bei der Besteigung unterstützen und ihnen bei der Errichtung der Lager im Gipfelbereich behilflich sein.

Der Neuseeländer George Lowe beginnt mit Hilfe seiner Gefährten den langen Aufstieg zum Südpass, kerbt im Laufe von zehn Tagen Stufe um Stufe ins Eis, befestigt Seile und Handläufe. Lager VII, auf 7.315 Metern Höhe, wird ab dem 17. Mai mit Vorräten versorgt, und vier Tage später erreichen die Männer den unterhalb des Gipfels gelegenen Südpass. Dort errichten Hilfstruppen Lager VIII. Am 26. Mai unternimmt die Seilschaft Bourdillon-Evans wie vorgesehen den ersten Besteigungsversuch. Am folgenden Tag erreichen die beiden Briten, trotz ihrer nur mangelhaft funktionierenden Sauerstoffgeräte, gegen 13 Uhr den Südgipfel des Mount Everest, auf 8.760 Metern Höhe, doch dann müssen sie aufgeben. Hillary und Tenzing Norgay starten am 28. Mai den zweiten Versuch. Mit Unterstützung einer kleinen Hilfstruppe gelangen sie bis auf 8.500 Meter Höhe. Der Neuseeländer und sein tapferer Sherpa bleiben allein auf einer winzigen, von Windböen leergefegten Plattform zurück. Sie stärken sich mit Sauerstoff, ein wenig Nahrung und heißem Zitronensaft. Am folgenden Morgen brechen sie um 6.30 Uhr auf und erreichen in weniger als drei Stunden später den Südgipfel. Nach einer weiteren Stunde, während

der die beiden nur langsam vorwärts kommen, müssen sie ein letztes Hindernis überwinden: eine Felsstufe von zwölf Metern Höhe. Was in den Alpen ein Kinderspiel ist, stellt auf 8.700 Metern Höhe eine unmenschliche Anstrengung dar! Hillary windet sich gefolgt von Tenzing Norgay zwischen den Felsen hindurch und nutzt jede Einkerbung, bis er schließlich auf dem Vorsprung steht. Nun müssen sie noch einige Schneekuppen überwinden, bevor sie endlich den Gipfel erreichen. Beide Männer stehen aufrecht auf dem Mount Everest, auf 8.848 Metern Höhe! Es ist der 29. Mai 1953, ihre Uhr zeigt 11.30 Uhr. Hillary und Tenzing Norgay schütteln sich die Hand, dann umschlingt der Sherpa mit seinen Armen die Schultern seines Freundes. Die beiden Bezwinger des Mount Everest ruhen sich einige Minuten auf dem Gipfel aus. Vergeblich versuchen sie, Spuren einer möglichen Besteigung durch die beiden verschwundenen Helden Mallory und Irvine 1924 zu suchen. Im Schnee kniend bietet der Sherpa den Göttern des *Chomolungma*, wie der Berg bei den Tibetern heißt, Opfergaben dar: eine Tafel Schokolade, Kekse und Bonbons. Hillary seinerseits gräbt ein Loch in den Schnee und legt ein kleines Kruzifix hinein, das ihm Colonel Hunt anvertraut hat. Er fotografiert seinen Freund, der langsam vier an seinem Eispickel befestigte Fahnen, mit den Farben Großbritanniens, Nepals, Indiens und der Vereinten Nationen, ausrollt.
Da die Sauerstoffvorräte zur Neige gehen, ist keine Zeit mehr zu verlieren. Die beiden verlassen den Gipfel. George Lowe, der in der Nähe des Südsattels Wache schiebt, bemerkt die beiden Helden und geht ihnen mit Wilfrid Noyce entgegen, um sie lauthals zu beglückwünschen und ihnen ein wenig heiße Suppe zu bringen. Die beiden erschöpften Männer haben kaum noch die Kraft, ihrer Freude Ausdruck zu geben. Hillary flüstert seinem Landsmann in einem Atemzug die Worte zu: „George, wir haben den Bastard endlich bezwungen!" *
Eine verschlüsselte Nachricht mit der Erfolgsmeldung erreicht drei Tage später London, wo *die Times* für den nächsten Tag – den 2. Juni 1953 – eine Sonderausgabe vorbereitet. Ein unglaublicher Zufall, da Großbritannien an diesem Tag jubelnd die Krönung Elisabeths II. feiert. Die Lautsprecher, die entlang der Fahrtstrecke der königlichen Kutsche aufgestellt sind, verkünden den Millionen Briten, die die Straßen Londons säumen, die Bezwingung des Mount Everest durch ihre Landsleute.

* „Well, George, we knocked the bastard off."

De Britten willen deze keer hun kans benutten. Het is 1953 en het jaar daarna krijgen de Fransen de gelegenheid om de Everest te beklimmen. Vervolgens is de beurt weer aan de Zwitsers. De verantwoordelijkheid voor de expeditie wordt toevertrouwd aan een militair, kolonel John Hunt, een erkende klimmer en een uitstekende organisator. Een aantal mannen wordt geselecteerd op basis van een expeditie in de lente van 1952 naar de Cho Oyu in de Himalaya, bedoeld om hun uithoudingsvermogen op grote hoogte te testen en twee modellen zuurstofapparaat uit te proberen. De keuze valt enerzijds op de Nieuw-Zeelander Edmund Hillary en twee Britten, Thomas Bourdillon en Michael Ward, die al deelnamen aan de oriëntatie-expeditie op de Everest in 1951, en anderzijds op de Nieuw-Zeelander George Lowe en de Engelsman Alfred Gregory. Aan deze ervaren kern worden andere getalenteerde klimmers toegevoegd, onder anderen Charles Evans, Michael Westmacott, Wilfrid Noyce, Charles Wylie en George Band. Later voegt een reporter van *The Times*, James Morris, zich bij de expeditie.
Begin maart 1953 zet zich vanuit Katmandu een konvooi van driehonderdvijftig dragers in beweging met zeven ton materiaal. Van de tientallen Sherpa's die zijn geselecteerd voor de klim, hebben er achtentwintig de taak om zware vracht omhoog te brengen naar de verschillende hooggelegen kampen. Hun leider is Tenzing Norgay, de opvallendste 'Tijger' van zijn generatie, die nu voor de vijfde keer van de partij is. Voor het eerst hebben de Engelsen besloten hem op te nemen in de klimploeg.
Na aankomst in het basiskamp geeft kolonel Hunt de alpinisten en Sherpa's drie weken de tijd om te wennen aan de hoogte door hen de naastgelegen toppen te laten beklimmen. Vervolgens voeren zij vanaf midden april met behulp van touwen, balken en metalen ladders verkenningen uit op de ijsval en de ontzagwekkende westelijke kam. Daarna worden de kampen opgezet onder extreem gevaarlijke en uitputtende omstandigheden. Kamp VI wordt ingericht op een hoogte van 7010 meter tegen de helling van de Lhotse, die grenst aan de Everest. Op 7 mei roept de expeditieleider zijn manschappen bijeen en ontvouwt zijn plan voor de beklimming. De eerste poging zal worden uitgevoerd door het koppel Bourdillon-Evans, de tweede door Tenzing en Hillary. De klimmers zullen worden ondersteund door een aantal mannen die hen zullen helpen de kampen dichter onder de top op te zetten.
De Nieuw-Zeelander George Lowe begint, geholpen door zijn teamgenoten, aan de lange klim via de zuidelijke pas. Twaalf dagen lang hakt hij trede na trede uit en brengt hij touwen plus zekeringen aan. Kamp VII op 7315 meter hoogte wordt bevoorraad vanaf 17 mei en vier dagen later is de zuidelijke pas, die in de top verzonken ligt, eindelijk bereikt. De ondersteunende manschappen installeren hier kamp VIII. Zoals gepland, doen Bourdillon en Evans op 26 mei de eerste beklimmingspoging. Om 13.00 bereiken de twee Britten de zuidelijke top van de Everest op 8760 meter, ondanks problemen met de zuurstofapparatuur. De tweede poging gaat op 28 mei van start. Hillary en Tenzing klimmen met een kleine groep helpers naar 8500 meter. De Nieuw-Zeelander en de onvolprezen Sherpa installeren zich vervolgens op een klein platform, dat wordt bestookt door rukwinden. Zij sterken zich met zuivere zuurstof, een sobere maaltijd en warm citroensap. De volgende ochtend vertrekken ze om halfzeven en minder dan drie uur later zijn ze op de zuidelijke top van de Everest. Na een uur van geringe vorderingen, staan de twee alpinisten voor een laatste beproeving: het beklimmen van een twaalf meter hoge, uitspringende rots. In de Alpen is dat een eenvoudige oefening, maar op meer dan 8700 meter een bijna onmenselijke opgave. Hillary, gevolgd door Tenzing, wringt zich gebruikmakend van de kleinste steunpunten tussen de rotsen door tot op het uitsteeksel. Dan resten nog slechts enkele sneeuwheuvels en is de top eindelijk bereikt. De twee mannen staan op 29 mei 1953 om 11.30 in de ochtend boven op de Everest, op een hoogte van 8848 meter. Hillary en Tenzing schudden elkaar de hand en de Sherpa slaat zijn armen om de schouders van zijn vriend. De twee overwinnaars van de Everest zullen enkele minuten op de top blijven. Tevergeefs zoeken zij naar eventuele bewijzen dat Mallory en Irvine, de helden die verdwenen in 1924, de top hebben bereikt. Geknield in de sneeuw brengt de Sherpa offers aan de goden van de *Chomolungma*: een reep chocolade, biscuits en bonbons. Op zijn beurt

maakt Hillary een kuil in de sneeuw en stopt daarin een klein kruis dat hem is toevertrouwd door kolonel Hunt. Hij maakt een foto van zijn vriend terwijl deze langzaam de vier vlaggen in de kleuren van Groot-Brittannië, Nepal, India en de Verenigde Naties uitrolt, die hij aan zijn ijsbijl had bevestigd.
Omdat de zuurstofreserves opraken, moeten ze de top snel verlaten. George Lowe, die dicht bij de zuidelijke pas op de uitkijk staat, merkt de twee op en gaat hen samen tegemoet met Wilfrid Noyce om hen uitbundig te feliciteren en een beetje warme soep te geven. De uitgeputte helden hebben nauwelijks nog de kracht om hun blijdschap kenbaar te maken. Met een zucht laat Hillary zijn landgenoot weten: 'Zo, die rotzak hebben we verslagen!'* Via een gecodeerd bericht komt de boodschap van de overwinning drie dagen later in Londen aan, waar *The Times* een speciale editie voorbereidt voor de volgende dag, 2 juni 1953. Luidsprekers langs het traditionele parcours van de koninklijke stoet melden de Britse overwinning op de Everest aan de duizenden Britten die zich hebben verzameld in de straten van Londen.
* 'Well, we knocked the bastard off !'

Esta vez, los británicos no quieren dejar pasar la oportunidad. Estamos en 1953, y en 1954 serán los franceses quienes tendrán derecho a escalar el Everest. Después, será nuevamente el turno de los suizos. Un militar, el coronel John Hunt, alpinista con experiencia, y sobre todo, organizador sin igual, tendrá bajo su responsabilidad esta expedición. Algunos hombres han sido seleccionados en una expedición realizada en la primavera de 1952 al Cho Oyu, en el Himalaya, destinada a poner a prueba sus capacidades en altitudes elevadas y a probar dos modelos de aparatos de oxígeno. Esta expedición está formada, por una parte, por el neozelandés Edmund Hillary y los británicos Thomas Bourdillon y Michael Ward, ya alistados para la misión de reconocimiento del Everest en 1951; por la otra, la integran otro neozelandés, George Lowe, y el inglés Alfred Gregory. A este núcleo de alpinistas curtidos se unen otros escaladores de talento, como Charles Evans, Michael Westmacott, Wilfrid Noyce, Charles Wylie y George Band. Un periodista del *Times*, James Morris, se unirá a la expedición posteriormente.
A principios del mes de marzo de 1953, los convoyes de tres cientos cincuenta portadores parten desde Katmandú con 7 trescientos de material. Entre las varias decenas de *sherpas* elegidos para la ascensión, 28 se encargarán de subir los pesados cargamentos a los diferentes campamentos a varias altitudes. Su jefe es Tenzing Norgay, el «tigre» más extraordinario de su generación, que en este momento intenta escalar el Everest por quinta vez. Y por primera vez, los ingleses deciden integrarlo en los equipos de asalto.
A la llegada al campamento base, el coronel Hunt deja 3 semanas a los alpinistas y a los *sherpas* para aclimatarse a la altitud multiplicando los ascensos de las cumbres cercanas. A continuación, a partir de mediados de abril, con ayuda de cuerdas, vigas y escaleras metálicas, efectúan los reconocimientos en la cascada de hielo y en la temible hondonada oeste. Después, los campamentos se montan en condiciones sumamente peligrosas y extenuantes. El campamento VI está instalado a 7010 m en la fachada del Lhotse, que linda con la vertiente del Everest. El 7 de mayo, el jefe de la expedición reúne a sus tropas y les desvela su plan de batalla: el primer intento será dirigido por la cordada Bourdillon-Evans y el segundo por Tenzing y Hillary. Los equipos de apoyo respaldarán a los grupos de asalto y los ayudarán a subir a los campamentos más cercanos a la cumbre.
El neozelandés George Lowe, ayudado por sus compañeros de equipo, empieza el largo ascenso hacia el Collado Sur, cortando paso tras paso, instalando cuerdas fijas y pasamanos durante aproximadamente diez días. Desde el 17 de mayo, el campamento VII, a 7315 m, se encuentra avituallado y, cuatro días más tarde, se alcanza por fin el Collado Sur, en la parte inferior de la cumbre. Los equipos de apoyo establecen allí el campamento VIII. El 26 de mayo, tiene lugar el primer asalto con la cordada Bourdillon-Evans, como estaba previsto. A las 13:00 del día siguiente, los dos británicos, pese a que los respiradores no funcionan demasiado bien, coronan la cima sur del Everest a 8760 m. El segundo asalto se pone en marcha el 28 de mayo. Hillary y Tenzing, ayudados por un pequeño equipo de apoyo, suben hasta 8500 m. El neozelandés y su valeroso *sherpa* permanecen solos sobre una minúscula plataforma barrida por las borrascas de viento. Se reconfortan respirando el oxígeno, comen frugalmente y beben zumo de limón caliente. A la mañana siguiente, parten a las 6:30 y, menos de 3 horas después, se encuentran sobre la cima sur del Everest. Tras una hora de lenta progresión, los dos alpinistas deben enfrentarse a una última prueba: un resalte rocoso de 12 metros de alto. Un ejercicio fácil en los Alpes, pero casi inhumano a más de 8.700 metros. Hillary, seguido de Tenzing, se contorsiona entre las rocas, utiliza cualquier asidero que encuentra hasta que llega a lo alto del saliente. Aún hay que atravesar algunas cúpulas de nieve para coronar por fin la cumbre. Los dos hombres se ponen en pie sobre el Everest, ¡a 8848 metros! Son las 11:30 del 29 de mayo de 1953. Hillary y Tenzing se estrechan la mano, el *sherpa* rodea con sus brazos los hombros de su amigo. Los dos vencedores del Everest permanecen unos minutos en la cumbre; buscan, en vano, restos del eventual paso de los héroes desaparecidos en 1924, Mallory e Irvine. Arrodillado en la nieve, el *sherpa* prepara unas ofrendas para las divinidades del Chomolungma: una barra de chocolate, galletas y caramelos. A su vez, Hillary cava un agujero en la nieve y deposita un pequeño crucifijo que le ha entregado el coronel Hunt. Toma una foto de su amigo, que lentamente ha desenrollado cuatro banderas sujetas en su piolet con los colores de Gran Bretaña, Nepal, India y las Naciones Unidas.
Dado que las reservas de oxígeno están próximas a agotarse, hay que abandonar la cumbre sin más demora. George Lowe, de guardia cerca del Collado Sur, los divisa y acude a su encuentro con Wilfrid Noyce para felicitarles clamorosamente y les da de sopa caliente. Los dos héroes, extenuados, apenas tienen fuerzas para manifestar su gozo. De un soplo, Hillary le espeta a su compatriota: «Bueno, George, ¡al final hemos tumbado a este cabrón!*» Un mensaje codificado que anuncia la victoria llega a Londres tres días más tarde, y el *Times* prepara una edición especial para el día siguiente, 2 de junio de 1953. Y lo que es una coincidencia extraordinaria es que ese mismo día Inglaterra celebra alborozada la coronación de la reina Isabel II. Los altavoces instalados a lo largo del recorrido de la carroza real anuncian la victoria británica sobre el Everest a los millones de ingleses reunidos en masa en las calles de Londres.
* «Well, we knocked the bastard off!»

The 1953 expedition crossing the Chanwati Khola.

Die Expedition von 1953 bei der Überquerung des Chanwati Khola.

De expeditie van 1953 steekt de Chanwati Khola over.

La expedición de 1953 cruzando el Chanwati Khola.

Hillary swimming in a river pool.

Hillary beim Schwimmen in einem Flussbecken.

Hillary neemt een bad in de rivier.

Hillary nadando en un río.

Bridge crossing the Chanwati Khola.

Brücke über den Chanwati Khola.

Brug over de Chanwati Khola.

Puente cruzando el Chanwati Khola.

Monks blowing horns at Thyangboche monastery.

Mönche im Kloster von Tengboche beim Blasen von Hörnern.

Monniken blazen op hoorns in het Thyangboche-klooster.

Monjes soplando cuernos en el monasterio Thyangboche.

Thyangboche monastery with Mount Everest in the distance

Kloster von Tengboche mit dem Mount Everest im Hintergrund

Het Thyangboche-klooster met de Everest op de achtergrond.

El monasterio Thyangboche, con el Monte Everest a lo lejos

Nepali children peek inside a tent at rear base

Nepalesische Kinder schauen in den Eingang eines Zelts an der hinteren Basis.

Nepalese kinderen kijken door een tentopening.

Niños nepaleses miran por la puerta de una tienda de campaña en la base trasera.

Stobart and Lowe skinning a yak at Camp I.

Stobart und Lowe beim Häuten eines Yaks in Lager I.

Stobart en Lowe villen een jak in kamp I.

Stobart y Lowe despellejando un yak en el campamento Camp I.

Sherpa porter tending a cooking fire.

Ein Sherpa-Träger beim Entfachen des Feuers.

Een Sherpa bekommert zich om het kookvuur.

Portador *sherpa* ocupándose del fuego para cocinar.

Buddhist monk at Thyangboche holding some beads.

Buddhistischer Mönch in Tengboche mit Perlenstrang in der Hand.

Boeddhistische monnik met gebedskralen in Thyangboche.

Monje budista sujetando un abalorio en Thyangboche.

Portrait of a smiling Sherpa boy.

Lächelnder Sherpa-Junge.

Portret van een lachende Sherpa-jongen.

Retrato de un niño *sherpa* sonriente.

John Hunt reading and smoking a pipe at a camp near Thyangboche.

John Hunt bei Lesen und Rauchen seiner Pfeife im Camp bei Tengboche.

John Hunt lezend en pijprokend in een kamp bij Thyangboche.

John Hunt leyendo y fumando en pipa en el campamento cerca de Thyangboche.

John Hunt and Tenzing Norgay organising paying the porters.

John Hunt und Tenzing Norgay bei der Bezahlung von Trägern.

John Hunt en Tenzing Norgay regelen de betaling van de dragers.

John Hunt y Tenzing Norgay organizando el pago de los portadores.

Hillary's Sherpa party loaded with supplies en route for Base Camp.

Hillarys und seine Gruppe schwer beladener Sherpas auf dem Weg zum Basislager.

Hillary's Sherpa-ploeg beladen met voorraden op weg naar het basiskamp.

El *sherpa* de Hillary cargado con provisiones en ruta hacia el campamento base.

This peak on the south side of Everest, which was unnamed at the time, used to be explored by the mountaineers by way of training.

Dieser damals unbenannte Gipfel auf der Südseite des Mount Everest wurde von den Bergsteigern zu Trainingszwecken bestiegen.

Deze, toen nog naamloze piek aan de zuidkant van de Everest werd bij wijze van training beklommen.

Este pico, en el lado sur del Everest, que en aquel entonces no tenía nombre, solía ser explorado por los escaladores a modo de entrenamiento.

John Hunt on Chukhung Peak.

John Hunt auf dem Chukhung Peak.

John Hunt op de Chukhung-piek.

John Hunt en el Pico Chukhung.

Tenzing Norgay training on Chukhung Peak.

Tenzing Norgay beim Training auf dem Chukhung Peak.

Tenzing Norgay oefent op de Chukhung-piek.

Tenzing Norgay entrenando en el Pico Chukhung.

Team members reach an acclimatisation peak in the Himalayas.

Mitglieder der Expedition erreichen einen Akklimatisierungsgipfel.

Een team bereikt een piek in de Himalaya waar de klimmers kunnen acclimatiseren.

Los miembros del equipo alcanzan un pico de aclimatación en el Himalaya.

Base camp on the Khumbu glacier.

Basislager auf dem Khumbu-Gletscher.

Basiskamp op de Khumbu-gletsjer.

Campamento base en el glaciar Khumbu.

Dr. Griffith Pugh shaving in the camp.

Dr. Griffith Pugh beim Rasieren im Lager.

Dokter Griffith Pugh scheert zich in het kamp.

El Dr. Griffith Pugh afeitándose
en el campamento.

Charles Evans cutting George Lowe's hair at Base Camp.

Charles Evans schneidet George Lowe im Basislager die Haare.

Charles Evans knipt George Lowes haar in het basiskamp.

Charles Evans cortando el pelo a George Lowe en el campamento base.

Sherpas and Sherpanis with tent boxes and equipment at Base Camp.

Sherpas und Sherpanis mit Zeltkästen und Ausrüstung im Basislager.

Sherpa-mannen en -vrouwen met tenten, kisten en klimuitrusting in het basiskamp.

Sherpas y sherpanis con tiendas de campaña y equipos en el campamento base.

Ice pinnacles surrounding Base Camp.

Eistürme um das Basislager.

Het basiskamp omringd door ijspieken.

Cumbres heladas alrededor del campamento base.

Charles Evans writing in his tent
at Base Camp.

Charles Evans beim Schreiben
in seinem Zelt im Basislager.

Charles Evans schrijvend
in zijn tent in het basiskamp.

Charles Evans escribiendo en su tienda
de campaña en el campamento base.

Base Camp on the Khumbu glacier, with
Lingtren behind.

Basislager auf dem Khumbu-Gletscher mit
dem Lingtren im Hintergrund.

Basiskamp op de Khumbu-gletsjer, met de
Lingtren op de achtergrond.

Campamento base en el glaciar Khumbu,
con Lingtren detrás.

Team member ascending ice formations in the Khumbu glacier.

Mitglieder des Teams beim Aufstieg über Eisformationen im Khumbu-Gletscher.

Een teamlid beklimt ijsformaties van de Khumbu-gletsjer.

Un miembro del equipo ascendiendo por las formaciones de hielo en el glaciar Khumbu.

A Sherpa steps across a crevasse above Camp II.

Ein Sherpa beim Überschreiten einer Gletscherspalte oberhalb von Lager II.

Een Sherpa stapt over een spleet boven kamp II.

Un sherpa atraviesa una grieta sobre el campamento II.

Team members reconnoitring the Icefall.

Mitglieder des Teams bei Erkundungen im Eisbruch.

Een team verkent de ijsval

Los miembros del equipo haciendo un reconocimiento en la cascada de hielo.

Team members reconnoitring the Icefall.

Mitglieder des Teams bei Erkundungen im Eisbruch.

Een team verkent de ijsval.

Los miembros del equipo haciendo un reconocimiento en la cascada de hielo.

Tenzing Norgay holding crampons and being watched by George Lowe, Thyangboche.

Tenzing Norgay mit Steigeisen in der Hand, neben sich George Lowe, in Tengboche.

Tenzing Norgay met sneeuwijzers naast een toekijkende George Lowe in Thyangboche.

Tenzing Norgay sujetando crampones observado por George Lowe en Thyangboche.

A Sherpa carrying equipment crossing a crevasse on a ladder between Camps II and III.

Ein mit Ausrüstung beladener Sherpa überquert mithilfe einer Leiter eine Gletscherspalte zwischen Lager II und III.

Een Sherpa met klimuitrusting gaat via een ladder naar de andere zijde van een kloof tussen kamp II en III.

Un *sherpa* llevando los equipos en el cruce de una grieta con una escalera entre los campamentos II y III.

Hillary crossing a ladder bridge over a crevasse in the Western Comb, above Camp II.

Hillary beim Überqueren einer Leiterbrücke über einer Gletscherspalte im Tal des Schweigens oberhalb von Lager II.

Hillary gaat via een ladderbrug over een kloof in de westelijke kam, boven kamp II.

Hillary cruzando un puente de escalera sobre una grieta en la Cresta Oeste, sobre el campamento II.

Sherpas carrying loads on the hazardous Icefall.

Sherpas beim Transport von Lasten in dem gefährlichen Eisbruch.

Bepakte Sherpa's op de verraderlijke ijsval.

Sherpas llevando cargas sobre la peligrosa cascada de hielo.

Two Sherpa porters wearing oxygen equipment and carrying ice-axes.

Zwei Sherpa-Träger mit Sauerstoffgeräten und Eispickeln.

Twee Sherpa's met zuurstofmaskers en ijsbijlen.

Dos portadores *sherpas* utilizando equipos de oxígeno y llevando piquetas.

Hillary assisting Sherpas with supply loads on the Icefall.

Hillary ist Sherpas im Eisbruch mit ihren Lasten behilflich.

Hillary helpt Sherpa's met hun voorraadlast op de ijsval.

Hillary ayudando a los *sherpas* con el cargamento de provisiones en la cascada de hielo.

A Sherpa carrying equipment along a rope ladder.

Ein mit Ausrüstung beladener Sherpa auf einer Strickleiter.

Een Sherpa met uitrusting op een touwladder.

Un *sherpa* llevando el equipo sobre una escalera de cuerda.

Ice formations in the Icefall, with Mount Everest in the distance.

Eisformationen im Eisbruch mit dem Mount Everest im Hintergrund

IJsformaties van de ijsval met de Everest op de achtergrond.

Formaciones de hielo en la cascada de hielo, con el Monte Everest a lo lejos.

Sherpas wearing crampons cross a log bridge over a crevasse, Western Cwm (Comb).

Sherpas mit Steigeisen bei der Überquerung einer aus einem Baumstamm gefertigten Brücke über eine Gletscherspalte, Tal des Schweigens (Western Cwm).

Sherpa's gaan gezekerd via een boomstambrug over een kloof, westerlijke Cwm (kam).

Sherpas con crampones cruzan un puente de troncos sobre una grieta, Cresta Oeste.

Large crevasse with ladder bridge, above Camp III.

Große Gletscherspalte mit Leiterbrücke, über Lager III.

Grote kloof met ladderbrug boven kamp III.

Grieta grande con puente de escalera, sobre el campamento III.

George Band leading the climbing of a block above Camp II.

Gruppe von Bergsteigern beim Aufstieg über einen Eisblock unter Führung George Bands.

George Band leidt de beklimming van een ijsblok boven kamp II.

George Band dirigiendo el ascenso de un bloque sobre el campamento II.

Stobart with cinematograph in the Western Cwm (Comb).

Stobart mit Filmkamera im Tal des Schweigens (Western Cwm).

Stobart met filmtoestel op de westerlijke Cwm (kam).

Stobart con la cámara filmadora en la Cresta Oeste.

Hillary with Sherpas on the Icefall.

Hillary mit Sherpas im Eisbruch.

Hillary met Sherpa's op de ijsval.

Hillary con *sherpas* en la cascada de hielo.

Team members on the Khumbu Icefall.

Mitglieder des Teams im Khumbu-Eisbruch.

Teamleden op de Khumbu-ijsval.

Los miembros del equipo en la cascada de hielo de Khumbu.

Sherpas on the Icefall climb ice formations.

Sherpas beim Aufstieg über Formationen im Eisbruch.

Sherpa's beklimmen ijsformaties van de ijsval.

Sherpas en la cascada de hielo escalando formaciones de hielo.

Noyce keeping a taut rope for a Sherpa.

Noyce hält einen Sherpa an einem gespannten Seil.

Noyce houdt het touw strak voor een Sherpa.

Noyce sujetando a un *sherpa* con una cuerda tirante.

Sherpas wearing crampons crossing a log bridge.

Sherpas mit Steigeisen bei der Überquerung einer Brücke aus Baumstämmen.

Sherpa's met stijgijzers gaan een boomstambrug.

Sherpas llevando crampones en el cruce de un puente de troncos.

Sherpa carrying a ladder section across a ladder bridge on the Icefall.

Sherpa beim Transport eines Leiterabschnitts über eine Leiterbrücke im Eisbruch.

Een Sherpa draagt een ladderdeel over een ladderbrug in de ijsval.

Sherpa llevando un tramo de escalera por un puente de escalera en la cascada de hielo.

Sherpa ascending a rope ladder.

Sherpa beim Aufstieg über eine Strickleiter.

Een Sherpa klimt in een touwladder.

Sherpa ascendiendo por una escalera de cuerda.

An expedition team member climbs steep ice above Camp VII and fixes an ice screw for safety.

Ein Expeditionsmitglied beim Aufstieg über eine Eiswand und bei der Befestigung einer Eisschraube zum Schutz oberhalb von Lager VII.

Een expeditielid beklimt een steile ijswand boven kamp VII en plaatst ijsankers voor de veiligheid.

Un miembro del equipo de expedición escalando una formación de hielo abrupta y fijando un tornillo de hielo para una protección segura sobre el campamento VII.

George Lowe assists Sherpas carrying supplies through the Khumbu Icefall, with Pumori (7,145m) in the distance.

George Lowe hilft Sherpas beim Transport von Vorräten durch den Eisbruch, im Hintergrund der Pumori (7145 m).

George Lowe helpt Sherpa's met het dragen van voorraden over de Khumbu-ijsval, met de Pumori (7145 m) op de achtergrond.

George Lowe ayuda a los *sherpas* que llevan provisiones a través de la cascada de hielo de Khumbu, con Pumori (7145 m) en la lejanía.

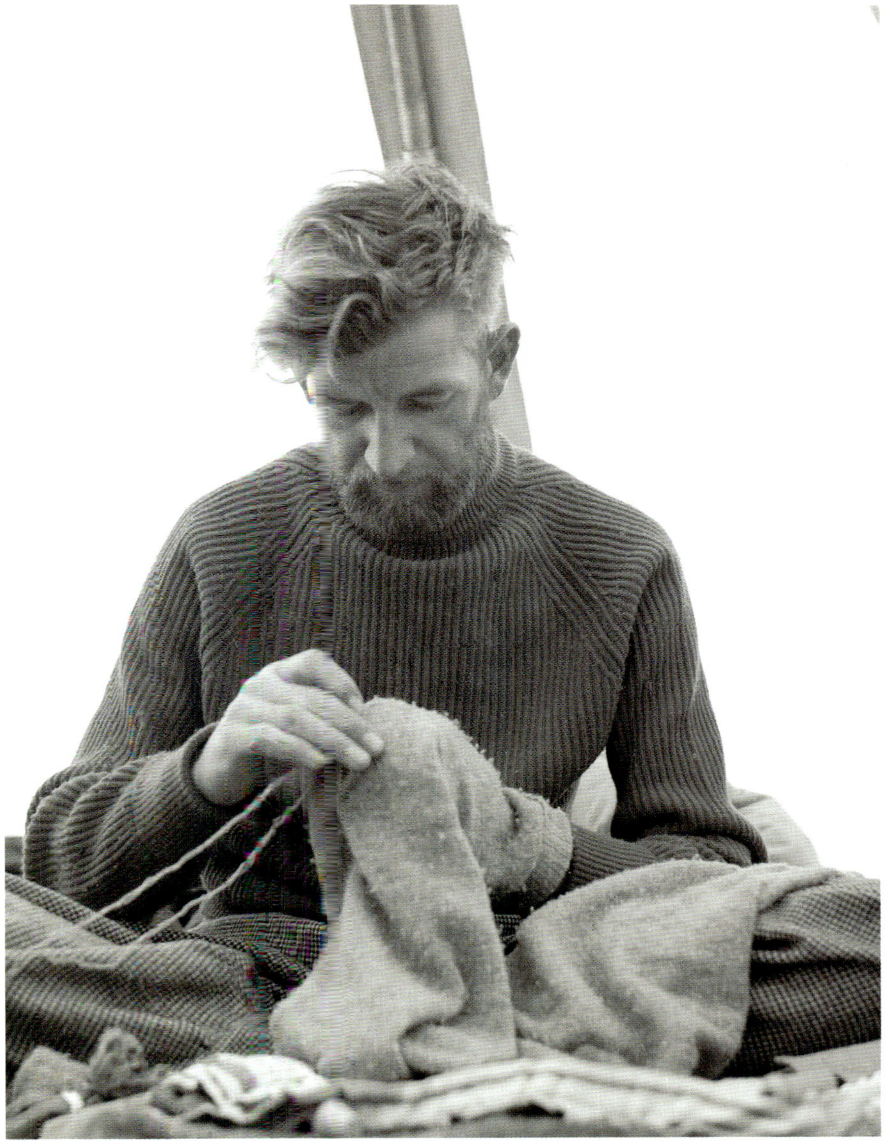

Lowe mending a jumper in a tent.

Lowe repareert een trui in een tent.

Lowe beim Flicken eines Pullovers im Zelt.

Lowe remendando un jersey en una tienda de campaña.

George Lowe eating in a tent, with a wireless radio beside him.

George Lowe eet in een tent, met naast zich een draadloze radio.

George Lowe beim Essen im Zelt, neben sich ein Funkgerät.

George Lowe comiendo en una tienda de campaña, con una radio inalámbrica a su lado.

Portrait of Mike Ward by Alfred Gregory.

Mike Ward, Aufnahme von Alfred Gregory.

Portret van Mike Ward gemaakt door Alfred Gregory.

Retrato de Mike Ward por Alfred Gregory.

Tom Stobart with his Bell Howell cinematograph at Camp IV.

Tom Stobart mit seiner Bell Howell-Filmkamera in Lager IV.

Tom Stobart met zijn Bell Howell-filmtoestel in kamp IV.

Tom Stobart con su cámara filmadora Bell Howell en el campamento IV.

Tenzing Norgay wearing crampons, climbing down an icy patch on the Lhotse Face.

Tenzing Norgay mit Steigeisen beim Abstieg über eine vereiste Stelle an der Lhotse-Wand.

Tenzing Norgay daalt met stijgijzers af van een ijswand op de Lhotse.

Tenzing Norgay llevando crampones descendiendo de un tramo helado en la cara oeste de Lhotse.

Lowe on wireless radio, with Hillary enjoying the conversation.

Lowe führt ein Gespräch über Funk, während Hillary gut gelaunt zuhört.

Lowe luistert naar de draadloze radio en Hillary heeft plezier in het gesprek.

Lowe con la radio inalámbrica, junto a Hillary disfrutando de la conversación.

Noyce with pipe.

Noyce mit Pfeife.

Noyce met pijp.

Noyce con su pipa.

Camp IV (Advanced Base Camp).

Lager IV (vorgeschobenes Basislager).

Kamp IV (vooruitgeschoven basiskamp).

Campamento IV (campamento base avanzado).

Sherpas sleeping in snow at Lake Camp.

Sherpas beim Schlafen im Schnee im Lager an einem See.

Sherpa's slapen in de sneeuw in het kamp bij het meer.

Sherpas durmiendo bajo la nieve en el campamento del lago.

Camp V at the foot of the Lhotse face looking towards the west ridge of Everest.

Lager V am Fuße der Lhotse-Wand mit Blick auf den Westgrat des Mount Everest.

Kamp V aan de voet van de Lhotse-wand uitkijkend op de westelijke kam van de Everest.

El campamento V al pie de la cara oeste del Lhotse mirando hacia la cresta oeste del Everest.

Noyce and Sherpa porters by the side of crevasse in the Western Cwm (Comb).

Noyce und Sherpa-Träger an einer Gletscherspalte im Tal des Schweigens (Western Cwm).

Noyce en Sherpa's op de rand van een kloof in de westerlijke Cwm (kam)

Noyce y portadores sherpa al lado de una grieta en la Cresta Oeste

Looking down into the Western Cwm (Comb) from the Lhotse Face. This comb is surrounded by Everest, Lhotse and Nuptse.

Blick in das Tal des Schweigens (Western Cwm) von der Lhotse-Wand. Das Tal des Schweigens ist vom Mount Everest, vom Lhotse und vom Nuptse umgeben.

Neerkijkend op de westerlijke Cwm (kam) vanaf de Lhotse-wand. Deze bergkam is omringd door de Everest, de Lhotse en de Nuptse.

Mirando hacía abajo en la Cresta Oeste desde la cara oeste del Lhotse. Esta cresta está rodeada por el Everest, Lhotse y Nuptse.

Sunset over the Lhotse Face. The Everest 1953 team placed Camps VI and VII here.

Sonnenaufgang über der Lhotse-Wand, an der die Mitglieder der Expedition von 1953 ihre Lager VI und VII aufschlugen.

Zonsondergang op de Lhotse-wand. Het Everest-team van 1953 plaatste kamp VI en VII daarop.

Atardecer sobre la cara oeste de Lhotse. El equipo del Everest de 1953 estableciendo los campamentos VI y VII allí.

The "Tigers" who reached the South Col with Noyce and Wylie.

Die „Tiger", die mit Noyce und Wylie den Südsattel erreichten.

De 'Tijgers' die de zuidelijke pas bereikten met Noyce en Wylie.

Los «tigres» que coronaron el Collado Sur con Noyce y Wylie.

The 1953 Mount Everest team.

Die Mitglieder der Mount Everest-Expedition von 1953.

Het Everest-team van 1953.

El equipo del Monte Everest de 1953.

Bourdillon and Evans leave Camp IV for their first attempt at the summit.

Bourdillon und Evans verlassen Lager IV zum ersten Besteigungsversuch.

Bourdillon en Evans verlaten kamp IV voor de eerste poging om de top te bereiken.

Bourdillon y Evans abandonan el campamento IV para el primer intento de coronar la cumbre.

George Lowe climbing the ridge from the South Col to the final camp.

George Lowe beim Aufstieg über den Grat auf dem Weg vom Südsattel zum letzten Lager.

George Lowe beklimt een richel vanaf de zuidelijke pas naar het laatste kamp.

George Lowe escalando una cresta desde el Collado Sur hasta el último campamento.

Bourdillon prepares the oxygen equipment for his assault with Evans.

Bourdillon maakt zijn zuurstofapparaat gereed voor zijn poging samen met Evans.

Bourdillon bei der Vorbereitung von Sauerstoffgeräten für seinen Besteigungsversuch mit Evans.

Bourdillon prepara las máscaras de oxígeno para su asalto con Evans.

Wilfrid Noyce ascending a snowy slope on Everest.

Wilfrid Noyce beklimt een sneeuwhelling van de Everest.

Wilfrid Noyce beim Aufstieg über einen verschneiten Hang am Mount Everest.

Wilfrid Noyce ascendiendo una pendiente nevada en el Everest.

The first tent of Camp VII.

Das erste Zelt von Lager VII.

De eerste tent van kamp VII.

La primera tienda de campaña el campamento VII.

Evans and Bourdillon resting
at Swiss Camp V.

Evans und Bourdillon bei der Rast
im Lager V der Schweizer.

Evans en Bourdillon rusten uit
in het Zwitserse kamp V.

Evans y Bourdillon descansando
en el campamento suizo V.

Noyce climbing steep ice above Camp VII.

Noyce beim Aufstieg über eine Eiswand oberhalb von Lager VII.

Noyce beklimt een steile ijswand boven kamp VII.

Noyce escalando sobre el hielo abrupto sobre el campamento VII.

Portrait of Sir John Hunt at the South Col, 26th May 1953.

Sir John Hunt am Südsattel, 26. Mai 1953.

Portret van Sir John Hunt in de zuidelijke pas op 26 mei 1953.

Retrato de Sir John Hunt en el Collado Sur, 26 de mayo de 1953.

From left to right: Hunt, Hillary, Tenzing Norgay, Ang Nyima, Gregory and Lowe at Camp IV.

Von links nach rechts: Hunt, Hillary, Tenzing Norgay, Ang Nyima, Gregory und Lowe in Lager IV.

In kamp IV (v.l.n.r.): Hunt, Hillary, Tenzing Norgay, Ang Nyima, Gregory en Lowe.

De izquierda a derecha: Hunt, Hillary, Tenzing Norgay, Ang Nyima, Gregory y Lowe en el campamento IV.

Tom Bourdillon at the South Summit.

Tom Bourdillon auf dem Südgipfel.

Tom Bourdillon op de zuidelijke top.

Tom Bourdillon en la Cumbre Sur.

 THE UNION JACK FLIES FROM THE ROOF OF THE WORLD 1953 – DER UNION JACK AUF DEM DACH DER WELT 1953

Bourdillon at the South Summit, photographed by Charles Evans.

Tom Bourdillon auf dem Südgipfel, Aufnahme von Charles Evans.

Bourdillon op de zuidelijke top, gefotografeerd door Charles Evans.

Bourdillon en la Cumbre Sur, fotografiado por Charles Evans.

Disappointed and exhausted, Charles Evans and Tom Bourdillon return to the South Col after their failed attempt.

Charles Evans und Tom Bourdillon kehren nach ihrem fehlgeschlagenen ersten Besteigungsversuch enttäuscht und erschöpft zum Südsattel zurück.

Charles Evans en Tom Bourdillon keren na hun mislukte poging teleurgesteld en uitgeput terug naar de zuidelijke pas.

Charles Evans y Tom Bourdillon, decepcionados y agotados, vuelven al Collado Sur tras su intento fallido.

Edmund Hillary and Tenzing Norgay at Camp IV, preparing for the final assault.

Edmund Hillary und Tenzing Norgay bei der Vorbereitung zu ihrem Besteigungsversuch in Lager IV.

Edmund Hillary en Tenzing Norgay bereiden zich in kamp IV voor op de laatste poging.

Edmund Hillary y Tenzing Norgay preparando el asalto final en el campamento IV.

Hillary putting on his specially designed high altitude boots.

Hillary beim Anlegen seiner eigens entwickelten Stiefel für große Höhen.

Hillary trekt laarzen aan die speciaal zijn ontworpen voor grote hoogte.

Hillary poniéndose sus botas diseñadas especialmente para altitudes elevadas.

Evans and Bourdillon back at Camp VII on the South Col after ascending the south summit of Everest.

Evans und Bourdillon nach ihrer Rückkehr in Lager VII auf dem Südsattel nach ihrem Aufstieg auf den Südgipfel des Mount Everest.

Evans en Bourdillon terug in kamp VII op de zuidelijke pas na afdaling van de zuidelijke top van de Everest.

Evans y Bourdillon a su regreso en el campamento VII en el Collado Sur tras el ascenso de la Cumbre Sur del Everest.

The remains of the Swiss Camp at an altitude of 8,290m, on the south-east ridge of Everest.

Die Überreste des schweizerischen Lagers in 8290 m Höhe auf dem Südostgrat des Mount Everest.

De overblijfsels van het Zwitserse kamp op 8290 meter hoogte op de zuidoostelijke kam van de Everest.

Los restos del campamento suizo a 8290 m en la cresta sureste del Everest.

Edmund Hillary and Tenzing Norgay approach the south-east ridge 28th May 1953.

Edmund Hillary und Tenzing Norgay bei der Annäherung an den Südostgrat, 28. Mai 1953.

Edmund Hillary en Tenzing Norgay naderen de zuidoostelijke kam op 28 mei 1953.

Edmund Hillary y Tenzing Norgay se acercan a la cresta sureste. 28 de mayo de 1953.

Edmund Hillary and Tenzing Norgay approach the south-east ridge at 8321m.

Edmund Hillary und Tenzing Norgay bei der Annäherung an den Südostgrat auf 8321 m Höhe.

Edmund Hillary en Tenzing Norgay naderen de zuidoostelijke kam op 8321 meter hoogte.

Edmund Hillary y Tenzing Norgay se acercan a la cresta sureste a 8321 m

Edmund Hillary on the south-east ridge of Everest.

Edmund Hillary auf dem Südostgrat des Mount Everest.

Edmund Hillary op de zuidoostelijke kam van de Everest.

Edmund Hillary en la cresta sureste del Everest.

Edmund Hillary and Tenzing Norgay approach 8,534m, at the site of Camp IX.

Edmund Hillary und Tenzing Norgay bei der Annäherung an den Standort von Lager IX in 8534 m Höhe.

Edmund Hillary en Tenzing Norgay naderen de plaats van kamp IX op ruim 8500 meter hoogte.

Edmund Hillary y Tenzing Norgay acercándose a los 8534 m, en el emplazamiento del campamento IX.

Edmund Hillary and Tenzing Norgay on the south-east ridge, about to leave for the South Col to establish Camp IX.

Edmund Hillary und Tenzing Norgay auf dem Südostgrat, kurz bevor sie den Südsattel verlassen, um Lager IX zu errichten.

Op de zuidoostelijke kam staan Edmund Hillary en Tenzing Norgay op het punt te vertrekken naar de zuidelijke pas om kamp IX te bereiken.

Edmund Hillary y Tenzing Norgay en la cresta sureste a punto de salir hacia el Collado Sur para establecer el campamento IX.

Edmund Hillary arrives at the site of Camp IX.

Edmund Hillary komt aan op de plaats van kamp IX.

Edmund Hillary bei der Ankunft am Standort des Lagers IX.

Edmund Hillary a su llegada al emplazamiento del campamento IX.

The summit ridge of Everest (showing the Hillary step), 29th May 1953.

De toprichel van de Everest (met de *Hillary step*), 29 mei 1953.

Der Gipfelgrat des Mount Everest mit dem Hillary Step, 29. Mai 1953.

La cresta de la cumbre del Everest (mostrando el Paso Hillary), 29 de mayo de 1953.

Tenzing Norgay on the summit of Mount Everest on 29th May 1953, waving his ice-axe on which are hung the flags of Britain, Nepal, The United Nations and India.

Tenzing Norgay auf dem Gipfel des Mount Everest (29. Mai 1953). Er bewegt seinen Eispickel hin und her, an dem Flaggen Großbritanniens, Nepals, der Vereinten Nationen und Indiens befestigt sind.

Tenzing Norgay op de top van de Everest op 29 mei 1953, zwaaiend met zijn ijsbijl waaraan de vlaggen van Groot-Brittannië, Nepal, de Verenigde Naties en India hangen.

Tenzing Norgay en la cumbre del Monte Everest el 29 de mayo de 1953, agitando su piqueta de la que cuelgan las banderas de Gran Bretaña, Nepal, las Naciones Unidas e India.

View from the South Summit showing Makalu and Kanchenjunga.

Blick vom Südgipfel auf den Makalu und den Kangchendzönga.

Uitzicht vanaf de zuidelijke top met de Makalu en de Kanchenjunga.

Vista desde la Cumbre Sur mostrando Makalu y Kanchenjunga.

View from the summit looking west (showing Pumori, Cho Oyo, Lingtren and the West Rongbuk glacier).

Blick vom Gipfel nach Westen (auf den Pumori, Cho Oyo, Lingtren und den westlichen Rongpu-Gletscher).

Uitzicht vanaf de top in westelijke richting (met de Pumori, de Cho Oyo, de Lingtren en de westelijke Rongbuk-gletsjer).

Vista desde la cumbre mirando hacia el oeste (mostrando Pumori, Cho Oyo, Lingtren y el glaciar Rongbuk oeste).

Footprints of Tenzing and Hillary descending from the summit ridge of Everest.

Fußspuren von Tenzing Norgay and Hillary beim Abstieg vom Gipfelgrat des Mount Everest.

Voetafdrukken van Tenzing en Hillary afdalend van de toprichel van de Everest.

Las pisadas de Tenzing y Hillary en la bajada hacia la cresta de la cumbre del Everest.

Team members return to Camp IV after the ascent.

Mitglieder des Teams bei ihrer Rückkehr in Lager IV nach der geglückten Besteigung.

Team keert terug naar kamp IV na de beklimming.

Los miembros del equipo vuelven al campamento IV tras el ascenso.

Hillary and Tenzing Norgay at Camp IV after their ascent of Everest.

Hillary und Tenzing Norgay im Lager IV nach der geglückten Besteigung des Mount Everest.

Hillary en Tenzing Norgay in kamp IV na hun beklimming van de Everest.

Hillary y Tenzing Norgay en el campamento IV tras su ascenso al Everest.

Edmund Hillary after his successful attempt on Everest, with Alfred Gregory and Tom Bourdillon at Advanced Base Camp.

Edmund Hillary nach seinem geglückten Versuch zur Besteigung des Mount Everest mit Alfred Gregory und Tom Bourdillon im vorgeschobenen Basislager.

Edmund Hillary na zijn geslaagde poging op de Everest, met Alfred Gregory en Tom Bourdillon in het vooruitgeschoven basiskamp.

Edmund Hillary tras su exitoso intento de culminar el Everest, con Alfred Gregory y Tom Bourdillon en el campamento base avanzado.

Tenzing Norgay and Edmund Hillary warm themselves with tea in the Western Cwm (Comb).

Tenzing Norgay und Edmund Hillary wärmen sich im Tal des Schweigens mit Tee auf.

Tenzing Norgay en Edmund Hillary warmen zich met thee op de westelijke Cwm (kam).

Tenzing Norgay y Edmund Hillary se calientan bebiendo té en la Cresta Oeste.

Edmund Hillary drinks a celebratory cup of tea at Camp IV after his ascent of Everest.

Edmund Hillary trinkt in Lager IV zur Feier seines Aufstiegs auf den Mount Everest eine Tasse Tee.

Edmund Hillary drinkt een feestelijke kop thee in kamp IV na zijn beklimming van de Everest.

Edmund Hillary bebiendo una taza de té en el campamento IV para celebrar su ascenso al Everest.

Charles Evans and Edmund Hillary after Hillary and Tenzing's ascent of Everest.

Charles Evans und Edmund Hillary nach Hillarys und Tenzing Norgays geglücktem Aufstieg auf den Mount Everest.

Charles Evans en Edmund Hillary na de beklimming van de Everest door Hillary en Tenzing.

Charles Evans y Edmund Hillary después del ascenso de Hillary y Tenzing al Everest.

Edmund Hillary being congratulated by James Morris, correspondent from *The Times*.

James Morris, der Korrespondent der *Times*, gratuliert Edmund Hillary.

Edmund Hillary wordt gefeliciteerd door James Morris, de *Times*-correspondent.

James Morris, corresponsal del *Times*, felicita a Edmund Hillary.

Tenzing Norgay flanked by two Sherpas with victory flags.

Tenzing Norgay, flankiert von zwei Sherpas mit Flaggen.

Tenzing Norgay met de overwinningsvlaggen, vergezeld van twee andere Sherpa's.

Tenzing Norgay flanqueado por dos *sherpas* con las banderas de la victoria.

Band, Evans, Ward and Stobart "Happy" on rum on Coronation Day, 2nd June 1953.

Band, Evans, Ward und Stobart mit Rum am Krönungstag, 2. Juni 1953.

Band, Evans, Ward en Stobart vrolijk aan de rum op *Coronation Day*, 2 juni 1953.

Band, Evans, Ward y Stobart "felices" bebiendo ron el Día de la Coronación, 2 de junio de 1953.

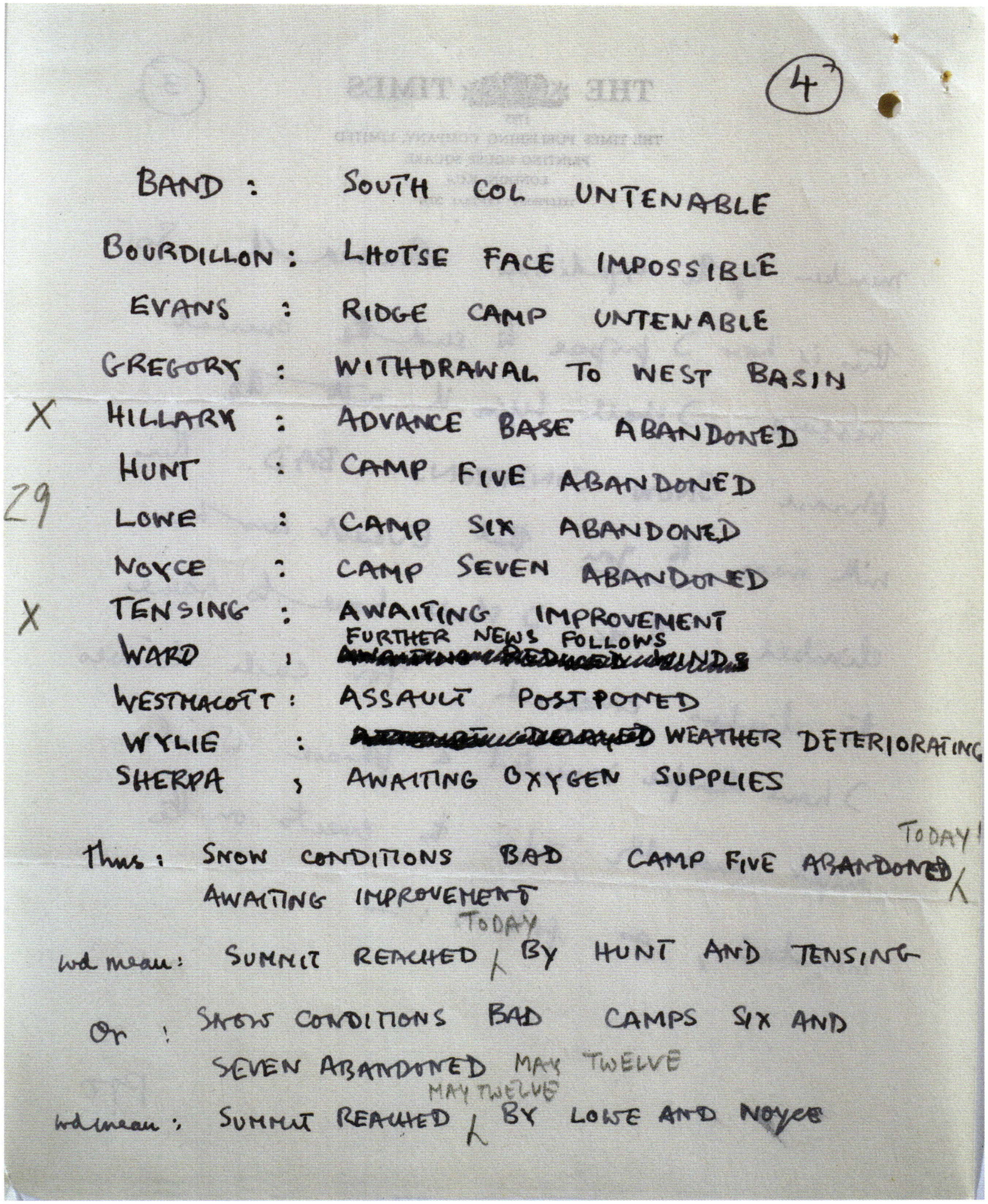

THE TIMES

4

BAND : SOUTH COL UNTENABLE

BOURDILLON : LHOTSE FACE IMPOSSIBLE

EVANS : RIDGE CAMP UNTENABLE

GREGORY : WITHDRAWAL TO WEST BASIN

X HILLARY : ADVANCE BASE ABANDONED

HUNT : CAMP FIVE ABANDONED

29 LOWE : CAMP SIX ABANDONED

NOYCE : CAMP SEVEN ABANDONED

X TENSING : AWAITING IMPROVEMENT

WARD : FURTHER NEWS FOLLOWS

WESTMACOTT : ASSAULT POSTPONED

WYLIE : WEATHER DETERIORATING

SHERPA : AWAITING OXYGEN SUPPLIES

thus : SNOW CONDITIONS BAD CAMP FIVE ABANDONED TODAY AWAITING IMPROVEMENT

wd mean : SUMMIT REACHED TODAY BY HUNT AND TENSING

Or : SNOW CONDITIONS BAD CAMPS SIX AND SEVEN ABANDONED MAY TWELVE

wd mean : SUMMIT REACHED MAY TWELVE BY LOWE AND NOYCE

Letter from James Morris (*Times* correspondent) to the *The Times* explaining the code words for the telegram that would be sent in the event of a successful ascent of Mount Everest.

Brief des Korrespondenten James Morris an *die Times* mit einer Erklärung der Codeworte für das Telegramm, das im Falle einer erfolgreichen Besteigung des Mount Everest gesendet werden sollte.

Brief van James Morris (*Times*-correspondent) aan zijn krant met uitleg van de codewoorden voor het telegram dat zou worden verstuurd ter gelegenheid van de overwinning op de Everest.

Carta de James Morris (corresponsal del Times) al *Times* explicando las palabras codificadas del telegrama que se enviaría en caso de que se consiguiera culminar el ascenso al Monte Everest.